PROGRAMMING
A PERSONAL COMPUTER

In memory of
NIELS IVAR BECH

PROGRAMMING
A PERSONAL COMPUTER

PER BRINCH HANSEN

PRENTICE-HALL, INC., Englewood Cliffs, New Jersey 07632

Library of Congress Cataloging in Publication Data

Brinch Hansen, Per (date)
    Programming a personal computer.

    Bibliography: p.
    Includes index.
    1. Edison (Computer program language) 2. Operating
systems (Computers) 3. Microcomputers—Programming.
I. Title.
QA76.73.E34B74 1983   001.64'2   82-23130
ISBN 0-13-730267-3
ISBN 0-13-730283-5 (pbk)

Editorial/production supervision: Nancy Milnamow
Manufacturing buyer: Gordon Osbourne

Printed in the United States of America

10 9 8 7 6 5 4 3 2

ISBN 0-13-730267-3
ISBN 0-13-730283-5 {PBK}

PRENTICE-HALL INTERNATIONAL, INC., *London*
PRENTICE-HALL OF AUSTRALIA PTY. LIMITED, *Sydney*
EDITORA PRENTICE-HALL DO BRASIL, LTDA., *Rio de Janeiro*
PRENTICE-HALL OF CANADA INC., *Toronto*
PRENTICE-HALL OF INDIA PRIVATE LIMITED, *New Delhi*
PRENTICE-HALL OF JAPAN, INC., *Tokyo*
PRENTICE-HALL OF SOUTHEAST ASIA PTE. LTD., *Singapore*
WHITEHALL BOOKS LIMITED, *Wellington, New Zealand*

CONTENTS

PREFACE

For a brief period, personal computers have offered programmers a chance to build small software systems of outstanding quality using the best available programming languages and design methods.

Personal computers attract a new generation of programmers for whom the ability to use software written for previous computers is of little or no interest. Consequently, computer manufacturers have the freedom to choose new programming languages and develop innovative computer architectures for personal computing.

The simple operating procedures and small stores of personal computers make it both possible and essential to limit the complexity of software.

For these reasons, personal computers provide a unique opportunity to improve software quality. This goal has indeed been achieved by the UCSD Pascal system [Bowles, 1980]. But it does not appear to be an industry-wide trend yet. Most operating systems for microcomputers are still written in assembly language.

The recent development of the complicated programming language Ada combined with new microprocessors with large stores will soon make the development of incomprehensible, unreliable software inevitable even for personal computers.

Before that happens, I would like to present an obvious alternative to

software designers: a software system that is powerful enough to support
the development of nontrivial programs on a personal computer and yet is
simple enough to be studied in detail at all levels of programming.

This book describes the *Edison system* which supports the development
of programs written in the programming language Edison, a Pascal-like
language designed for microprocessors. The Edison system was developed
on a PDP 11/23 microcomputer with floppy disks. It can, however, be
moved to other microprocessors.*

The main difficulty of software design is the human difficulty of understanding a massive amount of detail. A textbook ignores the trivia and con-
centrates on oversimplified (but effective) principles of design. In this book,
however, I cannot suppress the programming details, since my aim is to
demonstrate how you can build software that is understandable in all details.

The book explains how the programming language and the software
system were designed and implemented. It includes the program text of the
operating system and the compiler, both of which are written in Edison.
It also includes the text of the system kernel for the PDP 11 computers.

The book is not intended to be read from cover to cover unless you
wish to move the software system to another computer. As a new user of
the Edison system, you may wish to start with the system report (Chapter
5), which explains how the system is operated. Before you can write programs for the system, it is also necessary to read Chapters 2 and 3 on the
programming language Edison.

The text provides realistic case studies for nearly every undergraduate
course on computer programming:

> Systematic programming
> Data structures
> Programming languages
> Computer architectures
> Compilers
> Operating systems

The book is written for professional programmers and undergraduates
with a background in programming languages, compilers, and operating systems. The necessary background is described in the textbooks by Wirth
[1973, 1976a] and myself [Brinch Hansen, 1973]. If you know some of
this material, but not all of it, you may wish to skip those sections of the
text that are marked with an asterisk.

I have used the text in an undergraduate course at USC to give students
a feeling for how the principles studied in core courses on computer science
can be used in the design of a complete software system.

---

*Including the *IBM Personal Computer* (see p. 381).

My earlier book, *The Architecture of Concurrent Programs* [Prentice-Hall, 1977], describes a single-user operating system, called Solo, written in the programming languages Pascal and Concurrent Pascal. The Solo system was an experimental research effort to evaluate the usefulness of the monitor concept.

The Edison system is an engineering project aimed at further simplifying well-known ideas. It is written in a single programming language that is smaller than Pascal but more powerful than the combination of Pascal and Concurrent Pascal. The system runs on a microcomputer with only $2/3$ of the store and $1/10$ of the disk capacity used by the Solo system.

John Wiley and Sons kindly granted permission to reprint large parts of the papers:

> Edison—a multiprocessor language.
> The design of Edison.
> Edison programs.
> *Software—Practice and Experience*, April 1981.

I am grateful to Steve Goings, Nick Matelan, Vincent Prothro, and L. J. Sevin of Mostek Corporation for the opportunity to develop the programming language Edison. The language report was improved considerably by the constructive comments of Peter Naur. Helpful comments on the text were also provided by Dines Bjørner, Jon Fellows, David Gries, Tony Hoare, Peter Lyngbaek, Habib Maghami, and Harlan Mills.

The book is dedicated to the memory of *Niels Ivar Bech*, the originator of computer development in Denmark. Under Bech's inspired leadership, a generation of young Danes made unique contributions to computer programming, such as the Algol 60 Report, the Gier Algol compiler, and the RC 4000 multiprogramming system.

PER BRINCH HANSEN

1

SOFTWARE QUALITY

This book describes the Edison system, a personal software system for professional programmers. The system consists of a compiler, an operating system, a screen editor, a text formatter, and a few other programs, all of which are written in the programming language Edison.

We begin by examining the crucial role of *simplicity* in software design. The historian William McNeill [1967] puts it this way: "What cannot be understood becomes meaningless, and reasonable people quite properly refuse to pay attention to meaningless matters."

A professional programmer will inevitably push a small computer to its limit. I did that during the design of the Edison system. On a PDP 11 microcomputer, the system can compile the largest pass of the Edison compiler in a store of 28 K words, leaving only 200 words unused! This was not due to luck. I deliberately extended the operating system with useful functions until the store limit was reached.

During the design of nontrivial user programs, a programmer must also be acutely aware of the system limits. Otherwise, such programs may not be able to run on a small computer. In some applications, it may even be necessary to adapt the system to a different kind of backing store.

None of these things are possible unless the software system can be fully understood by a programmer.

The details of software can be mastered only if the designer strives for the utmost simplicity.

Although the practical demands of software design make simplicity essential, a more profound reason is to be found in the nature of creative work. The joy of discovery and the pleasure of making something work are the most powerful drives in science and engineering. To sustain this motivation, a software engineer must look for astonishing simplicities and beautiful patterns of design.

Simplicity is a measure of the human effort needed to build, understand, and use a system. This will be our measure of simplicity: *A personal software system is simple if it takes no more than a day to learn to use it, a month to understand it in detail, and a year to build it.* The attraction of personal computing is that one person can master it all!

In the following, I suggest some guidelines of design that will help make a software system simple.

1.1 SIMPLICITY OF USE

Three design rules are essential to help even the most casual user of a software system:

(1) *Define the system purpose clearly.*

The Edison system supports the development and documentation of Edison programs on a personal computer with an alphanumeric display terminal, a dual floppy disk drive, and a printer. The system enables a single user to invoke the following operations from the terminal:

> Text input
> Text storage
> Text editing
> Text formatting
> Text printing
> Program compilation
> Program storage
> Program execution

(2) *Describe the operating conventions precisely.*

Although a professional programmer should be able to understand a personal software system in complete detail, he or she should, of course, also be able to ignore the programming details and depend solely on an accurate description of the system commands and their effect. The Edison system report is such a description (Chapter 5).

(3) *Make the system easy to use.*

All operations performed by the Edison system are invoked by similar commands. The user need only remember the name of an operation and type it on the terminal. The system will then remind the user of the parameters required to define the operation completely.

Minor typing mistakes are corrected by means of a uniform set of line editing conventions used throughout the system. A text editor enables the user to go back and forth across a text file and make corrections, insertions, and deletions on the screen using a small set of editing commands with conventions that are very similar to ordinary typing.

1.2 SIMPLICITY OF PROGRAMMING

The following design rules make it much easier for a user to add new programs to a system and understand the existing programs. These rules also simplify the task of building the system itself.

(1) *Keep the system small.*

If software is developed for a small machine by a single person in one year, it is bound to be small. It is therefore advisable to do just that and no more for a personal computer. Needless to say, a small system can do only a small number of things. But that cannot be helped.

(2) *Use the same language throughout.*

This book describes a software system of about 10,000 lines of program text. If you wish to understand it in one month, you must study 500 lines every day (excluding weekends). The least the designer can do to reduce this burden is to use the same programming language throughout the whole system.

The Edison system consists of an operating system, a compiler, a screen editor, a text formatter, a print program, and a PDP 11 assembler. All these programs are written in the programming language Edison.

The only program that is written in assembler language is a system kernel (of 1800 words) which interprets the code generated by the compiler. The kernel was first written and tested in Edison and was then translated manually into assembler language using the Edison statements as comments.

(3) *Hide machine details.*

Most computers differ only in irrelevant details, and few of them are well suited for systematic implementation of programming languages. It is therefore quite reasonable to ignore machine details wherever possible. This can be done only by using an abstract programming language in which store addresses, registers, and bit patterns are replaced by the concepts of variables, expressions, and values.

In addition, one can make the compiler produce abstract code for an ideal machine tailored to the programming language and then interpret that code with reasonable efficiency by means of a small machine-dependent program (the system kernel).

(4) *Use uniform interfaces.*

One of the most challenging programming tasks is to design a file system that enables all programs to use the floppy disks efficiently while hiding the details of space allocation and data access. A floppy disk drive is several orders of magnitude slower than a microprocessor. Since the properties of such a device severely limit the performance of the whole system, they cannot be ignored. The best one can hope for is to find a uniform set of procedures for handling the disk which can be implemented once and for all by the operating system and invoked by all other programs.

However, a uniform interface between the operating system and all other programs contributes to simplicity only if it is small. The Edison operating system implements a set of 33 procedures which enable other programs to use the terminal, the disks, and the printer.

1.3 SIMPLICITY OF PROGRAMMING LANGUAGE

In most cases, a wise software designer will choose an existing programming language and will not attempt to design a new one. In either case, I offer the following advice:

(1) *Keep the language small.*

To determine whether or not a programming language is small, you need only look at the language report and the compiler. The reports defining the programming languages Pascal and Edison, are less than 50 pages long. The Edison compiler written in Edison consists of 4200 lines of program text.

You can make a new programming language small by starting with a good existing language, such as Pascal, and *omitting* all language features that are not absolutely essential. You may have to *refine* the remaining features of the language to be able to express some of the eliminated concepts concisely. But any *extensions* of the language should be minimal.

(2) *Define the language precisely.*

The main value of an abstract programming language is its ability to hide hardware and software details. However, a programmer can safely ignore the properties of the computer, the operating system, and the compiler only if the language report describes the effect of each language feature precisely in system-independent terms. The difficulties of writing such a report are discussed in Chapter 2.

1.4 OTHER SOFTWARE PROPERTIES

The previous discussion of simplicity may seem very unbalanced. Other properties of software are obviously important also:

(1) *Reliability*

Experience has shown that small software systems can be made more reliable than the hardware they run on. But if any errors remain, it is obviously much easier to find them if the system is simple and well documented. So simplicity and reliability go hand in hand.

(2) *Efficiency*

Efficient execution is obtained by choosing language constructs that can be implemented in a straightforward way on existing computers and by performing simple optimizations of the code during compilation. However, the main contribution to efficiency is a well-designed file system that minimizes the movements of disk heads.

(3) *Extensibility*

The ability to extend a software system with new programs is supported by the design of a uniform program interface.

(4) *Portability*

A system that executes machine-independent code can be moved to other computers by rewriting the kernel. To make the kernel as small as possible, one must choose a small programming language.

So, in many cases, simplicity contributes directly to other desirable software properties. Software properties that are in serious conflict with simplicity must, however, be sacrificed.

Other discussions of software quality are to be found in Hoare [1972a] and Brinch Hansen [1977].

2

PROGRAMMING LANGUAGE DESIGN

2.1 BACKGROUND

The development of the programming language Pascal was a landmark in software technology [Wirth, 1971]. A programmer could now for the first time use an abstract notation to describe both data types and operations. This machine-independent notation made it possible for a single programmer in one year to write a portable compiler that was both understandable and correct.

Faced with a dramatic decrease in hardware costs and a steady rise of software costs, it was inevitable that the computer industry eventually would adopt this superior programming tool to support the new microprocessor technology.

Since Pascal was first developed, two significant breakthroughs have been made in software technology:

(1) It is now widely recognized that the ability to group data structures and operations into *program modules* greatly clarifies the meaning of large programs.

(2) The ability to write *concurrent programs* in an abstract language is becoming essential for a new generation of multiprocessor architectures based on microprocessors.

The invention of the monitor concept led to the development of a new generation of programming languages which support both modularity and concurrency [Brinch Hansen, 1973] [Hoare, 1974]. The programming languages Concurrent Pascal and Modula have had a dramatic impact on our ability to develop simple and correct operating systems and real-time systems for minicomputers [Brinch Hansen, 1975, 1977] [Wirth, 1977]. But it must be admitted that these languages were based on somewhat complicated concepts.

Edison is an attempt to combine the significant gains of recent software technology into a programming language that is simpler than Pascal and which supports modular construction of both sequential and concurrent programs for microcomputers.

The simplicity of Edison was achieved by eliminating many well-known language concepts and by separating issues that were previously intertwined. This chapter describes the considerations behind the design of Edison. It also discusses the linguistic problems of writing a concise language report. I assume that you are already familiar with Pascal.

2.2 DATA TYPES

The most significant advance made by Pascal was the introduction of a set of data types that made system programming in an abstract programming language practical. Nevertheless, some of Pascal's data types are complicated and imprecisely defined.

In Edison, I have tried to simplify and clarify the issues concerning data types.

2.2.1 The Type Concept

The type concept can best be illustrated by looking at the standard types of Edison: the integers, booleans, and characters.

(1) *A type consists of a finite set of values.*

The type integer consists of a finite set of successive whole numbers

$$\ldots, -2, -1, 0, 1, 2, \ldots$$

The type boolean consists of the truth values

false, true

The type character consists of a finite set of characters

..., 'a', 'b', 'c', ...

(2) *Each type has a name.*

The standard types are named

int   bool   char

(3) *Each value is of one and only one type.*

Or, to put it differently, the types are disjoint sets of values.

(4) *Every constant, variable, and expression is of a fixed type.*

The type of an operand limits its possible values during program execution. The operand type can be determined from the program text without executing it.

The type of a constant is given by either its syntax or its name:

15   'a'   false

or by its declaration

const max = 100

The type of a variable is given by its declaration, for example

var x: int

The type of an expression can be determined from the types of its operands and from the known types of the operator results.

(5) *Every operation applies to operands of fixed types and yields results of fixed types.*

As an example, a comparison of two integer values for equality yields a boolean result.

The type concept of Pascal has the same properties, except (2) and (3). This leads to conceptual difficulties as discussed in Sections 2.2.3 and 2.2.16.

2.2.2 Elementary Types

The types integer, boolean, and character are of a similar nature. Each of these types consists of a finite, *ordered* set of values. This is essentially the definition used in the revised Pascal report, in which these types are called scalar types [Jensen and Wirth, 1975]. (Unfortunately, the report also considers type real as a scalar type, which gives the unintended impression elsewhere in the report that array indices can be of type real.)

In Edison, these types are called *elementary types* and their similarity to the integers is described as follows: The successive values of an elementary type can be mapped onto a finite set of successive integers known as *ordinal values.*

The ordinal value of an elementary value x is denoted int(x). For any integer value, say 5, the ordinal value is the integer itself, that is,

$$int(5) = 5$$

For the boolean values, we have

$$int(false) = 0 \qquad int(true) = 1$$

The ordinal values of the characters are system dependent. For the ASCII character set, some examples of ordinal values are

$$int('a') = 97 \qquad int('b') = 98 \qquad int('c') = 99$$

The *inverse mapping* of integers onto booleans is defined as follows:

$$bool(0) = false \qquad bool(1) = true$$

and similarly for the characters

$$char(97) = 'a' \qquad char(98) = 'b' \qquad char(99) = 'c'$$

The familiar problem of converting an integer value x in the range 0 to 9 to a digit of type character is solved by the mapping

$$char(x + int('0'))$$

Pascal uses a similar notation

$$chr(x + ord('0'))$$

but cannot describe the inverse mapping bool(x), where x is an integer expression.

The types integer, boolean, and character are standard types in the Edison language. Other elementary types known as *enumerations* can be introduced by type declarations, such as

$$\textbf{enum task (flow, scan, log)}$$

This declaration introduces an enumeration type named task consisting of three successive values named flow, scan, and log.

These values have the ordinal values

$$\text{int(flow)} = 0 \qquad \text{int(scan)} = 1 \qquad \text{int(log)} = 2$$

The inverse mapping of integers onto task values is defined as follows:

$$\text{task}(0) = \text{flow} \qquad \text{task}(1) = \text{scan} \qquad \text{task}(2) = \text{log}$$

In Pascal, the same type is declared like this:

$$\textbf{type task} = \text{(flow, scan, log)}$$

The inverse mapping cannot be described in Pascal.

In Pascal, the predecessor and successor of a scalar value x are denoted pred(x) and succ(x), for example

$$\text{pred('b')} \qquad \text{succ(scan)}$$

In Edison, these values are defined by the following mappings:

$$\text{char(int('b')} - 1) \qquad \text{task(int(scan)} + 1)$$

Although this notation is less elegant, it does eliminate two standard functions from the language.

The *arithmetic operators*

$$+ \qquad - \qquad * \qquad \textbf{div} \qquad \textbf{mod}$$

apply to integer values and yield integer results (as in Pascal).

The *boolean operators*

$$\textbf{not} \qquad \textbf{and} \qquad \textbf{or}$$

apply to boolean values and yield boolean results (as in Pascal).

These operators have their conventional meaning.
The *ordering relations*

$$= \qquad <> \qquad < \qquad <= \qquad > \qquad >=$$

apply to operands of the same elementary type and yield boolean results (as
in Pascal). These relations have their conventional meaning for integers. The
ordering of other elementary values is the same as the ordering of their
ordinal values; that is, $x < y$ if, and only if, $int(x) < int(y)$, and similarly
for the other relations.

The only contribution of Edison to these well-known concepts is to
define mappings between the values of any elementary type and the integers
(and vice versa). This idea is used to define the properties of all elementary
types in terms of the properties of the integers.

2.2.3 Subrange Types

The subrange types of Pascal can be used to introduce types that are
either disjoint, contained in other subranges, or even overlapping, as illustrated by these examples:

> **var** x1: 1 .. 10; x2: 11 .. 20; x3: 5 .. 9; x4: 0 .. 15

This raises complicated issues, such as: Is the expression x1 + x2 valid, and
if so, what is its type (1 .. 10, 11 .. 20, 1 .. 20, or perhaps 12 .. 30)? Is a
value of type 1 .. 10 also of type 0 .. 15? Are some of the values 0 .. 15 also
of type 1 .. 10, while others are also of type 11 .. 20? Are the values of
these subrange types in general compatible with the integer values, or are
they distinct types? None of these questions are answered by the Pascal
report.

The elimination of subrange types from Edison makes these issues
irrelevant.

2.2.4 Reals

Edison does not include the type real because it is not needed for system programming and text processing. The inclusion of reals would only
have added more details to this work without contributing to its main goal:
the design of understandable software. It is, however, a debatable decision
which makes the system impractical for engineering computations.

2.2.5 Type Declarations

In Pascal, type declarations begin with a name, for example

> **type** T1 = **record** x: char;   y: integer **end**;
> T2 = **array** [1 . . 10] **of** char

The compiler must therefore scan three symbols

> Type name = Word symbol

before it can determine whether a declaration introduces a record or an array type. This is an ugly exception in a compiler that otherwise only needs to look at a single symbol to determine the syntactic form of the next sentence in a program text.

Error recovery during compilation is also complicated by this syntax. After a syntax error, such as

> **type** T1 = **record** x: char;   y: integer ned;
> T2 = **array** [1 . . 10] **of** char

the compiler is unable to determine where the record declaration ends and the array declaration begins. The transcribed word symbol **end** will be interpreted as a misplaced field name *ned*, and so will the type name T2 that follows the semicolon. The result is a burst of misleading error messages referring to all uses of variables of type T2.

In Edison, each type declaration begins with a word symbol (instead of a name), for example

> **record** T1 (x: char;   y: int)
> **array** T2 [1:10] (char)

After a syntax error, such as

> **record** T1 (x: char;   y: int]
> **array** T2 [1:10] (char)

the compiler will skip the right bracket and correctly recognize the word **array** as the beginning of a new type declaration.

It is true that assignments and procedure calls suffer from the same problem of error recovery since they begin with names and also may contain names as operands. But the accidental erasure of a statement during compilation is not as serious as the erasure of a declaration since other statements cannot refer to the missing one by name.

It is characteristic of a superior tool like Pascal that its notation is felt to be so natural that there seems to be no reason for a programmer to look for a better one. So it was without much thought that I originally used Pascal's notation for type declarations in Edison. As I was testing the first Edison compiler written in Pascal, the problems of error recovery became apparent. But even then it took a while before I was mentally prepared to propose an alternative syntactic notation.

2.2.6 Records

The declaration of a *record type* named time takes the form

record time (hour, minute, second: int)

in Edison. A value of this type consists of three subvalues (or *fields*) named hour, minute, and second. The fields are of type integer.

A *record constructor* of the form

time(10, 55, 2)

denotes a value of type time in which the fields have the values 10, 55, and 2. The fields are listed in their order of declaration (that is, hour, minute, and second).

A record variable of type time, such as

var now: time

consists of three *field variables* denoted

now.hour   now.minute   now.second

(as in Pascal).

It is a peculiar omission of Pascal that, although a data type is defined as a set of values, the language has no notation for record and array values! A record value can be computed only one field at a time, for example

now.hour := 10;   now.minute := 55;   now.second := 2

In Edison, this is expressed by a single assignment

now := time(10, 55, 2)

Two record values of the same type may be tested for equality and inequality. If all the corresponding fields are equal, the record values are also equal; otherwise, they are not.

The fields of a record value may be of different types, for example

record job (kind: task; title: text)

2.2.7 Arrays

An *array type* named lastday, which defines the number of days for each month of the year, may be declared as follows in Edison:

array lastday [1:12] (int)

A value of this type consists of 12 subvalues (or *elements*) of type integer. The elements are identified by *indices* in the range 1 to 12.

An *array constructor* of the form

lastday(31, 28, 31, 30, 31, 30, 31, 31, 30, 31, 30, 31)

denotes a value of type lastday. The elements of the array value are listed in the order of their indices.

An array variable x of type lastday

var x: lastday

consists of 12 *element variables* denoted

x[1]   x[2]   . . .   x[12]

(as in Pascal).

Since Pascal does not have array constructors, an array value must be computed element by element, for example

```
x[1] := 31;  x[2] := 28;  x[3] := 31;  x[4] := 30;
x[5] := 31;  x[6] := 30;  x[7] := 31;  x[8] := 31;
x[9] := 30;  x[10] := 31;  x[11] := 30;  x[12] := 31
```

The absence of record and array constructors in Pascal makes the use of constant tables so awkward that one soon adopts a programming style in which decisions are made by case statements rather than table lookup. The ability to initialize tables in Edison by a single assignment statement, such as

$$x := \text{lastday}(31, 28, 31, 30, 31, 30, 31, 31, 30, 31, 30, 31)$$

should once again make table-driven decision logic an attractive alternative.

The elements of an array type may be of any type, but their indices must be a finite set of successive values of the same elementary type.

Other possible array types are:

array schedule ['a':'z'] (job)
array table [flow:log] (text)

2.2.8 Text Strings

With one exception (text strings), the fixed length of array types in Pascal has never bothered me in the design of operating systems and compilers. But text strings pose special problems that are cleverly hidden by ad hoc means in Pascal.

By their nature, text strings are of different lengths, for example

'tape'   'Edison'

How then does one write a procedure that outputs a text string to some device (or file) one character at a time? In Pascal you can try the following:

```
procedure writetext(value: text);
var i: integer;
begin i := 1;
    while i <= n do
    begin write(value[i]);   i := i + 1 end
end
```

where

type text = **array** [1 .. n] **of** char

Now, if n = 4, the call

writetext('tape')

is valid, but the call

writetext('Edison')

is not, because the second textstring contains six characters.

You could, of course, write a procedure that accepts strings of the same length but only outputs the characters that precede a given delimiter (say, a period):

```
procedure writetext(value: text);
var i: integer;  c: char;
begin i := 1;  c := value[1];
   while c <> '.' do
   begin write(c);  i := i + 1;  c := value[i] end
end
```

If n = 10, this procedure can be called as follows:

  writetext('tape.^^^^^ ')   writetext('Edison.^^^ ')

using the character ^ (or a space) as a filler to make the text strings of length 10. But this artificial convention is very annoying for longer strings (say, of length 80).

Why, then, is this not regarded as an intolerable problem in Pascal? Because Pascal includes a standard procedure named write which is cleverly designed to accept strings of any length, for example

  write('tape')   write('Edison')

But this procedure cannot be written in the language itself!

Since Edison is also used for writing operating systems, a standard procedure, such as write, cannot be built into the language. It must indeed be possible in Edison to program a file system that includes a write procedure. Such a procedure must therefore be programmed in the language itself.

In designing the array constructors of Edison, these problems were carefully considered. In general, an array constructor must contain an expression for every element of the array type—unless it is a string type! A *string constructor* of type text may contain fewer than 10 characters, for example

  text('t', 'a', 'p', 'e', '.')

This is an abbreviation for the five given characters followed by five spaces. The constructor above may be further abbreviated as follows:

  text('tape.')

2.2.9 Control Characters

A graphic character, such as *, is denoted '*' in Pascal and Edison. But how does one represent a control character, such as *bell*? In the ASCII character set, the bell character is character number 7, which is denoted

$$chr(7)$$

in Pascal. But the standard function chr cannot occur in a constant declaration. So control characters cannot be named in Pascal.

In Edison, the bell character can be declared as

const bell = char(7)

but the name *bell* cannot be used within a character string, such as

'Edisonbell'

because it is indistinguishable from the graphic letters b, e, l, l. It can, however, be included as follows in a string constructor:

text('Edison', bell)

2.2.10 Sets

The conceptual problems associated with subrange types have already been discussed (Section 2.2.3). Similar problems are apparent in the set concept of Pascal when subranges are used to define the possible members of a set type, as in

type T1 = **set of** 1 . . 10;
T2 = **set of** 5 . . 15

Are sets of type T1 and T2 compatible with one another in set operations?

The omission of a type name in front of a set constructor makes it impossible to determine whether a set value, such as

[6, x + y, 9]

is of type T1 or T2. This problem is even more evident in the case of the empty set

[ ]

Consequently, a Pascal compiler cannot always check whether operands are of compatible types (Section 2.2.16).

The elimination of subrange types and the use of typed constructors in Edison remove these ambiguities.

A *set type* named charset is declared as follows:

set charset (char)

The values of this type are all the possible subsets of the characters (including the empty set).

A *set constructor* of the form

charset('0', '1', '2', '3', '4', '5', '6', '7', '8', '9')

denotes a value of type charset. The members of this set value are the characters from '0' to '9'. The constructor above can be abbreviated as

charset('0123456789')

The *empty set* of characters is denoted

charset

The relation

x in y

is true if the elementary value x is a member of the set value y; otherwise, it is false (as in Pascal).

Two set values of the same type may be tested for equality and inequality. If both set values have the same members, they are equal; otherwise, they are not.

The *set operators*

+   −   *

denote the union, difference, and intersection of two set values of the same type.

Other possible set types are

set intset (int)
set boolset (bool)
set taskset (task)

The members of a set value must be of the same elementary type and must fall within a finite range which is system dependent. In the Edison system, a set member must have an ordinal value in the range 0:127. This range was chosen to permit unrestricted use in the system programs of sets of the 128 ASCII characters.

2.2.11 Retyping

Type checking is an invaluable technique for detecting programming errors that would otherwise have very obscure, machine-dependent effects. There is, however, an occasional need to bypass type checking, particularly within the operating system.

Consider a floppy disk that is divided into sectors of 64 words each. An Edison procedure that reads a sector with a given number can be declared as follows in Edison:

```
proc readsector(sectorno: int; var value: sector)
begin . . . end
```

Since the language forces you to declare the data type of a sector, you may, for example, write

```
array sector [1:64] (int)
```

Unfortunately, a single declaration cannot capture all the intended uses of disk sectors. The declaration above is fine for a sector that holds 64 words of compiled code. But if a sector is part of a text file, it should be declared as a string of 64 characters. And if it is part of a disk catalog, it should be described by yet another declaration.

It would seem that we need a new type which is the union of several other types. But even if we could write something like

```
union sector (intsector, charsector, . . . , catalogsector)
```

within the operating system, we would still be unable to anticipate all the future uses programmers will make of sectors in their own programs.

It must therefore be admitted that we are dealing with a very machine dependent property of a peripheral device which cannot be hidden by means of abstract notation. What we need is simply a notation that defines the physical length of a disk sector and makes a sector value compatible with any other value that occupies the same amount of storage on a given machine.

One possibility is to introduce a machine dependent data type, called a block, and declare a sector as

```
block sector (64)
```

Another possibility is to use the notation

$$x \; : \; T2$$

to indicate that a variable (or an expression) x of a type T1 is temporarily considered to be of another type T2 of the same length. This form of *retyping* is used in Edison.

If a sector of a disk catalog is declared as a variable x of some record type

> **record** catalogsector (. . .)
> **var** x: catalogsector

then x is temporarily considered to be of the type sector in a procedure call of the form

> readsector (n, x:sector)

*2.2.12   Variant Records

The Concurrent Pascal compiler, which is written in Pascal, makes extensive use of the variant records and pointers of Pascal [Hartmann, 1977]. Since these concepts are both complicated and insecure to use, I decided to write an Edison compiler without using them. The resulting compiler is much easier to understand (Chapter 10). Evidently, these programming tools were used previously only because they were there.

Only in one part of the compiler did I feel the need for variant records. During semantic analysis, a name index is used to retrieve the attributes of a named entity from a table. Since the attributes depend on the kind of entity the name refers to, the name table is best described as an array of variant records of the following Pascal type:

```
nameattr =
  record link: integer
    case kind: namekind of
      constant:
        (consttype, constvalue: integer);

            . . .

      procparam, procedur:
        (proclevel, procaddr, proctype, param: integer)
  end
```

In Edison, the name table is described as an array of elements of the type

> **record** nameattr (kind: namekind; link: int;
> none1, none2, none3, none4, none5: int)

The variants of the type are described by separate record types

> **record** constattr (constkind: namekind;
> constlink, consttype, constvalue,
> none6, none7, none8: int)
> . . .
> **record** procattr (prockind: namekind;
> proclink, proclevel, procaddr, proctype,
> param, none11)

The records above are padded with fields to make them all of the same length.

The compiler first uses a name index x to select a general name description of type nameattr. If the kind field is equal to constant, the name description is then retyped to be of type constattr, as illustrated by the following program piece:

> **var** x, value: int
>
> if names[x].kind = constant **do**
> value := names[x]:constattr.constvalue
> . . .

I cannot recall any other system program that requires the use of variant records. If they are that rare in practice, dynamic retyping seems preferable to introducing a very complicated data type in Edison with a matching set of constructors and control statements. But if the use of variant records is more frequent than I thought, their elimination from Edison must be regarded as a mistake. Until experimental data are available from a wide range of applications, the elimination of variant records seems a worthwhile experiment.

*2.2.13 Pointers

The pointers of Pascal have been omitted from Edison for the same reason that variant records were eliminated. It is a complicated concept that appears to be a concession to the current practice of programming even though its full implications are not well understood. The need to define cyclical data structures in terms of different record types that can point to one another breaks the general rule that a type must be declared before it can be used as a subtype of another type. Furthermore, like the tag fields of variant records, pointer variables must be initialized to nil automatically to enable a processor to detect the use of a meaningless pointer. Otherwise, the effect of an assignment can even change the code of a program (just as in assembly language). No other kind of variable poses this serious problem.

The dynamic allocation of storage accessed through pointers is quite complicated, particularly when it is combined with the storage allocation of concurrent processes. And there is no secure way to release the storage again and make sure that it can no longer be accessed through existing pointer values. Since the aim of Edison is utter simplicity rather than a compromise dictated by tradition, the pointer types of Pascal could only be excluded from the language.

2.2.14   Files

In Pascal, data files are described by type declarations of the form

Type name = **file of** Type

The file procedures put, get, reset, and rewrite are standard procedures in the language. In practice, this means that the implementation details of files are hidden from Pascal programmers. This is fine for most programming applications. However, since Edison is also an operating system design language, a file system must be programmed in the language itself and cannot be built into the language (Section 2.2.8). That is why file types are not part of the Edison language.

2.2.15   Type Synonyms

The syntactic rules of Pascal make type definitions of the form

type temperature = integer;
speed = integer

legal, but the language report does not define the meaning of this. Are temperature and speed the same types as the standard type integer? In that case, the use of type synonyms serves no purpose since the addition of temperatures to speeds is now a valid operation (because they are just integers). If, on the other hand, temperature and speed are distinct types, then we have conceptual confusion in the language. For although the types are now incompatible, we would presumably expect the arithmetic operations and the ordering relations to apply to both of them. But the set of values to which these operations apply is per definition the set of integers. And to introduce several different kinds of incompatible "integers" nullifies in one stroke one of humankind's most important concepts.

Since the syntax of Edison does not include the rule

$$\text{Type name} = \text{Type name}$$

the problem never arises.

The conceptual clarity and operational security that is gained from the use of types is considerable. But as all abstractions, types derive their power from an oversimplified view of the security problem: All integer values are considered compatible irrespective of the physical or conceptual properties they represent. The type concept cannot capture the subtle distinctions between temperatures and speeds, just as it cannot describe the constraints among related values of the same type, such as the requirement that the sum of free and used pages on a disk must equal the total number of available pages.

2.2.16 Type Compatibility

Most operations on a pair of data values are valid only if the values are of the same type. Unfortunately, the precise meaning of type compatibility is not defined in the Pascal report.

The Concurrent Pascal report states that two types are compatible if one of the following conditions is satisfied [Brinch Hansen, 1977]:

(1) Both types are defined by the same type declaration, for example

> **type** T = **array** [1 . . 80] **of** char
> **var** x, y: T

(2) Both types are defined by the same variable declaration, for example

> **var** x, y: **array** [1 . . 100] **of** integer

(3) Both types are subranges of a single elementary type, which is type integer in the example

> **var** x: 1 . . 10; y: 5 . . 15

(4) Both types are strings of the same length, for example

> 'disk'   'tape'

(5) Both types are sets of compatible base types, for example

> [1, 5, 9]   [6, 14]

(6) The empty set is compatible with any set.

Although this clarifies the matter, it is not particularly simple to remember or implement.

The following rules are unnecessary in Edison:

Rule 2: There are no nameless types in Edison.

Rule 3: There are no subrange types in Edison.

Rules 4-6: In Edison, each string constructor includes the name of its type, and so does a set constructor. Even the empty set has a type name.

That leaves only rule 1, which can be made more precise.

Every data type in Edison has a name—either a standard name (int, char, bool), or a name introduced by a type declaration. So it is tempting to say that two types are compatible if, and only if, they have the same name. A given name can, however, be declared with different meanings in different blocks. Consequently, the issue of type compatibility is settled by the following simple rule: *Two types are the same only if they have the same name and the same scope* (Section 2.4.4).

2.3 SEQUENTIAL STATEMENTS

In the following, we discuss the choice of statements for sequential programming (except for procedure calls, which are described in Section 2.4.5). The main goal is still to omit features from Pascal and refine the remaining ones.

2.3.1 Empty Statements

Pascal has no notation for the empty statement. It is indicated by writing nothing. This is impractical for two reasons:

First, the compiler cannot tell the difference between an empty statement and a statement that was omitted by mistake. Consequently, no error message can be produced in the latter case.

Second, it is very difficult to describe something that cannot be written down. A proof rule which states that the execution of an empty statement will leave any assertion P about the variables unchanged looks very strange indeed:

$$P \ \{ \ \} \ P$$

In Edison, the empty statement is denoted

skip

2.3.2 Assignments

An assignment statement of the form

Variable symbol := Expression

denotes assignment to a variable of a value given by an expression (as in Pascal).

Examples:

$$i := i + 1$$

$$now.minute := (now.minute + 1) \textbf{ mod } 60$$

$$x[2] := 28$$

2.3.3 If Statements

A Pascal statement of the form

if B then S

specifies that a statement S is to be executed only if a boolean expression B has the value true.

Example:

if c = lf then display(cr)

This statement can be refined in several ways:

A programmer who is already dealing with numerous details should not have to remember that a boolean expression is followed by the word **then** in an if statement and by the word **do** in a while statement:

while B do S

An if statement often denotes conditional execution of a *statement list* of the form

S1; S2; ... ; Sn

In Pascal, a statement list SL must be enclosed by the words **begin** and **end**:

if B then begin SL end

Example:

> if lineno **mod** pagelimit = 1 **then**
> **begin** write(ff); write(nl); write(nl) **end**

In Edison, these two variants of the if statement are combined into a statement of the form

> **if B do SL end**

Examples:

> if c = lf **do** display(cr) **end**

> if lineno **mod** pagelimit = 1 **do**
>   write(ff); write(nl); write(nl)
> **end**

Pascal also includes an if statement of the form

> **if B then S1 else S2**

which denotes the execution of one of the statements S1 and S2 depending on whether the boolean expression B has the value true or false.
Example:

> if sym = name1 **then** oldname
> **else** syntax(succ)

Since the else statement S2 may be another if statement, a Pascal programmer will often use a construct of the form

> **if B1 then begin SL1 end**
> **else if B2 then begin SL2 end**
>   . . .
> **else begin SLn end**

Example:

> if ch = '>' **then**
> **begin** emit(notequal1); next(ch) **end**
> **else if** ch = '=' **then**
> **begin** emit(notgreater1); next(ch) **end**
> **else** emit(less1)

In Edison this is expressed more elegantly by a statement of the form

> if B1 do SL1
> else B2 do SL2
>
> . . .
>
> else Bn do SLn end

This denotes a single choice among one or more statement lists SL1, SL2, ..., SLn, depending on the values of boolean expressions B1, B2, ..., Bn.

The   boolean expressions are evaluated one at a time in the order written until one is found to have the value true or until all of them have been found false. If the value obtained from an expression is true, the statement list that follows the expression is executed; otherwise, none of the statement lists are executed.

Examples:

> if sym = name1 do oldname
> else true do syntax(succ) end

> if ch = '>' do emit(notequal1); next(ch)
> else ch = '=' do emit(notgreater1); next(ch)
> else true do emit(less1) end

In an attempt to eliminate empty options, I have resisted the temptation to introduce an abbreviation for the clause

> else true do

The if statement of Edison is similar to the guarded command

> if B1 → SL1 | B2 → SL2 | . . . | Bn → SLn fi

proposed by Dijkstra [1975]. But in contrast to guarded commands, the if statements of Edison are deterministic since the boolean expressions are evaluated in the order written (and not in unpredictable order).

Programs, such as compilers, that accept both correct and incorrect input often describe a choice among several different actions on valid inputs followed by a single action to be taken on invalid input, for example:

> if mode = constant do
>   constant_factor(typ, endfactor)
> else mode in typekinds do
>   constructor(type, endfactor)
> else mode in varkinds do
>   variable_factor(typ, endfactor)

      else mode **in** prockinds **do**
         function__call(typ, endfactor)
      else true **do**
         kinderror2(x, typ);   nextsym
      end

If the order in which the expressions are evaluated is unknown (as it is for guarded commands), the final expression in this example must be changed from *true* to the following monstrosity:

      (mode <> constant) **and**
      not (mode in typekinds) **and**
      not (mode in varkinds) **and**
      not (mode in prockinds)

In Edison, the execution of an if statement has no effect if all the boolean expressions yield the value false. For guarded commands, Dijkstra assumed that this would cause a program failure. If a programmer wishes to provoke such a failure, it can be done by ending an if statement as follows:

      . . . **else** true **do** halt **end**

where halt is a procedure that causes program failure when executed. The language Edison-11 for the PDP 11 computers includes a standard procedure halt.

2.3.4   While Statements

The while statement of Pascal

      while B do S

specifies that a statement S is to be executed repeatedly as long as a boolean expression B has the value true.
     Example:

      while c <> '.' **do**
      begin write(c); i := i + 1; c := value[i] **end**

In Edison, a while statement has the form

      while B do SL end

where SL is a statement list.

Example:

>**while** c <> '.' **do**
>   write(c); i := i + 1; c : = value[i]
>**end**

The general form of a while statement has the same syntactic form as an if statement:

>**while** B1 **do** SL1
>**else** B2 **do** SL2
>   . . .
>**else** Bn **do** SLn **end**

This denotes a repeated choice among one or more statement lists SL1, SL2, . . . , SLn, depending on the values of boolean expressions B1, B2, . . . , Bn.

The expressions are evaluated one at a time in the order written until one is found to have the value true or until all of them have been found false. If the value obtained from an expression is true, the statement list that follows the expression is executed and afterward the process is repeated. When all the expressions are false, the execution of the while statement is finished.

The well-known algorithm for finding the greatest common divisor of two natural numbers x and y can be described by the following while statement:

>**while** x > y **do** x := x - y
>**else** x < y **do** y := y - x **end**

In Pascal, this algorithm can only be expressed by a combination of while and if statements:

>**while** x <> y **do**
>   **if** x > y **do** x := x - y
>   **else** y := y - x

Another beautiful example of the general while statement is found in the Edison compiler in a procedure that recognizes the syntax of a variable symbol that consists of a variable name possibly followed by one or more field names, index expressions, or type names (indicating a retyping of the variable), for example:

>names[x]:constattr.constvalue

When the initial variable name has been recognized, the compiler proceeds as follows:

```
while sym = period1 do
    field_selector(endvar)
else sym = lbracket1 do
    indexed_selector(endvar)
else sym = colon1 do
    type_transfer(endvar)
end
```

The while statement of Edison is similar to the guarded command

$$\text{do } B1 \rightarrow SL1 \mid B2 \rightarrow SL2 \mid \ldots \mid Bn \rightarrow SLn \text{ od}$$

[Dijkstra, 1975]. But, in contrast to guarded commands, the while statements of Edison are deterministic since the boolean expressions are evaluated in the order written.

2.3.5 Case Statements

The case statement of Pascal,

```
case expression of
    constant1:  S1;
    constant2:  S2;
        . . .
    constantn:  Sn
end
```

was originally part of Edison as well, but was later removed. The experience of writing the Edison compiler showed that a case statement often is used to describe actions on symbols that are grouped together, as in

```
case ch of
    'a', 'b', . . . , 'z': name;
    '0', '1', . . . , '9': numeral;
        . . .
end
```

The same clarity and efficiency can be achieved by using a combination of if statements and sets representing the necessary symbol classes, for

example:

>
> if ch **in** letters **do** name
> **else** ch **in** digits **do** numeral
>
> . . .
>
> **end**

This grouping reduces the number of cases to eight in the lexical analysis of the compiler.

The syntactic and semantic analyses of the Edison compiler use recursive descent and include one procedure for each syntactic form of the language. Since a given procedure is prepared only to recognize a small number of symbols (corresponding to the syntactic form it represents), an if statement combined with sets is again quite efficient. Several examples described earlier illustrate this point (Sections 2.3.3 and 2.3.4).

The code generator is the only part of the compiler that inputs one symbol at a time and immediately uses it to branch to one of about 60 procedures. In that one case, I had to resort to an awkward construct of the form

>
> **if** op $<$= construct2 **do**
>   **if** op = add2 **do** add
>   **else** op = also2 **do** alsox(a, b)
>   **else** op = and2 **do** andx
>   **else** op = assign2 **do** assign(a)
>   **else** op = blank2 **do** blank(a)
>   **else** op = cobegin2 **do** cobeginx(a, b, c)
>   **else** op = constant2 **do** constant(a)
>   **else** op = construct2 **do** construct(a) **end**
> **else** op $<$= endproc2 **do**
>   **if** op = difference2 **do** difference
>
> . . .

to obtain fast compilation. But that was fewer than 70 lines in a compiler of 4200 lines and hardly worth the addition of another kind of statement to the language.

2.3.6 Repeat Statements

There are no repeat statements in Edison. The repeat statement of Pascal,

> **repeat** SL **until** B

can be represented in Edison either by the statements

> **SL;   while not B do SL end**

or by the following program piece:

> **var** again: bool
> **begin** again := true;
>   **while** again **do**
>   SL; again := **not** B
>   **end**
> **end**

2.3.7 For Statements

There are no for statements either in Edison. The for statement of Pascal,

> **for** i := 1 **to** n **do** S

can be written either as

> i := 0;
> **while** i < n **do** i := i + 1; S **end**

or as

> i := 1;
> **while** i < = n **do** S; i := i + 1 **end**

in Edison. It may seem that the two representations of the for statement are not equivalent since the final value of the control variable i will be n in the first version and n + 1 in the second. Although the Pascal report is silent on this issue, the more informal user report states that "the final value of the control variable is left undefined upon normal exit from the for statement." This rule is introduced precisely to give the language implementor the freedom to choose the most efficient implementation for a given machine.

The decreasing variant of the for statement in Pascal,

> **for** i := n **downto** 1 **do** S

can be represented similarly in Edison.

*2.3.8 With Statements

The with statement of Pascal appears to be used mostly to assign values to all the fields of a record variable, as in the following example:

```
with names[nameno] do
begin
    kind := mode;
    minlevel := scope;
    maxlevel := origin;
    originalname := x
end
```

In Edison this is expressed more concisely by means of an assignment statement and a record constructor.

```
names[nameno] := nameattr(mode, scope, origin, x)
```

So there are no with statements either in Edison.

2.3.9 Goto Statements

The goto statement of Pascal was excluded from Concurrent Pascal in 1975 and has never been missed since.

2.4 PROCEDURES

The procedure concepts of Edison and Pascal are very similar.

2.4.1 Procedure Declarations

The procedure declaration

```
proc writetext(value: text)
var i: int;  c: char
begin i := 1; c := value[1] ;
    while c <> '.' do
        write(c); i := i + 1; c := value[i]
    end
end
```

describes a procedure named writetext. The *value parameter* named value is a local variable that is assigned the value of an expression when the procedure is called. The *procedure body* consists of declarations of *auxiliary entities* used by the procedure and a statement part which describes a sequence of operations on the parameters and auxiliary entities. In this example, the auxiliary entities are named i and c.

Another procedure declaration is shown below:

```
proc readint(var x:  int)
var c:  char
begin x := 0;  read(c);
    while c in digits do
        x := 10 * x + (int(c) - int('0'));
        read(c)
    end
end
```

The *variable parameter* named x denotes a variable that is selected when the procedure is called. During the execution of the procedure body, every operation on the variable parameter stands for the same operation performed on the selected variable.

2.4.2 Functions

The following procedure declaration describes a function of type integer:

```
proc gcd(x, y:  int):  int
begin
    while x > y do x := x - y
    else x < y do y := y - x end;
    val gcd := x
end
```

During the execution of the body, the value of the function named gcd is held in a local variable denoted

$$val\ gcd$$

This is a notational improvement over Pascal in which a function name is used to denote two different concepts: If a function name occurs on the left side of an assignment operator, for example

$$gcd := x$$

it denotes the value of a function. But if it occurs in an expression, the name denotes a function call.

In Pascal, a function can only be of an elementary type. In Edison, it can be of any type.

In spite of these refinements, I would omit functions if I had to design yet another language. The problem is that the function concept is simple only if the function calls have no side effects on global variables. But, in general, this crucial restriction cannot be enforced by a compiler.

Since function calls can occur in any expression, any language concept in which an expression may occur becomes complicated. Consequently, the following definitions of well-known language concepts are no longer correct:

"The evaluation of an expression computes a single value."

"The execution of an assignment statement assigns the value of an expression to a variable."

In short, the possibility of using impure functions complicates the meaning of even the most elementary operations. Functions should therefore be removed from the language.

The fact that functions are very useful when properly used is beside the point. The meaning of a language concept should remain simple under all circumstances.

2.4.3 Programs

A Pascal program begins with a heading of the form

> **program** Program name (Parameter list)

In Edison, a program has the form of a procedure declaration:

> **proc** Program name (Parameter list)

During the compilation of a program, a compiler needs to know the types of the program parameters. So an Edison program generally consists of a procedure declaration preceded by declarations of constants and data types, for example

```
const namelength = 12
array name [1:namelength] (char)
      . . .
proc edit(title:  name . . . )
```

An Edison program is a precompiled procedure that can be called by another program. The calling program will typically be an operating system written in Edison.

How does an Edison program perform input/output, say on a terminal? In Pascal, this is done by calling standard procedures. As explained earlier, this approach is unacceptable in Edison.

The solution to this problem is to enable an Edison program to call procedures that are defined inside an operating system written in Edison. These procedures must be declared as parameters of the Edison program, for example:

proc edit(title: name;
    proc accept(**var** value: char);
    proc display(value: char);
      . . .)

The *procedure parameters* named accept and display denote two procedures that are selected when the edit program is called by an operating system. During the execution of the program, every call of a procedure parameter stands for the same call of the selected procedure.

In designing Edison based on my experience with Concurrent Pascal, I tried to replace specialized mechanisms with more general ones that can be combined freely. This approach led to the adoption of the following rule: *Whenever a mechanism is needed for a particular purpose, the most general variant of that mechanism will be selected.*

Since programs are procedures that must be able to call procedure parameters, procedure parameters should be allowed in any procedure (and not just in programs).

The procedure readint described earlier calls another procedure named read to input the next digit of an integer value (Section 2.4.1). If we assume that the latter procedure is written for a particular kind of peripheral device, the given procedure can only be used to read numbers from that device.

But if we redeclare the procedure as follows:

proc readint(**proc** read(**var** c: char); **var** x: int)

the input medium can be selected when the procedure is called, for example:

readint(accept, driveno)

Generality pays off in unexpected ways!

In Pascal, a procedure P may also have a procedure parameter Q:

procedure P(procedure Q)

But since the declaration of Q does not include a parameter list, the concept is both impractical and unsafe to use. It is impractical because the parameters of Q are assumed to be value parameters only, and unsafe because a compiler cannot check whether the number and types of arguments in a call of Q are correct. This deficiency alone makes Pascal unsuitable for operating system design.

2.4.4 Scope Rules

Edison procedures may be *nested* arbitrarily. Each procedure acts as a *block*. The named entities declared within the procedure are *local* to the procedure and can be used only within the procedure body.

In general, the *scope* of a named entity extends from the declaration of the entity to the end of the block in which the declaration appears. The scope does not include inner blocks in which the same name is declared with other meanings.

A given name can be declared with only one meaning in the same block. Modules introduce further scope rules (Section 2.5).

Although Pascal is block structured, it is not clear from the report whether this means that the scope of a named entity is the entire block in which the entity is declared or whether the entity is known from the point of its declaration to the end of the given block [Jensen and Wirth, 1975].

The former interpretation is used in the Algol 60 report from which the block concept originates [Naur, 1962]. The latter meaning is implemented by most Pascal compilers and is the one described in the Edison report.

The requirement that a named entity must be declared before it is used makes it possible for a compiler to build a name table and verify that all names are used correctly during a single scan of the program text. In most cases this convention is quite natural since we are used to reading text in the order in which it is written. Occasionally, however, programmers are mystified by the compiler's refusal to accept an Edison program with the following structure:

```
array line [1:80] (char)
   . . .
proc program(
   proc writetext(value:  line))
array line [1:80] (char)
var x:  line

   . . .
begin . . . writetext(x) . . . end
```

The compiler insists that the statement

writetext(x)

contains a type error. The problem is an inadvertent use of two declarations of the type called line in nested blocks that are separated by more than 100 lines of text and which do not appear on the same page of text.

To the compiler these declarations introduce two different data types with the same name. The scope of the first line type extends from its declaration in the outer block up to the declaration of the second line type in the inner block. The second line type is valid in the rest of the program. This makes the parameter of the procedure writetext of the first type while the argument x of the procedure call is of the second type.

The record fields in Pascal do not follow the normal scope rules. If two variables x and y are declared as follows:

var x: **record** y, z: **char end**; y: boolean

the name y denotes a boolean variable when it stands alone but refers to a character field when it occurs in the variable symbol x.y. Although this convention seems natural enough when it is illustrated by example, it is nevertheless an exception that adds to the complexity of an already quite subtle set of naming rules.

In looking at the first Edison compiler I found that its most complicated part, the semantic analysis, introduced about 400 distinct names, of which fewer than 40 were field names of records. I decided that anyone who can invent 360 different names can surely invent another 40. Consequently, in Edison the scope of a field name (like any other name) extends from its declaration to the end of the block that contains the declaration. Although a field name y can only be used in a field variable symbol of the form x.y, it cannot be redeclared with another meaning in the same block.

Later I discuss the difficulties of explaining scope rules precisely in prose.

2.4.5 Procedure Calls

A procedure call of the form

Procedure name (Argument, . . . , Argument)

denotes execution of a procedure with a set of arguments. Each argument is either an expression, a variable, or another procedure.

Examples:

> writetext(text('Edison.'))
> gcd(189, 215)
> readint(accept, driveno)

A procedure may call itself recursively and may also be called simultaneously by concurrent processes (Section 2.6). Each call creates a fresh instance of the parameters and auxiliary variables. These entities exist only while the procedure body is being executed.

2.4.6 Library Procedures

An Edison program may include library procedure declarations of the form

> **lib** Procedure heading [Expression]

This describes a procedure body held on a backing store. When the program calls the library procedure, the expression is evaluated and the result is used to retrieve the procedure body from the library and execute it.

In the following example, the expression is a call of a function named load that returns the value of a program file with a given name:

> **lib proc** program(title: name;
>   **proc** accept(**var** value: char);
>   **proc** display(value: char);
>   . . .)
> [load(title)]

When this procedure is called as follows:

> program(name('edit'), accept, display, . . .)

it executes a program file named edit.

Notice that the Edison language makes no a priori assumptions about the structure of a given file system. These assumptions are only made in the function load, which is programmed in the language itself.

Library procedures have the form of complete programs. It is therefore possible in Edison to write programs that invoke the execution of other programs to an arbitrary depth. Library procedures may also be used as arguments in procedure calls.

The two features that make Edison suitable for operating system design are library procedures and procedure parameters (Section 2.4.3). There are no library procedures in Pascal.

2.5 MODULES

The invention of syntactic structures to describe self-contained parts of larger programs is one of the major achievements of software research. In Concurrent Pascal, these structures are called processes, monitors, and classes. In Modula and Edison they are known as modules.

2.5.1 Abstract Data Types

One of the main purposes of a program module is to implement the concept of an abstract data type—a data type that can be operated on only by a fixed set of operations. In Concurrent Pascal, abstract data types are implemented by means of a secure variant of Simula classes [Dahl, 1972]. In Edison I decided to use a very different idea inspired by Modula [Wirth, 1977].

Consider the problem of unpacking integer values from a sequence of disk pages. In Modula this can be done by means of the following module (Algorithm 2.1). The define clause shows that this module exports an entity named next to the surrounding block. The use clause indicates that the module uses (or imports) entities named page, pagelength, and get from the surrounding block.

The data structure of the module consists of two local variables which assume the value of a disk page and the index of the last value unpacked from that page.

```
module symbolinput;
    define next;
    use page, pagelength, get;

    var data: page;  index: integer;

    procedure next(var value: integer);
    begin
      if index = pagelength then
        get(data); index := 0
      end;
      index := index + 1;
      value := data[index]
    end next;

begin get(data); index := 0
end symbolinput
```

Algorithm 2.1

The procedure named next gets another disk page from the disk (if necessary) and unpacks the next integer value from the page. The initial operation described at the end of the module gets the first page from the disk and sets the index to zero.

The compiler ensures that the only operation performed on the data structure (following the initial operation) is the well-defined operation called next. This kind of module is appealing because it ensures the integrity of the data structure entirely by means of scope rules: The variables named data and index are local to the module and are unknown outside the module. The protection of the data structure is achieved at compile time without run-time support.

In Edison the same module looks as shown in Algorithm 2.2. The define clause has been replaced by an asterisk in front of the exported procedure (a notation borrowed from Pascal Plus [Welsh, 1980]). This simplifies the visual image of the module a bit and makes it unnecessary for the compiler to check whether all the entities mentioned in the define list are indeed declared within the module. On the negative side one must now scan the module visually to discover the operation it implements. The imported entities are known simply by virtue of the ordinary scope rules of nested blocks. So there is no use clause either in Edison.

This kind of module is an ideal structuring tool when it controls access to a single instance of a data structure that is hidden inside the module, as in this example. The initial operation ensures that the data structure is brought into a consistent initial state before it is operated on by the surrounding block.

```
module "symbol input"

    var data: page;  index: int

    *proc next(var value:  int)
    begin
      if index = pagelength do
        get(data); index := 0
      end;
      index := index + 1;
      value := data[index]
    end

begin get(data); index := 0 end
```

Algorithm 2.2

The module concept is less convenient when several instances of an abstract data type are needed. Algorithm 2.3 shows an Edison module that implements push and pop operations on stacks of integer values.

module

       array table [1:100] (int)
      *record stack (contents: table; size: int)

      *proc push(var x: stack; y: int)
        begin x.size := x.size + 1;
          x.contents[x.size] := y
        end

      *proc pop(var x: stack; var y: int)
        begin y := x.contents[x.size] ;
          x.size := x.size − 1
        end

      *proc newstack(var x: stack)
        begin x.size := 0 end

    begin skip end

Algorithm 2.3

In the surrounding block one or more stacks can be declared:

      var s, t: stack

and used as follows

      push(s, 15)   pop(t, value)

The initial operation of the module can no longer guarantee that all stacks are empty to begin with (since the stacks are declared in the surrounding block after the module). The surrounding block must do that by performing the operations

      newstack(s)   newstack(t)

on the stacks before using them to push and pop integer values.

Now, if the asterisk in front of the record type named stack would export not only the record type, but also its fields, it would be possible to perform meaningless operations on stacks outside the module, for example

$$s.size := -3$$

The rule that record fields cannot be exported from modules was introduced in Edison to ensure that the module procedures describe the only possible operations on stacks (apart from assignments and comparisons of the values of whole stacks).

In Concurrent Pascal, a stack can be described more elegantly by the type declaration shown in Algorithm 2.4.

```
type stack =
class

  var contents: array [1 .. 100] of integer;
    size:  0 .. 100;

  procedure entry push(y:  integer);
  begin size := size + 1;
    contents[size] := y
  end;

  procedure entry pop(var y:  integer);
  begin y := contents[size];
    size := size - 1
  end;

begin size := 0 end
```

Algorithm 2.4

An instance of this data type is declared and used as follows:

$$var\ s:\ stack$$

init s   s.push(15)   s.pop(value)

But the class concept is more complicated both to explain and implement because it combines the concepts of data types, procedures, and modules into a single, indivisible unit. By contrast, the module concept of Edison merely modifies the scope of a set of named entities of any kind. With the exception of fields, any named entity can be exported from a module by placing an asterisk in front of its declaration.

*2.5.2 Monitors

The significance of the monitor concept was that it imposed modularity on synchronizing operations used by concurrent processes. A monitor introduces an abstract data type and describes all the operations on it by means of procedures that can be called by concurrent processes. If several processes attempt to execute monitor procedures simultaneously, these procedures will be executed one at a time in unspecified order [Brinch Hansen, 1973] [Hoare, 1974].

In Concurrent Pascal, a message buffer for transmitting characters from one process to another can be declared as shown in Algorithm 2.5.

```
type buffer =
monitor

    var slot: char;  full: boolean;
        sender, receiver:  queue;

    procedure entry put(c:  char);
    begin if full then delay(sender);
        slot := c;  full := true;
        continue(receiver)
    end;

    procedure entry get(var c:  char);
    begin if not full then delay(receiver);
        c := slot;  full := false;
        continue(sender)
    end;

begin full := false end
```

Algorithm 2.5

The buffer is represented by a message slot of type character and a boolean indicating whether it is full or empty. Two variables of type queue are used to delay the sending and receiving processes until the buffer is empty and full, respectively.

Initially, the buffer is empty. The procedure named put delays the calling process (if necessary) until there is room in the buffer for another message. When that condition is satisfied, a character is placed in the buffer, making it full. Finally, the receiving process is continued if it is waiting for the message. (If the receiver queue is empty, the continue operation has no effect.)

The get operation is similar to the put operation.

Since the operations on the monitor variables must be performed one at a time, the following rules apply to queues: When a process delays its completion of a monitor operation, another process can perform a monitor operation. And when a process continues the execution of a delayed process, the former process immediately returns from the monitor procedure in which the continue operation was executed.

The whole monitor concept is a very intricate combination of shared variables, procedures, process scheduling, and modularity.

Here is Modula's variant of the monitor concept for a single buffer instance (Algorithm 2.6). Although monitors and queues are called interface modules and signals in Modula, the concepts are essentially the same.

```
interface module buffer;
    define get, put;

    var slot: char;  full: boolean;
        nonempty, nonfull:  signal;

    procedure put(c:  char);
    begin if full then wait(nonfull) end;
        slot:= c;   full := true;
        send(nonempty)
    end put;

    procedure get(var c:  char);
    begin if not full then wait(nonempty) end;
        c := slot;   full := false;
        send(nonfull)
    end;

    begin full := false end buffer
```

Algorithm 2.6

Now, I originally proposed process queues as an engineering tool to reduce the overhead of process scheduling on a single-processor computer [Brinch

Hansen, 1972]. Each queue is used to delay a process until the monitor variables satisfy a particular condition, such as

not full   or   full

When a process delays itself in a queue until a condition holds, it depends on another process to continue its execution when the condition is satisfied.

In 1972, Tony Hoare published a much more elegant mechanism for process scheduling in the form of the *conditional critical region*

with v **when** B **do** S

which delays a process until a variable v satisfies a condition B and then executes a statement S. The conditional regions on a given variable v are executed strictly one at a time in some order [Hoare, 1972b].

This beautiful concept requires a process to reevaluate a boolean expression B periodically until it yields the value true. The fear that this reevaluation would be too costly on a single processor motivated the introduction of queues (also called signals or conditions) as an engineering compromise between elegance of expression and efficiency of execution.

With the new inexpensive microprocessor technology now available, I feel that the much simpler concept of conditional critical regions should be preferred. Occasional inefficiency is of minor importance on a microprocessor.

Hoare's original proposal made it possible for operations on different shared variables, such as

with v1 **when** B1 **do** S1

and

with v2 **when** B2 **do** S2

to take place simultaneously. For Edison I decided to use the simplest form of the conditional critical region

when B **do** SL **end**

where SL is a statement list of the form S1; S2; . . . ; Sn. The execution of all *when statements* takes place strictly one at a time. If several processes need to evaluate (or reevaluate) scheduling conditions simultaneously, they will be able to do so one at a time in some fair order (for example, cyclically).

Measurements of concurrent systems have shown that in a well-designed system each process spends most of its time operating on local data and only a small fraction of its time exchanging data with other processes. The additional overhead of expression evaluation will therefore most likely be quite acceptable. This performance issue can, of course, be settled only by measurements of running Edison programs. But it is an intellectual gamble that I feel quite comfortable about.

A monitor in Edison is simply a module in which the procedure bodies consist of single when statements as illustrated by the buffer example (Algorithm 2.7).

Notice that Edison does not include the monitor concept. A monitor is constructed by using a programming style that combines the simpler concepts of modules, variables, procedures, and when statements. In addition, processes are no longer required to manipulate scheduling queues, since the when statements implement the necessary delays of processes. This form of a monitor is very close to the original proposal, which I called a "shared class" [Brinch Hansen, 1973].

Once this module has been programmed correctly, the compiler will ensure that the buffer is accessed only by the synchronized get and put operations. The module is now as secure as any monitor.

```
module "buffer"

    var slot: char;  full: bool

    *proc put(c: char)
    begin
       when not full do
          slot := c;  full := true
       end
    end

    *proc get(var c: char)
    begin
       when full do
          c:= slot;  full := false
       end
    end

begin full := false end
```

Algorithm 2.7

But the programmer is no longer tied to the monitor concept, but can use simpler concepts, such as semaphores (Algorithm 2.8).

module

      ***record** semaphore (value: int)

      ***proc** wait(**var** s: semaphore)
      begin
        when s.value $>$ 0 **do**
          s.value := s.value – 1
        end
      end

      ***proc** signal(**var** s: semaphore)
      begin
        when true **do**
          s.value := s.value + 1
        end
      end

      ***proc** newsem(**var** s: semaphore; n: int)
      begin s.value := n **end**

    begin skip end

Algorithm 2.8

Semaphores can then be used to implement a multislot buffer in which sending and receiving can take place simultaneously from different slots (Algorithm 2.9).

If the mutually exclusive operations are as simple as wait and signal (rather than entire monitor procedures), the conditional critical regions may well be more efficient in some cases than conventional monitors with scheduling queues.

```
module

    const n = 10 "slots"
    array table [1:n] (char)
    var ring: table;  head, tail: int;
        full, empty: semaphore

*proc put(c:  char)
  begin wait(empty);  ring[tail] := c;
      tail := tail mod n + 1;  signal(full)
  end

*proc get(var c:  char)
  begin wait(full);  c := ring[head];
      head := head mod n + 1;  signal(empty)
  end

begin head := 1;  tail := 1;
    newsem(full, 0);  newsem(empty, n)
end
```

Algorithm 2.9

*2.6 PROCESSES

In the RC 4000 multiprogramming system I dealt with the complexities of processes that may appear and disappear at any time during program execution [Brinch Hansen, 1970]. In Concurrent Pascal, I tried the opposite approach of processes that exist forever after their creation. This works quite well for operating systems and real-time programs which perform the same tasks over and over. In addition, it simplifies store allocation dramatically.

For Edison I selected a compromise between these two extremes. Processes described by a *concurrent statement* of the form

```
        cobegin 1 do SL1
        also 2 do SL2
            . . .
        also n do SLn end
```

can appear and disappear dynamically—but only at the same time! The concurrent statement was published with the following structure by Dijkstra in 1968:

```
        parbegin S1; S2; . . . ; Sn parend
```

I merely replaced the semicolons (which normally denote sequential execution) with the word **also** (to indicate simultaneity).

The process constants 1, 2, . . . , n were introduced to make it possible to select a particular processor in a multiprocessor system (usually because the given processor is the only one that is connected to a particular peripheral device). On a single-processor computer the process constants can either be ignored or used to define the storage requirements of processes. (If they are ignored, the simplest implementation strategy is to divide the available storage space evenly among the processes.)

Consider now two processes that exchange a sequence of characters terminated by a period through a buffer. In Concurrent Pascal the producer process can be declared as follows:

```
type producer =
process (buf:  buffer);
var x:  char;
begin read(x);
   while y <> '.' do
   begin buf.put(x);   read(x) end;
   buf.put(x)
end
```

To vary the theme a bit, the consumer will be programmed in Modula:

```
process consumer;
var y:  char;
begin get(buf, y);
   while y <> '.' do
      write(y);   get(buf, y)
   end;
   write(y)
end consumer
```

In both cases, a process is described by a special kind of module. These syntactic forms enable compilers to check that one process does not refer to the variables of another process—an extremely dangerous kind of programming error.

In Edison, the same operational security can be achieved by adopting a programming style in which processes are described by procedures called by concurrent statements (Algorithm 2.10). Since each procedure call creates a fresh instance of the local variables of the given procedure, and since these variables are accessible only to the calling process, this solution is as secure as any.

```
proc producer
var x:  char
begin read(x);
   while x <> '.' do
      put(x); read(x)
   end;
   put(x)
end

proc consumer
var y:  char
begin get(y);
   while y <> '.' do
      write(y);   get(y)
   end;
   write(y)
end

cobegin 1 do producer
also 2 do consumer end
```

Algorithm 2.10

On the other hand, the programmer can also write concurrent programs, such as the following, in Edison:

```
var x, y:  char
begin read(x);
   while x <> '.' do
      y := x;
      cobegin 1 do write(y)
      also 2 do read(x) end
   end;
   write(x)
end
```

Since the compiler provides no assistance in checking whether these processes refer simultaneously to the same variables without proper synchronization, such programs must be written with extreme care.

The added flexibility (and insecurity) of Edison compared to Concurrent Pascal will be viewed by some as a step backward and by others as a challenge. To me it is simply an experiment that will either confirm or contradict my current feeling that programming languages cannot be expected to support complex abstractions, but should instead make it reasonably convenient to adopt programming styles that use simpler concepts to construct the more complex ones. Needless to say, this makes the design of a programming language a delicate balance between the anarchy of assembly language and the straightjacket of highly specialized languages.

*2.7 INPUT/OUTPUT

In Concurrent Pascal, all input/output is handled by standard procedure calls of the form

$$io(\text{variable, operation, device})$$

The calling process is delayed until the operation is completed. In the meantime, other processes can continue to use the rest of the computer. The advantage of this approach is that a data transfer is just another sequential operation that takes a finite time and produces a reproducible result. Another benefit of making input/output an indivisible operation for a single process is that peripheral interrupts become irrelevant to the programmer. They are handled completely at the machine level as part of the implementation of the input/output operations.

The disadvantage of using a single standard procedure for low-level input/output is that the system kernel for the language must contain a separate piece of code for each kind of peripheral device. This means that industrial programmers must be prepared to extend the kernel (which is a nontrivial task since peripheral interrupts interact with the processor multiplexing).

In Modula, Niklaus Wirth offered a more practical solution in the form of *device modules* combined with device processes and device registers. The whole concept was tailored to the PDP 11 computers to enable programmers to write device procedures in the language itself. Algorithm 2.11 shows a device module that outputs one character at a time on a screen. The module consists of a device process, named driver, which is connected to an exported procedure, named display, through a set of variables used as a character buffer.

The standard procedure *doio* delays the device process until the screen produces an interrupt with the octal number 64B. Since the doio operation can be performed only by a device process and, since a device process must be hidden within a device module, the module defined above appears to be the simplest possible way of displaying a character on the screen. It does not seem to be possible to eliminate a device process and let a user process control the peripheral directly. This example shows that Modula (like Concurrent Pascal) attempts to support and enforce a particular programming style by means of very specialized language constructs.

```
device module screen [4];
    define display;
    var slot: char;  full: boolean;
        nonempty, nonfull: signal;

    procedure display(c: char);
    begin
        if full do wait(nonfull) end;
        slot := c; full := true; send(nonempty)
    end put;

    process driver [64B];
    var status [177564B]: bits;  buffer [177566B]: char;
    begin
        loop
            if not full do wait(nonempty) end;
            buffer := slot;  full := false;
            status[6] := true; doio; status[6] := false;
            send(nonfull)
        end
    end driver;

begin full := false; driver end screen
```

Algorithm 2.11

The Edison language implemented for the PDP 11 computers is called Edison-11. Since the language is designed to support inexpensive microprocessors, I decided to anticipate this use and ignore interrupts completely on the PDP 11 (even at the machine level).

In Edison-11, input/output is controlled by standard procedure calls of the form

place(device address, value)
obtain(device address, variable)
sense(device address, value)

The operation place(x, y) assigns the integer value y to the device register with the byte address x. The operation obtain(x, y) assigns the value of the device register with the byte address x to the integer variable y. The operation sense(x, y) compares the integer value y to the value of the device register with the byte address x. If some of the corresponding bits of the two values are both equal to one, the operation yields the value true; otherwise, it yields the value false.

Edison-11 also includes octal numerals of the form

#177564

to denote device addresses. This option is necessary because the computer manufacturer does not use the decimal system in the computer manuals. Why, I do not know.

A process described by a concurrent statement in Edison-11 can output a character directly on the screen by calling the following procedure:

```
proc display(c:  char)
const status = #177564;   buffer = #177566;
   ready = #200
begin
   when sense(status, ready) do
      place(buffer, int(c))
   end
end
```

The effect of executing the when statement is to delay the output until the status register shows that the device is ready.

A PDP 11 computer executes one process at a time. This continues until the process either terminates or attempts to execute a when statement in which the boolean expressions yield the value false. The waiting processes are executed in cyclical order in Edison-11. The simplicity of process scheduling makes the overhead of process switching five times shorter than in Concurrent Pascal (which is interrupt driven). The Edison-11 implementation ignores all interrupts.

The input or output of nonelementary data types requires the use of a standard function call

addr(y)

which yields the byte address of a variable y of any type. The operation place(x, addr(y)) assigns the address of the variable y to the device register with the address x. This operation is necessary to transfer data between the variable y and a block-oriented device, such as a disk or magnetic tape.

2.8 LANGUAGE DESCRIPTION

In 1967, the designer of the programming language Pascal, Niklaus Wirth, wrote that "the definition of a language, comprising its syntax specifying the set of well-formed sentences, and its semantics defining the meaning of these sentences, should not extend over more than 50 pages." The Edison report is comparable in size to the reports that define its predecessors: Algol 60 (43 pages), Pascal (38 pages), Concurrent Pascal (34 pages), and Modula (29 pages). The Edison report is 50 pages long. (The sizes of these reports are measured in pages of 50 lines each.)

The shortness of a language report is, of course, of no help unless it is written with complete clarity. As Wirth put it: "In programming, we are dealing with complicated issues, and the more complicated the issue is, the simpler the language must be to describe it. Sloppy use of language—be it English, German, Fortran, or PL/1—is an unmistakable symptom of inadequacy" [Wirth, 1976b].

The only language report that has been widely recognized as a model of clarity is the Algol 60 report written by Peter Naur. In 1967, Donald Knuth wrote that "the most notable feature of the Algol 60 report was the new standard it set for language definition." Unfortunately, as Tony Hoare said, the Algol 60 report was a considerable improvement over its successors [Hoare, 1973].

Even though the Pascal language was far more successful than Algol 60, Nico Habermann severely criticized Wirth for the imprecision of the Pascal report and pointed out that it was hiding some conceptual inconsistencies in the definition of data types [Habermann, 1973]. Peter Naur pointed out that the Concurrent Pascal report, which I wrote, suffered from similar problems.

The task of writing a language report that explains a programming language with complete clarity to its implementors and users may look deceptively easy to someone who hasn't done it before. But in reality it is one of the most difficult intellectual tasks in the field of programming.

In writing the Edison report I have benefited greatly from the constructive criticism of Peter Naur. Naur made almost no comments about my choice and design of language features. His main concern was the clarity of the report. I would write a complete draft of the language report and Naur would then point out what the weaknesses were and suggest broadly how they might be removed in my next draft. The following describes the stages of development which the Edison report went through over a period of two years.

The first Edison report of January 1979 used *syntax graphs* of the form shown in Fig. 2.1, with an explanation such as the following:

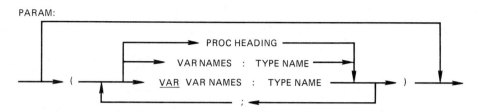

Fig. 2.1 A syntax graph.

"Each parameter declaration introduces a name to represent the parameter and specifies its type or procedure heading.

"A value parameter is a local variable which is assigned the value of an expression before the procedure is executed.

"A variable parameter denotes a variable which is bound to the procedure before it is executed. The symbol **var** *distinguishes a variable parameter from a value parameter.*

"A procedure parameter denotes another procedure which is bound to the given procedure before the latter is executed."

About this report, Naur wrote the following:

"The weaknesses that will be described in most cases are such that may cause only little difficulty to a reader who is familiar with, for example, reports on the language Pascal, and who is generous in his willingness to rely on his own ability to fill in open holes by guesses and to remove inconsistencies. With the view taken all such holes and inconsistencies are unacceptable and should be removed, as far as possible.

"There is a poor connection between the formal syntactic description and the prose explanation."

I had used syntax graphs because they enable a programmer to see quite complex structures at a glance. Unfortunately, when a complicated concept is presented under a single name, the substructures of the graph have no names and cannot easily be referred to in the text. So, although the text refers to the concept of a "parameter declaration," the graph does not reveal what it is. The reader must also guess what the syntax of value, variable, and procedure parameters looks like. Note also that rather than explaining the meaning of certain concepts (such as variable parameters) the first report would use suggestive (but undefined) terms such as "binding."

In the second Edison report of July 1979 a parameter list was defined as follows (now using an extended *Backus–Naur form* instead of syntax graphs):

Parameter list:
    Parameter group [';' Parameter group] *
Parameter group:
    Value parameter group # Variable parameter group
Value parameter group:
    Parameter name [',' Parameter name] * ':' Type name
Variable parameter group:
    'var' Parameter name [',' Parameter name] *
       ':' Type name
Parameter name:
    Name

(In this version of the language I had tentatively excluded the use of procedures as parameters of other procedures.)

These syntactic forms were now explained as follows:

"A parameter list consists of a sequence of parameter groups. Each parameter group is either a value parameter group or a variable parameter group.

"A value parameter group introduces one or more names, called parameter names, to denote value parameters. Each value parameter is a local variable that is assigned the value of an argument before the procedure block is executed.

"A variable parameter group introduces one or more names to denote variable parameters. Each variable parameter denotes a variable argument which is selected before the procedure block is executed. During the execution of the procedure block all operations performed on the variable parameter stand for the same operations performed on the variable argument. The variable parameter is said to be bound to the variable argument during the execution of the procedure block."

The concept of a parameter list is now presented as the composition of four simpler concepts. Each concept is described by a syntactic rule that introduces a name for the concept and defines its syntax. The prose explanation carefully follows the syntactic rules and explains their meaning using the same terminology. As a minor detail the meaning of variable binding is now explained.

The idea of using an abundance of simple syntactic rules to introduce names for most concepts, so that the text can refer directly to these definitions, had not occurred to me previously. But once you realize that syntactic rules can be used to define terminology (and not just syntax), the job of writing a language report becomes far more well defined. When the syntactic rules become very trivial the syntax graphs lose their visual appeal and appear bulky and clumsy. So I returned to the BNF notation, which has the great advantage that it can be included in program texts as comments.

Later, when I wrote the Edison compiler, I found that the syntactic rules used in the report were so short that each of them conveniently could be recognized by a single procedure with the same name as the syntactic rule. Each procedure is now preceded by the corresponding syntactic rule written as a comment in BNF notation.

About the second report, Naur wrote this:

"The report is a vast improvement over the previous version in clarity, consistency, and completeness. The remaining weaknesses, described below in detail, are to a large extent concerned merely with finer matters of conceptual clarity."

After this pleasant introduction, Naur goes on to enumerate 79 conceptual problems. The first of these is that "a number of weaknesses of the description can be traced to a general disinclination to accept abstract notions, not uniquely associated with syntactic entities of the language, as well-defined useful constituents of the language and its description."

The conceptual difficulties of trying to describe all concepts purely in terms of their notation are both philosophical and practical. If, for example, the notion of data value is purely notational, it is quite difficult to explain why the relation

$$\text{'A'} = \text{char}(65)$$

is true for the ASCII character set. But the matter becomes quite simple if both symbols are viewed as different notations for the same abstract concept—the first capital letter of the alphabet.

In the third report of January 1980 the distinction between fixed values and the notation used to represent them in the language was made as follows: "A constant is a fixed value of a fixed type," and "A constant symbol denotes a constant."

The distinction between an *abstract concept* and the *symbol* that denotes the concept is immediately obscured when a syntactic rule is given the same name as the abstract concept. In the second Edison report, a variable used as an operand was described by a syntactic rule named variable:

Variable:
Whole variable # Subvariable

The report explained that "a variable denotes either a whole variable or a subvariable." For a purist this is already unsatisfactory. Does the term "variable" in that sentence refer to the abstract concept of a variable that exists during program execution, or does it refer to one of the symbols in the program text described by the syntactic form named variable? For the writer of the language report it becomes downright awkward to describe what action a processor takes when a variable is used as an operand in a program. If we stick strictly to the rule of using the name introduced by the syntactic rule, the result is the following cryptic sentence: "The evaluation of a variable causes the processor to locate the variable in the current context."

In the third report, the matter was settled by making a distinction between a variable (which is a named entity that may assume any of the values of a known type) and a variable symbol (which denotes a variable used as an operand). It was now easy to explain that "the evaluation of a variable symbol involves locating the corresponding variable in the current context."

The failure to make this conceptual distinction pervades most language reports. In the Pascal, Concurrent Pascal, and Modula reports one finds syntactic forms named constant, number, type, and variable instead of the more appropriate terms constant symbol, numeral, type definition, and variable symbol (or similar ones).

After reading both the first and second drafts of the Edison report, Naur felt that "the central concept of types is not properly introduced, while the many different aspects of it are scattered around in an unsystematic and confusing manner." In the third version of the report I tried to clarify the *type concept* and its relation to the abstract notions of *value* and *operation*. I did not, however, succeed in organizing the report into sections each describing all the aspects of a single type in one place.

The problem is that the type concept pervades the whole language. To explain even a simple type, such as boolean, in all its aspects, one must discuss constants, ranges, variables, expressions, functions, and statements as they relate to boolean values. Now that is practically the whole language right there. So even to begin this section, one has to assume that the reader already understands all these concepts in general. And then one has to do it all over again for integers, characters, enumerations, arrays, records, and sets. It ends up being a very repetitive report in which the same story is told seven times. And that is, of course, because the language is designed in such a way that all the types have very similar properties which are described by very similar syntax.

After spending about 25 full working days trying to write a report along those lines I gave up and wrote another one instead (the third version). As a compromise, I now described several facets of each kind of type in the same section: namely, the introduction of a new data type by means of a type declaration, the representation of values of the type by constants or constructors, and the meaning of the operators that apply to these values.

The sections on data types were followed by sections describing the general properties of variables, expressions, statements, and procedures.

The concept of *scope* is explained quite concisely in the Algol 60 report:

"Every block automatically introduces a new level of nomenclature. This is realized as follows: Any identifier occurring within the block may through a suitable declaration be specified to be local to the block in question. This means (a) that the entity represented by this identifier inside the block has no existence outside it and (b) that any entity represented by this identifier outside the block is completely inaccessible inside the block.

"Identifiers occurring within a block and not being declared to this block will be non-local to it, i.e. will represent the same entity inside the block and in the level immediately outside it."

"Since a statement of a block may again itself be a block the concepts local and non-local must be understood recursively."

"No identifier may be declared more than once in any one block head."

One may complain about the complexity of block structure but not, I think, about the precision with which it is explained in the Algol 60 report. In the Pascal report written 10 years later the explanation of the same concept is much more incomplete:

"All identifiers introduced in the formal parameter part, the constant definition part, the type definition part, the variable-, procedure or function declaration parts are local *to the procedure declaration which is called the* scope *of these identifiers. They are not known outside their scope."*

This explanation fails to distinguish between a name and the entity it denotes. Since a name can be used with different meanings in different blocks, it is not the name itself that is unknown outside a given block but the use of the name to denote a given entity declared inside the block. In short, it is named entities (rather than names) which have scopes. I too failed to make that distinction in the earlier Edison reports.

More important, the explanation above from the Pascal report does not explain which entity a name denotes when it is declared with different meanings in nested blocks. To paraphrase an earlier remark, such weaknesses of the Pascal report have fortunately caused little difficulty for readers who are already familiar with the Algol 60 report.

The Concurrent Pascal and Modula reports also do not succeed in explaining scope rules precisely. This is much more unfortunate since these languages introduce new forms of modularity which serve primarily to change the traditional scope rules of block-structured languages. My present attempts to explain these rules are contained in the section "Named Entities" in the Edison report.

Having deprived myself of the opportunity to gloss over ill-understood issues in the Edison report, it was quite embarrassing to explain the effect of executing processes described by *concurrent statements*. Although a programmer may have no difficulty understanding a particular concurrent statement, the language designer faces the much harder task of explaining in a few paragraphs the meaning of every conceivable use of this idea.

Unfortunately, one can only make a simple statement about the most trivial (and uninteresting) use of concurrent processes, which is the following: "If concurrent processes only operate on private variables and disjoint, common variables then the effect of executing a concurrent statement is the same as the effect of executing the process statements one at a time in any order."

As soon as processes begin to communicate, one needs the whole apparatus of the Gries–Owicki theory to reason about the effects of using semaphores, buffers, monitors, and so on [Owicki, 1976]. Even so, processes must satisfy very rigid assumptions for the theory to apply. Although one can design language features (such as monitors) which enable a compiler to check that some of these assumptions are satisfied, one cannot expect a programming language to capture all aspects of well-behaved concurrent programs. And even if one could, it would not be very helpful to repeat the entire theory behind these concepts in a language report.

The difficulty of explaining what concurrent processes really do will, of course, arise in any report that describes a concurrent programming language. In yet another appeal to the generous reader the Concurrent Pascal and Modula reports evade the issue by the suggestive use of undefined phrases to the effect that "all processes are executed concurrently." In writing the Edison report I decided to make the difficulty explicit by the following statement:

> *"If concurrent processes operate on intersecting, common variables then the effect of executing a concurrent statement is generally unpredictable since nothing is known about the order in which the processes operate on these variables. However, by restricting the operations on intersecting variables to well-defined disciplines under the control of modules, procedures, and when statements it is possible to formulate concurrent statements that make predictable use of such variables. The theories used to reason about concurrent statements, when statements, and common variables are beyond the scope of this report."*

In effect, the report says that one can write meaningless Edison programs that will produce unpredictable results. But it does not prescribe how to avoid doing this. This is surely a startling property of a programming tool. The report does, however, say that when this happens even the most basic programming concepts can lose their meaning:

"The meaning of variable retrieval and assignment defined earlier is valid only if these operations are performed one at a time on a given variable. Concurrent processes can ensure that this assumption is satisfied by performing all operations on intersecting, common variables within when statements."

The execution of recursive procedures and concurrent statements will generally create multiple instances of named entities, such as variables. Furthermore, procedures used as parameters of other procedures can have side effects on some of these variable instances (and not necessarily the most recent ones!). In such cases, the language report must make it possible to decide which variable instance a process refers to at any given time.

In the fourth version of the Edison report (September 1980) the dynamic meaning of names is explained in terms of the so-called context of a process. This concept is introduced at the beginning of the report as follows:

"When a process executes a statement it operates on known entities selected from a set of entities called the current context of a process."

(A language implementor might say more loosely that a context is an abstract description of that part of a stack that is currently accessible to a process by following the chain of static links.)

Subsequent sections of the report then explain how the initial context of an executed program is established and how it is changed by the execution of procedure calls and concurrent statements.

A key idea is to associate contexts with procedures as well as processes. When a procedure body is executed by a process the current context of the process is attached as an attribute to all the local procedures declared in the body. If one of these procedures is called directly by the process, its execution will take place in the context associated with the procedure. And if the procedure and its current context are bound to a parameter of another procedure, the rule above still applies: When a procedure parameter is called, it is executed in the context currently associated with the procedure parameter.

So the effect of any procedure call is now explained by a single rule.

This concludes the discussion of the linguistic difficulties that a language designer is faced with during the writing of a language report. The writing of the Edison report was far more difficult and time consuming than the selection of the language features and the design of the first compiler.

The remarkably few shortcomings of Algol 60 and Pascal have also been discussed by Knuth [1967] and Welsh [1977]. The reports by Hoare [1973] and Wirth [1976b] contain many useful hints on programming language design.

3

THE EDISON LANGUAGE REPORT

3.1 LANGUAGE OVERVIEW

This report defines the programming language Edison. The language is suitable both for teaching the principles of concurrent programming and for designing reliable real-time programs for a multiprocessor system.

The overriding concern in the design of Edison was to achieve simplicity in the design of medium-sized programs of 1000 to 2000 lines of text. This aim led to the selection of a small number of abstract concepts for modular programming. In particular, the issues of modularity, concurrency, and synchronization were separated into distinct language features.

An Edison program describes operations on named entities called constants, variables, and procedures. The constants and variables have data values of fixed types. The types determine the possible values of these entities and restrict the operations that can be performed on them.

The data types integer, boolean, and character are standard types. Other types are introduced by enumerating their values or by describing how the values are composed from other values. The composition methods for new types are the well-known arrays, records, and sets. Every type has a name, and two operands are of the same type only if their types are denoted by the same name and have the same scope.

The computation of new data values from existing values is described by expressions in which the operands are constants, variables, and function calls, while the operators are the conventional arithmetic, boolean, set, and relational operators. The computation of composite values in terms of other values is described by expression lists called constructors.

Statements describe operations such as the assignment of values to variables and the execution of procedures. The if, while, and when statements describe a choice among substatements to be executed depending on the truth values of expressions. The concurrent statement denotes simultaneous execution of several substatements as concurrent processes. Process synchronization is controlled by when statements. The execution of a when statement delays a process until an expression is true and then performs an operation on the common variables shared by the processes. Concurrent processes can only execute when statements one at a time.

The named entities and statements of a program are grouped into blocks of two kinds, called procedures and modules. Blocks can be combined to form other blocks in a nested fashion.

A procedure is a group of named entities and statements that describe an operation on operands of fixed types. The operands (known as parameters) may vary from one execution of the procedure to another. Each parameter is either a variable or another procedure. The named entities introduced by a procedure are local to the procedure and cannot be used outside it. Each execution of the procedure creates a fresh instance of its parameters and local variables. These entities disappear again when the execution of the procedure terminates.

A module is a group of named entities that fall into two categories: (1) local entities that can be used only within the module, and (2) exported entities that can be used both within the module and within the immediately surrounding block. The module entities exist as long as the entities of the immediately surrounding block. A module serves to ensure that its local entities are operated on only by well-defined procedures which are exported from the module to the immediately surrounding block. To ensure that the local variables are initialized before they are used, a module includes a statement part that is executed when the module entities are created.

3.2 SYMBOLS AND SENTENCES

The programming language Edison is a formal notation in which programs can be written. The programs are texts composed of symbol sequences known as sentences.

The language is described in terms of syntactic forms. A syntactic form is a named class of symbols or sentences with common properties. The definition of a syntactic form consists of syntactic rules that define how sentences of the form are composed and semantic rules that define the meaning of these sentences.

3.2.1 Syntactic Rules

A syntactic rule described in a variant of the Backus–Naur notation has the form

$$N:\ E$$

where N stands for the name of a syntactic form and E stands for a syntax expression that defines the corresponding class of sentences. The name N consists of a capital letter possibly followed by small letters and spaces.

Example of a syntactic rule:
   Parameter group:
      ['var'] Variable group # Procedure heading

A syntax expression has the form

$$T1\ \#\ T2\ \#\ \ldots\ \#\ Tn$$

where T1, T2, . . . , Tn stand for syntax terms that define classes of sentences. A sentence of this form is composed by writing a sentence belonging to any one of the classes.

Example of a syntax expression:
   ['var'] Variable group # Procedure heading

A syntax term has the form

$$F1\ \ F2\ \ \ldots\ \ Fn$$

where F1, F2, . . . , Fn stand for syntax factors that define classes of sentences. A sentence of this form is composed by writing a sentence of each class in the order shown.

Example of a syntax term:
   ['var'] Variable group

A syntax factor has one of four forms:

(1)   [E] *

This form is an abbreviation for the syntax expression Empty # E # EE # EEE

. . . , where the name Empty denotes the empty sentence and E denotes a syntax expression. A sentence of this form is composed by writing either nothing or a finite sequence of sentences of the class E.

Example of a syntax factor:
> [Letter # Digit # '_'] *

(2)   [E]

This form is an abbreviation for the syntax expression Empty # E. A sentence of this form is composed by writing either nothing or a sentence of the class E.

Example of a syntax factor:
> ['var']

(3)   N

where N denotes the name of a syntactic form. A sentence of this form is composed according to the syntactic rule named N.

Example of a syntax factor:
> Variable group

(4)   'C1 C2 . . . Cn'

where C1, C2, . . . , Cn denote characters. A symbol of this form is composed of the characters written in the order shown. In particular, the syntax factors '#', ':', '[',']', '*', and '"' denote the characters #, :, [,], *, and ' used as program symbols.

Example of a syntax factor:
> 'var'

3.2.2 Characters

Character:
> Graphic character # New line character

Graphic character:
> Letter # Digit # Special character # Space

Letter:
> 'a' # 'b' # 'c' # 'd' # 'e' # 'f' # 'g' # 'h' # 'i' #
> 'j' # 'k' # 'l' # 'm' # 'n' # 'o' # 'p' # 'q' # 'r' #
> 's' # 't' # 'u' # 'v' # 'w' # 'x' # 'y' # 'z'

Digit:
> '0' # '1' # '2' # '3' # '4' # '5' # '6' # '7' # '8' # '9'

Special character:
> '"' # '"' # '(' # ')' # '*' # '+' # ',' # '-' # '.' #
> ':' # ';' # '<' # '=' # '>' # '[' # ']' # '_'

Characters are used to form basic symbols (Section 3.2.3). A graphic character is represented by a graphic picture or the deliberate omission thereof (a space). A new line character marks the end of each line of text.

The character set may be extended with more letters and special characters. In particular, the letters may be extended with capital letters. The meaning of capital letters is explained in Sections 3.2.3 and 3.4.

3.2.3 Basic Symbols

Basic symbol:
    Special symbol # Word symbol # Name # Numeral #
    Graphic symbol
Special symbol:
    '+' # '-' # '*' # '=' # '<>' # '<' # '<=' # '>' # '>=' #
    ':=' # '(' # ')' # '[' # ']' # '.' # ',' # ':' # ';'
Word symbol:
    'also' # 'and' # 'array' # 'begin' # 'cobegin' #
    'const' # 'div' # 'do' # 'else' # 'end' # 'enum' #
    'if' # 'in' # 'lib' # 'mod' # 'module' # 'not' #
    'or' # 'post' # 'pre' # 'proc' # 'record' # 'set' #
    'skip' # 'val' # 'var' # 'when' # 'while'

The basic symbols are either special symbols, word symbols, names (Section 3.4), numerals (Section 3.7.1), or graphic symbols (Section 3.7.5).

The special symbols and the word symbols have fixed meanings which will be defined later.

Any capital letter used in a word symbol is considered equivalent to the corresponding small letter. In this report the word symbols are printed in boldface type.

3.2.4 Separators

Separator:
    Space # New line character # '"' Comment '"'
Comment:
    [Character] *

The character " cannot occur within a comment.

Any basic symbol preceded by one or more separators stands for the basic symbol itself. Two adjacent word symbols or names must be separated by at least one separator.

Example:
    "This is a comment"

3.2.5　Character Strings

Character list:
　　''' Graphic character '''
　　　　[',' ''' Graphic character '''] *
Character string:
　　''' Graphic character [Graphic character] *'''

A character list denotes a sequence of graphic characters. Character lists are used in constructors (Section 3.12).

A character string is an abbreviation for a character list that contains the same sequence of graphic characters.

Examples of character lists:
　　' '
　　'E', 'd', 'i', 's', 'o', 'n'
Examples of character strings:
　　' '
　　'Edison'

3.3　PROGRAMS AND EXECUTION

A program is a description of one or more related data processes, each process taking place in a number of separate steps. In each step a well-defined action (an operation) is performed on a set of entities (the operands).

The act of following a program text and performing the operations described by it is called the execution of the program (and its operations). A person or device that executes a program (or part of it) is called a processor.

The operands of a program generally denote data values that either remain fixed (constants) or change during the execution (variables).

The operations are generally rules for deriving new data values (results) from previous data values given by operands. Operations may also use data values to determine the order in which subsequent operations are to be executed.

The execution of an operation will have one of three outcomes:

(1) *Termination.* After a finite time the processor completes the operation.

(2) *Failure.* After a finite time the processor detects that the operation is meaningless and cannot continue the execution of the program.

(3) *Cycling.* The processor executes the same cycle of operations endlessly.

The execution of certain operations may be influenced by properties that are not fully described in this report since they vary from processor to processor. Such properties are said to be system dependent.

A program may prescribe a sequence of operations to be carried out strictly one at a time. Such a sequence is known as a process. A program may also allow several processes to take place simultaneously. They are known as concurrent processes.

3.4 NAMED ENTITIES

Name:
    Letter [Letter # Digit # '_'] *

Any capital letter used in a name is considered equivalent to the corresponding small letter. The word symbols cannot be used as names. Apart from that, names may be chosen freely.

A name denotes an entity used in a program. The entity is either a constant (Section 3.6), a data type (Section 3.5), a record field (Section 3.9), a variable (Section 3.13), or a procedure (Section 3.16).

Examples:
    char
    s
    table
    matrix1
    rc4000a
    end_of_file

3.4.1 Standard Names

Standard name:
    'bool' # 'char' # 'false' # 'int' # 'true'

The standard names denote the standard types bool, char, int, and the truth values false, true (Section 3.7). These names can be used throughout a program without being declared.

3.4.2 Declarations

Declaration:
    Constant declaration list # Type declaration #
    Variable declaration list # Procedure declaration #
    Module declaration

A declaration introduces names to denote program entities and describes some of their properties. The entities are either constants (Section 3.6.1), types (Section 3.5.1), variables (Section 3.13.1), procedures (Section 3.16), or modules (Section 3.4.4).

The use of a name within a program to denote an entity must be preceded by a declaration that introduces the name and describes the entity it stands for (unless the name is a standard name). A declaration of an entity is generally valid within one block only (Section 3.4.3). Outside this block the same name can be declared and used with other meanings.

3.4.3 Blocks, Scopes, and Contexts

A block is a piece of program text consisting of (1) declarations of named entities, and (2) statements that define operations on these entities. The only possible kinds of blocks are procedures (Section 3.16), modules (Section 3.4.4), and programs (Section 3.17).

Generally, a block Q can be a part of another block P, in which case P is said to contain Q. The block Q is then called an inner block of P, while P is called a surrounding block of Q. In general a program will consist of a hierarchy of nested blocks.

The innermost block in which a declaration of a named entity appears is called the origin of that declaration.

The scope of a named entity x is that part of the program text in which the name x may be used to denote that entity. A named entity is said to be known within its scope.

The scope generally extends from the declaration of the entity to the end of its origin, with the further additional rules:

(1) If the origin is a module M, the scope may be extended to the end of the immediately surrounding block B. The entity is then said to be exported from M to B (Section 3.4.4).

(2) If the same name is declared with another meaning in an inner block of the origin, the scope does not include the inner block.

A given name can be declared with only one meaning in the same block. And a name cannot be exported to a surrounding block in which the same name is declared with another meaning.

The meaning of a name used at some point in a block is determined by the following rules:

(1) *Local entity.* If the use of the name is preceded by a declaration in the same block of an entity of that name, the use of the name denotes that entity.

(2) *Exported entity.* If the use of the name is preceded by a module in the same block from which a declared entity of that name is exported to the block, the use of the name denotes that entity.

(3) *Global entity.* If neither of the above apply, the name has the same meaning that it has in the immediately surrounding block at the point where the given block begins.

When several processes are executed concurrently, or when a single process calls one or more procedures recursively, several instances of a named entity may exist simultaneously. At any given moment, however, a process can operate only on a single instance of every entity that is known to the process at that moment.

When a process executes a statement it operates on known entities selected from a set of entities called the current context of the process. The context consists of (1) an instance of every entity declared in the procedures surrounding the statement, and (2) an instance of every entity declared in the modules contained in these procedures.

When a process refers to a known entity an instance of that entity is located in the current context of the process in accordance with the scope rules.

Throughout this report the phrase "the current context" refers to the current context of the process that performs a given operation.

The dynamic changes of contexts are explained further in Sections 3.4.4, 3.15.3, 3.15.7, and 3.17.

3.4.4 Modules

A module is a block that introduces two kinds of named entities known as local and exported entities. The module also describes an initial operation on these entities.

The local entities can be used only within the module. The exported entities can be used both within the module and within the block that immediately surrounds the module.

A module is contained either in a procedure or in another module. When a procedure body is executed an operation known as module initialization is performed on all modules declared within the procedure body.

The initialization of a module M takes place in three steps:

(1) The local and exported entities declared in M are created and added to the current context.

(2) The modules declared in M are initialized one at a time in the order written.

(3) The initial operation of M is performed.

When the execution of the procedure terminates, the entities of the module (and those of its inner modules) disappear again.

Module declaration:
    'module' [Local declaration # Exported declaration] *
        Statement part
Local declaration:
    Declaration
Exported declaration:
    '*' Declaration
Statement part:
    'begin' Statement list 'end'

A module declaration describes a module by means of declarations of local and exported entities and by a statement part that describes the initial operation by means of a statement list (Section 3.15).

An export symbol * in front of a module declaration has no effect. Exported entities are discussed further in Sections 3.6.1, 3.7.6, 3.9, 3.10, 3.11, 3.13.1, and 3.16.

Example:

> **module**
>   **const** max = 10
>   **array** stack [1:max] (int)
>   **var** lifo : stack;   size : int
>
>   *__proc__ push(x : int)
>   **begin** size := size + 1; lifo[size] := x **end**
>
>   *__proc__ pop(**var** x : int)
>   **begin** x := lifo[size] ; size := size – 1 **end**
>
>   *__proc__ empty : bool
>   **begin val** empty := (size = 0) **end**
>
> **begin** size := 0 **end**

3.5 VALUES, OPERATIONS, AND TYPES

Data are physical phenomena chosen by convention to represent facts or ideas. The same fact or idea can be represented by a variety of different data. The common notion of data representing the same fact or idea will be called a value.

Data values are grouped into classes called types. A type is a named set of values. Each value is of one and only one type.

The operands that yield data values during execution are constants (Section 3.6), variables (Section 3.13), and expressions (Section 3.14).

Any value yielded by an operand during execution will be of one and only one type. The operand type can be determined from the program text without executing it.

Standard operations on values are denoted by symbols called operators. New operations are described in terms of previously defined operations by means of procedures (Section 3.16).

Every operation applies to operands of fixed types and delivers results of fixed types.

The types integer, boolean, and character are standard types—types that are available without being declared. All other types must be introduced by means of type declarations.

3.5.1 Type Declarations

Type declaration:
    Enumeration type declaration # Record type declaration #
    Array type declaration # Set type declaration

A type declaration describes a new type which is either an enumeration type (Section 3.7.6), record type (Section 3.9), array type (Section 3.10), or set type (Section 3.11).

3.6 CONSTANTS

A constant is a fixed value of a fixed type.

Constant symbol:
    Numeral # Truth symbol # Character symbol #
    Enumeration symbol # Constant synonym

A constant symbol denotes a constant and is either a numeral (Section 3.7.1), a truth symbol (Section 3.7.3), a character symbol (Section 3.7.5), an enumeration symbol (Section 3.7.6), or a constant synonym (Section 3.6.1).

3.6.1 Constant Declarations

Constant declaration list:
    'const' Constant declaration
        [';' Constant declaration] *

Constant declaration:
    Constant synonym '=' Constant symbol
Constant synonym:
    Name

Every constant declaration introduces a name, called a constant synonym, to denote a constant. A constant declaration cannot be of the form x = x, where x is the synonym.

The scope rules (Section 3.4.3) apply to declared constants. A constant c declared in a module is exported to the immediately surrounding block by exporting the constant declaration list that introduces c (Section 3.4.4).

Example:
    const namelength = 12; on = true; last = '.';
        nl = char(10); lf = nl

3.7 ELEMENTARY TYPES

An elementary type consists of a finite set of successive values, called elementary values.

The values of any elementary type can be mapped onto a finite set of successive integer values (and vice versa). The integer value that corresponds to an elementary value x is called the ordinal value of x and is denoted int(x).

The elementary types comprise the standard types integer, boolean, and character as well as the enumeration types introduced by type declarations.

3.7.1 Type Integer

The standard type integer is an elementary type denoted by the standard name int. The integer values are a finite set of successive whole numbers, including both positive and negative values. The range of integers is system dependent. For any integer value x we have int(x) = x.

Numeral:
    Digit [Digit] *

A numeral is a conventional decimal notation for a nonnegative integer value. Negative integer values must be denoted by expressions (Section 3.14).

Examples:
    0
    1351

3.7.2 Arithmetic Operators

The arithmetic operators apply to operands of type integer and yield a result of type integer. When applied to two operands of type integer, the operators +, –, *, **div**, **mod** denote addition, subtraction, multiplication, division, and modulo, respectively. The results of x **div** y and x **mod** y are the truncated quotient of x divided by y and the remainder of x **div** y. They satisfy the relation

$$x = (x \ \mathbf{div} \ y) * y + x \ \mathbf{mod} \ y$$

When applied to a single operand of type integer, + and – are conventional sign operators.

An arithmetic operation terminates if the result is within the range of integers; otherwise, it fails.

3.7.3 Type Boolean

The standard type boolean is an elementary type denoted by the standard name bool.

Truth symbol:
    'false' # 'true'

The truth symbols are standard names that denote the boolean values. The boolean values have the ordinal values int(false) = 0 and int(true) = 1.

3.7.4 Boolean Operators

The boolean operators **not, and, or** denote negation, disjunction, and conjunction, respectively. They apply to one or two operands of type boolean and yield a result of type boolean according to the following rules:

not false = true	**not** true = false
x **and** false = false	x **and** true = x
x **or** false = x	x **or** true = true

where x denotes an arbitrary boolean value. A boolean operation always terminates.

3.7.5 Type Character

The standard type character is an elementary type denoted by the standard name char. The set of characters and their ordinal values are system dependent (Section 3.2.2).

Character symbol:
    Graphic symbol # Control symbol
Graphic symbol:
    ''' Graphic character '''
Control symbol:
    'char' '(' Numeral ')'

A character symbol denotes a value of type character. A graphic symbol 'c' denotes the graphic character c. A control symbol char(n) denotes the character with the ordinal value n.

Examples:
    'a'
    '0'
    ','
    char(10)

3.7.6 Enumeration Types

Enumeration type declaration:
    'enum' Type name '(' Enumeration symbol list ')'
Enumeration symbol list:
    Enumeration symbol [',' Enumeration symbol] *
Type name:
    Name
Enumeration symbol:
    Name

An enumeration type declaration introduces a name, called a type name, to denote an elementary type and introduces a list of names, called enumeration symbols, to denote the successive values of the type.

The values of an enumeration type enum $T(c_0, c_1, \ldots, c_n)$ have the ordinal values $int(c_0) = 0$, $int(c_1) = 1, \ldots, int(c_n) = n$.

The scope rules (Section 3.4.3) apply to an enumeration type and its values. An enumeration type declared in a module can be exported together with its values to the immediately surrounding block (Section 3.4.4).

Examples:
>   **enum** task(flow, scan, log)
>   **enum** filekind(empty, scratch, ascii, code)

3.7.7 Elementary Constructors

Elementary constructor:
>   Type name '(' Expression ')'

An elementary constructor denotes a mapping of the values of one elementary type onto the values of a (usually different) elementary type. The type name must denote an elementary type and the expression must be of an elementary type.

The elementary constructor int(x) denotes the ordinal value of an elementary value x of type T. If y is the ordinal value of x, that is, int(x) = y, then T(y) = x. For a value y of any elementary type we have T(y) = T(int(y)).

Examples:
>   int(slot)
>   bool(1 – x)
>   char(x + int('0'))
>   task(x)

3.7.8 Elementary Relations

The relational operators =, <>, <, <=, >, and >= denote the relations equal, not equal, less, not greater, greater, and not less. These operators apply to two operands of the same elementary type and yield a result of type boolean.

These operators have their conventional meaning for operands of type integer: they yield the value true if the operand values satisfy the relations, and the value false if they do not. If x and y are values of another elementary type, then x = y has the same value as int(x) = int(y), and similarly for the other relations.

These operations always terminate.

3.8 RANGES

A range is a finite set of successive elementary values of the same type from a lower bound x to an upper bound y both included (where x <= y). The type of the values is known as the range type.

Range symbol:
    Lower bound ':' Upper bound
Lower bound:
    Constant symbol
Upper bound:
    Constant symbol

A range symbol denotes a range. The bounds are denoted by constant symbols which must be of the same elementary type (the range type).

Ranges are used to define the possible index values of array types (Section 3.10).

Examples:
    1 : namelength
    false : true
    'a' : 'b'
    flow : log

3.9 RECORD TYPES

A record type consists of a finite set of values, called record values. Each record value consists of a finite sequence of other values known as fields. Each field is of some known type. The set of record values consists of all the possible sequences of the possible field values.

Record type declaration:
    'record' Type name '(' Field list ')'
Field list:
    Field group [';' Field group]*
Field group:
    Field name [',' Field name]* ':' Field type
Field name:
    Name
Field type:
    Type name

A record type declaration introduces a type name to denote a record type. The field list introduces names, called field names, to denote the fields. A group of fields have the known type given by another type name, called the field type.

A record type declaration cannot use its own type name as a field type. The scope rules (Section 3.4.3) apply to a record type and its fields. A record type declared within a module can be exported to the immediately surrounding block (Section 3.4.4), but the corresponding field names remain local to the module and cannot be exported from it.

Examples:
    record semaphore(count : int)
    record time(hour, minute, second : int)
    record attributes(kind : filekind;
       address : int; protected : bool)
    record entry(id : name; attr : attributes)

3.9.1 Record Constructors

Record constructor:
    Type name '(' Expression list ')'
Expression list:
    Expression [',' Expression] *

A record constructor denotes a record value of the type given by the type name. The expression list must contain one expression for each field of the record type. The order in which the expressions are listed in the record constructor and the order in which the field names are listed in the record type declaration define a one-to-one correspondence between the expressions and the fields. The expressions must be of the same types as the corresponding fields.

The result of executing a record constructor is a record value in which the fields are the values obtained by evaluating the corresponding expressions in the order written. The execution terminates if the evaluation of the expressions terminates.

Examples:
    semaphore(0)
    time(x, y + 5, 0)
    attributes(code, x, true)
    entry(name('edit'), attributes(code, x, true))

3.9.2 Record Relations

The relational operators = and $<>$ apply to operands of the same record type and yield a result of type boolean. Two record values x and y of the same type are equal (denoted x = y) if all the corresponding fields of the values are equal. The relation x $<>$ y has the same value as **not** (x = y).

These operations always terminate.

3.10 ARRAY TYPES

An array type consists of a finite set of values, called array values. Each array value consists of a finite sequence of other values known as elements. The elements are of the same known type. The set of array values consists of all the possible sequences of the possible element values.

The elements are distinguished by their position in the array value. The positions are denoted by the successive values in a range known as the index range. The position of an element is called its index value.

An array type with n elements of type character is called a string type of length n.

Array type declaration:
    'array' Type name '[' Index range ']'
        '(' Element type ')'
Index range:
    Range symbol
Element type:
    Type name

An array type declaration introduces a name to denote an array type. The index range is given by a range symbol (Section 3.8). The known type of the elements is given by another type name, called the element type.

An array type declaration cannot use its own type name as the element type. The scope rules (Section 3.4.3) apply to an array type. An array type declared within a module can be exported to the immediately surrounding block (Section 3.4.4).

Examples:
    array name [1 : namelength] (char)
    array poll [false : true] (int)
    array timetable ['a' : 'b'] (time)
    array namelist [flow : log] (name)

3.10.1 Array Constructors

Array constructor:
    Type name '(' Expression list ')'

An array constructor denotes an array value of the type given by the type name. The expression list (Section 3.9.1) must contain one expression for each element of the array type (unless the array type is a string type). The order in which the expressions are listed in the array constructor and the order in which the array elements are arranged by the index values define a one-to-one correspondence between the expressions and the elements. The expressions must be of the element type given by the array type declaration.

An array constructor for a string type of length n must contain m expressions of type character (where $1 <= m <= n$). This is an abbreviation for an array value consisting of the character values given by the m expressions followed by n – m spaces.

The result of executing an array constructor is an array value in which the elements are the values obtained by evaluating the corresponding expressions in the order written. The execution terminates if the evaluation of the expressions terminates.

Examples:
```
name('do', nl, c)
poll(x + 1, y)
timetable(time(12, 30, 0), time(x, y + 5, 0))
namelist(name('flow'), name('scan'), name('log'))
```

3.10.2 Array Relations

The relational operators = and $<>$ apply to operands of the same array type and yield a result of type boolean. Two array values x and y of the same type are equal (denoted x = y) if all the corresponding elements of the values are equal. The relation x $<>$ y has the same value as **not** (x = y).

These operations always terminate.

3.11 SET TYPES

A set type consists of a finite set of values, called set values. Each set value consists of a finite (possibly empty) set of other values. These other values are known as the members of the set value. The members are of the same known elementary type, called the base type.

A member must have an ordinal number in the range 0:setlimit, where the upper bound is a system-dependent integer value called the set limit (Sections 3.7 and 3.8).

The range of possible members is called the base range of the set type. The set of set values consists of all the possible subsets (including the empty one) that can be formed from the values in the base range.

Set type declaration:
    'set' Type name '(' Base type ')'
Base type:
    Type name

A set type declaration introduces a type name to denote a set type. The known base type is given by another type name and must be elementary.

The scope rules (Section 3.4.3) apply to a set type. A set type declared within a module can be exported to the immediately surrounding block (Section 3.4.4).

Examples:
> set intset(int)
> set boolset(bool)
> set charset(char)
> set taskset(task)

3.11.1 Set Constructors

Set constructor:
> Type name ['(' Expression list ')']

A set constructor denotes a set value of the type given by the type name. The expression list (if any) consists of one or more expressions of the base type given by the set type declaration (Section 3.9.1).

The result of executing a set constructor is a set value in which the members are the values obtained by evaluating the expressions in the order written. The evaluation fails if any of the expression values are outside the base range.

A set constructor without an expression list denotes the empty set, which has no members.

Examples:
> intset
> boolset(x = y)
> charset('0123456789')
> taskset(scan, log)

3.11.2 Set Relations

The relational operator **in** applies to operands v and x, where x denotes a set value of type T and v denotes an elementary value of the base type. The relation v **in** x is true if the value v is a member of the set x. The evaluation of the relation fails if the value of v is outside the base range. The empty set T has no members, that is, (v **in** T) = false for all values v in the base range.

The relational operators = and <> apply to operands x and y of the same set type. The relation x = y is true if (v **in** x) = (v **in** y) for all values v in the base range. The relation x <> y has the same value as **not** (x = y). These operations always terminate.

3.11.3 Set Operators

The set operators +, –, and * denote union, difference, and intersection, respectively. They apply to operands x and y of the same set type and yield a result of that type.

For any value v in the base range of the set type

v in (x + y)	means	(v in x) or (v in y)
v in (x – y)	means	(v in x) and not (v in y)
v in (x * y)	means	(v in x) and (v in y)

These operations always terminate.

3.12 CONSTRUCTORS

Constructor:
     Elementary constructor # Record constructor #
     Array constructor # Set constructor

A constructor denotes a mapping of one or more values of fixed types onto a value of a (usually different) type. It is either an elementary constructor (Section 3.7.7), a record constructor (Section 3.9.1), an array constructor (Section 3.10.1), or a set constructor (Section 3.11.1).

3.13 VARIABLES

A variable is a named entity that may assume any of the values of a known type. The value of a variable may be used in expressions (Section 3.14) to compute other values and may be changed by means of assignments (Section 3.15.2).

A variable of a record or array type consists of a group of other variables known as subvariables. A variable of an elementary type or a set type has no subvariables. A variable that is not a subvariable of any other variable is called a whole variable.

3.13.1 Variable Declarations

Variable declaration list:
     'var' Variable group [';' Variable group] *

Variable group:
  Variable name [',' Variable name] * ':' Type name
Variable name:
  Name

Every variable group in a variable declaration list introduces one or
more names, called variable names, to denote whole variables of the known
type given by the type name.

Other whole variables known as parameters and function variables are
introduced by procedures (Section 3.16).

The scope rules (Section 3.4.3) apply to every whole variable. A whole
variable v declared in a module is exported to the immediately surrounding
block by exporting the variable declaration list that introduces v (Section
3.4.4).

Example:
  var x, y, size: int; full, free: bool; c, slot: char;
      job: task; s: semaphore; file: entry;
      answers: poll; schedule: timetable; tasks: namelist;
      months: intset; digits: charset

3.13.2 Variable Operands

Variable symbol:
  Whole variable symbol # Subvariable symbol #
  Retyped variable symbol
Whole variable symbol:
  Variable name # Function variable symbol
Subvariable symbol:
  Field variable symbol # Indexed variable symbol

A variable symbol denotes a whole variable, a subvariable, or a retyped
variable (Section 3.13.5) used as an operand.

A whole variable is denoted by a known variable name or by a function
variable symbol (Section 3.16.3).

A subvariable is denoted by a field variable symbol (Section 3.13.3) or
an indexed variable symbol (Section 3.13.4).

The evaluation of a variable symbol involves locating the corresponding
variable in the current context. This is called variable selection. The selection
of a whole variable always terminates. The selection of a subvariable is described later.

If a variable symbol occurs within an expression (Section 3.14) the corresponding variable is first selected and then a copy of its value is obtained. This is called variable retrieval. The retrieval terminates if the selection does.

Examples of whole variable symbols:
    x
    s
    file
    answers
    schedule
    tasks
    val empty

3.13.3 Field Variables

A variable of a record type is called a record variable. It contains a subvariable for each field of the record type. The subvariables are known as field variables. Their types are the corresponding field types given by the record type declaration.

Field variable symbol:
    Record variable symbol '.' Field name
Record variable symbol:
    Variable symbol

A field variable symbol v.f consists of a record variable symbol v followed by a field name f.
    A field variable is selected in two steps:

(1) The record variable is selected.

(2) The field variable given by the field name is selected within the record variable.

The selection of the field variable terminates if the selection of the record variable does.
    If v denotes a record variable of type T, the relation

$$v = T(v.f1, v.f2, \ldots , v.fm)$$

is true, where v.f1, v.f2, . . . , v.fm denote the values of the field variables of v.

Examples:
       s.count
       schedule[c].second
       file.attr.kind

3.13.4 Indexed Variables

A variable of an array type is called an array variable. It contains a sub-variable for each element of the array value. The subvariables are known as indexed variables. Their type is the element type given in the array type declaration.

Indexed variable symbol:
       Array variable symbol '[' Index expression ']'
Array variable symbol:
       Variable symbol
Index expression:
       Expression

An indexed variable symbol v[e] consists of an array variable symbol v followed by an index expression e. The index expression is an expression of the same type as the index range given in the array type declaration.

An indexed variable is selected in three steps:

(1) The array variable is selected.

(2) The index expression is evaluated to obtain an index value.

(3) The indexed variable corresponding to the index value is selected within the array variable.

The selection of an indexed variable terminates if the selection of the array variable terminates and if the evaluation of the index expression yields an index value within the index range. The selection fails if the index value is outside the index range.

If v denotes an array variable of type T, the relation

$$v = T(v[e1], v[e2], \ldots, v[em])$$

is true, where v[e1], v[e2], . . . , v[em] denote the values of the indexed variables of v.

Examples:
    answers[false]
    schedule[c]
    tasks[job] [x + 1]
    file.id[12]

3.13.5 Retyped Variables

In most computers data values are held as binary numerals known as stored values. The following describes a system-dependent operation that applies only to computers in which stored values of the same type occupy the same amount of storage.

If the stored values of two types occupy the same amount of storage the types are said to be of the same length.

An operation known as retyping maps the values of one type onto another type of the same length in such a way that the corresponding values of the two types have the same stored values.

If x denotes a variable of type T1, then x : T2 denotes the same variable considered to be of another type T2 of the same length. The variable x : T2 is called a retyped variable.

A selection of possible subvariables of x : T2 proceeds as if x were of type T2.

A retrieval of x : T2 yields a value of type T2 with the same stored value as the value of x.

An assignment (Section 3.15.2) to x : T2 of a value y of type T2 assigns a value to x with the same stored value as the value of y.

Retyped variable symbol:
    Variable symbol ':' Type name

A retyped variable is denoted by a variable symbol followed by a known type name.

Example:
    schedule[c] : attributes

3.14 EXPRESSIONS

Expression:
    Simple expression:
        [Relational operator Simple expression]
Relational operator:
    '=' # '<>' # '<' # '<=' # '>' # '>=' # 'in'

Simple expression:
    [Sign operator] Term #
    Simple expression Adding operator Term
Sign operator:
    '+' # '-'
Adding operator:
    '+' # '-' # **'or'**
Term:
    [Term Multiplying operator] Factor
Multiplying operator:
    '*' # **'div'** # **'mod'** # **'and'**
Factor:
    Simple operand # '(' Expression ')' #
    'not' Factor # Retyped factor
Simple operand:
    Constant symbol # Constructor #
    Variable symbol # Procedure call

An expression denotes a rule for computing a value of a fixed type known as the expression type. An expression consists of operands denoting values and operators denoting operations on the values. Parentheses may be used to prescribe the order in which the operators are to be applied to the operands. The execution of an expression is known as its evaluation.

An operator denotes a standard operation on the values of one or two operands. The same operator may stand for several different operations depending on the operand types. The execution of an operator yields a single value as described in Sections 3.7.2, 3.7.4, 3.7.8, 3.9.2, 3.10.2, 3.11.2, and 3.11.3.

Each operator restricts the operands to which it may be applied to belong to certain types only. The syntactic rules for expressions, which describe no restrictions arising from types, include many forms that are invalid.

The value of an expression is found either as the value of a simple expression or by applying a relational operator to the values of two simple expressions.

The value of a simple expression is found either as the value of a term, or by applying a sign operator to the value of a term, or by applying an adding operator to the values of another simple expression and a term.

The value of a term is found either as the value of a factor, or by applying a multiplying operator to the values of another term and a factor.

The value of a factor is found either as the value of a simple operand, or another expression, or by applying a not operator to the value of another factor, or by evaluating a retyped factor (Section 3.14.1).

The value of a simple operand is found either as the value of a constant (Section 3.6), a constructor (Section 3.12), a variable (Section 3.13.2), or a procedure call (Section 3.15.3).

Examples of simple operands:
    false
    attributes(code, x, true)
    schedule[c] .second
    gcd(189, 215)

Examples of factors:
    . . . all the examples above . . .
    (1 <= x)
    not full
    s : int

Examples of terms:
    . . . all the examples above . . .
    5 * x **div** y
    (1 <= x) **and** (x <= namelength)

Examples of simple expressions:
    . . . all the examples above . . .
    - 10
    x + y - 1

Examples of expressions:
    . . . all the examples above . . .
    1 <= x
    c **in** digits

3.14.1 Retyped Factors

If x denotes a value of type T1, then x : T2 denotes a value of type T2 with the same stored value as the value of x. The types T1 and T2 must be of the same length (Section 3.13.5). The operand x : T2 is called a retyped factor. Its value is system dependent.

Retyped factor:
    Factor ':' Type name

A retyped factor consists of a factor followed by a known type name.

Example:
    s : int

3.15 STATEMENTS

Statement:
      Skip statement # Assignment statement #
      Procedure call # If statement #
      While statement # When statement #
      Concurrent statement
Statement list:
      Statement [';' Statement] *

A statement denotes one or more operations and determines (at least partially) the order in which these operations are to be executed. A statement is either a skip statement (Section 3.15.1), an assignment statement (Section 3.15.2), a procedure call (Section 3.15.3), an if statement (Section 3.15.4), a while statement (Section 3.15.5), a when statement (Section 3.15.6), or a concurrent statement (Section 3.15.7).

A statement list denotes execution of a sequence of statements.

The statements of a statement list are executed one at a time in the order written.

Examples of statement lists:
      full := false
      send(x);   read(x)

3.15.1 Skip Statements

Skip statement:
      'skip'

The word symbol **skip** denotes the empty operation. The execution of a skip has no effect and always terminates.

3.15.2 Assignment Statements

Assignment statement:
      Variable symbol ':=' Expression

An assignment statement denotes assignment of a value given by an expression to a variable. The variable and the expression must be of the same type.

An assignment statement is executed in three steps:

(1) The variable is selected.

(2) The expression is evaluated to obtain a value.

(3) The value is assigned to the variable.

An assignment to a subvariable of a whole variable assigns a value to the subvariable without changing the values of the remaining subvariables.

If v denotes a record variable of type **record** T (f1 : T1; f2 : T2; ...; fm : Tm), then

v.f1 := e1	means	v := T(e1, v.f2, ... , v.fm)
v.f2 := e2	means	v := T(v.f1, e2, ... , v.fm)
	. . .	
v.fm := em	means	v := T(v.f1, v.f2, ... , em)

where f1, f2, ... , fm are the field names of the record type T, while e1, e2, ... , em are expressions of the field types T1, T2, ... , Tm.

Similarly, if v denotes an array of the type **array** T [i1 : im] (Te) then

v[i1] := e1	means	v := T(e1, v[i2], ... , v[im])
v[i2] := e2	means	v := T(v[i1], e2, ... , v[im])
	. . .	
v[im] := em	means	v := T(v[i1], v[i2], ... , em)

where i1, i2, ... , im are the index values of the array type T, while e1, e2, ... , em are expressions of the element type Te.

Examples:
```
x := x + 1
c := char(x + int('0'))
full := false
job := log
val empty := (size = 0)
file := entry(name('edit'), attributes(code, x, true))
s.count := s.count + 1
schedule[c] := time(12, 30, 0)
```

3.15.3 Procedure Calls

Procedure call:
　　Procedure name ['(' Argument list ')']

Argument list:
    Argument [',' Argument] *
Argument:
    Value argument # Variable argument # Procedure argument
Value argument:
    Expression
Variable argument:
    Variable symbol
Procedure argument:
    Procedure name

A procedure call denotes execution of a known procedure given by the procedure name (Section 3.16).

The argument list denotes operands that may be operated on by the procedure. The argument list must contain one argument for each parameter of the procedure. The order in which the arguments are written in the procedure call and the order in which the parameters are listed in the procedure declaration define a one-to-one correspondence between the arguments and the parameters.

Each argument is either a value argument, a variable argument, or a procedure argument.

A value argument must correspond to a value parameter and must be an expression of the same type as the corresponding parameter.

A variable argument must correspond to a variable parameter and must be a variable symbol of the same type as the corresponding parameter.

A procedure argument must correspond to a procedure parameter and must be the name of a procedure with the same heading as the corresponding parameter (apart from the choice of procedure and parameter names).

The execution of a procedure call takes place in six steps:

(1) The parameters of the procedure called are created one at a time in the order listed:

A value parameter is created as a fresh variable which is assigned the value obtained by evaluating the corresponding value argument.

A variable parameter is created by selecting the corresponding variable argument.

A procedure parameter is created by selecting the corresponding procedure argument and selecting a context associated with the argument (as described below).

(2) A new current context is formed from a context associated with the procedure called extended with the parameters.

The procedure body is then executed as described in steps (3) to (5):

(3) The auxiliary entities declared in the procedure body are created and added to the current context. The initial values of the auxiliary variables are undefined.

(4) The local modules of the procedure are initialized one at a time in the order written. This extends the current context further as described in Section 3.4.4. The current context is then also attached as an attribute to all procedures declared in the body (and to all procedures declared in the local modules of the body).

(5) The statement part of the procedure body is executed.

(6) The old context used prior to the call is reestablished as the current context.

During the execution of the procedure body every operation on a variable parameter stands for the same operation performed on the corresponding variable argument. And every call of a procedure parameter stands for the same call of the corresponding procedure argument in the context associated with the argument. These parameters are said to be bound to the corresponding arguments during the execution of the procedure body.

When a procedure call is used as a statement, it must refer to a general procedure (Section 3.16.1).

When a procedure call is used as an operand in an expression, it must refer to a function (Section 3.16.3). The execution of a function computes a value of a fixed type given by the procedure declaration.

Examples:
    init
    receive(x)
    gcd(189, 215)

3.15.4 If Statements

If statement:
    'if' Conditional statement list 'end'
Conditional statement list:
    Conditional statement ['else' Conditional statement] *
Conditional statement:
    Boolean expression 'do' Statement list
Boolean expression:
    Expression

An if statement denotes a single execution of a conditional statement list.

A conditional statement list denotes execution of one of several conditional statements (or none of them). Each conditional statement consists of an expression of type boolean and a statement list.

The execution of an if statement consists of executing the conditional statement list once.

The execution of a conditional statement list consists of first evaluating the boolean expressions one at a time in the order written until one yielding the value true is found or until all have been found to yield the value false. If the value obtained from an expression is true, the statement list that follows the expression is executed; otherwise, none of the statement lists are executed. In the latter case, the statement lists are said to be skipped.

Examples:
    if x mod y <> 0 do send(x) end

    if job = flow do flow—analysis
    else job = scan do alarm—scanning
    else job = log do data—logging
    else true do error end

3.15.5 While Statements

While statement:
    'while' Conditional statement list 'end'

A while statement denotes one or more executions of a conditional statement list (Section 3.15.4).

The execution of a while statement consists of executing the conditional statement list repeatedly until all the statement lists are skipped.

If statement lists continue to be executed forever, the execution cycles.

Examples:
    while x <> last do send(x); read(x) end

    while x > y do x := x - y
    else x < y do y := y - x end

3.15.6 When Statements

When statement:
    'when' Synchronized statement 'end'
Synchronized statement:
    Conditional statement list

A when statement consists of a conditional statement list known as a synchronized statement. This is a mechanism that can be used to give concurrent processes exclusive access to common variables when their values satisfy certain conditions.

A process executes a when statement in two phases:

(1) *Synchronizing phase.* The process is delayed until no other process is executing the critical phase of a when statement.

(2) *Critical phase.* The synchronized statement is executed as described in Section 3.15.4. If the statement lists are skipped, the process returns to the synchronizing phase; otherwise, the execution of the when statement is terminated.

Each synchronizing phase of a process lasts a finite time provided only that the critical phases of all other concurrent processes terminate.

Concurrent processes are discussed further in Section 3.15.7.

Examples:
        when true do s.count := s.count + 1 end

        when s.count $>$ 0 do s.count := s.count – 1 end

        when free do x := 1; free := false
        else x $>$ 0 do x := x + 1 end

3.15.7 Concurrent Statements

Concurrent statement:
        'cobegin' Process statement list 'end'
Process statement list:
        Process statement ['also' Process statement] *
Process statement:
        Process constant 'do' Statement list
Process constant:
        Constant symbol

A concurrent statement denotes execution of a process statement list. The process statement list consists of process statements to be executed simultaneously. Each process statement describes a process by means of a constant symbol (the process constant) and a statement list. The type and meaning of process constants are system dependent. They may, for example, be used to specify the amount of storage required by a process or the processor that must perform the process.

The execution of a concurrent statement consists of executing the process statements simultaneously. The relative ordering of operations performed by different processes is unspecified. The execution of such operations may generally overlap in time (unless they are described by when statements). The execution of a concurrent statement terminates when all the concurrent processes terminate.

When a process reaches a concurrent statement the current context of that process becomes the initial context of each of the concurrent processes.

The variable instances in the initial context of the processes are called common variables because they can be operated on by all the processes. The common variables enable processes to exchange values during their execution.

When a process calls one or more procedures, its initial context is extended with variable instances that are inaccessible to the other processes. They are called the private variables of the process.

Two common variables are said to be disjoint if they are different variable instances or if none of them is a subvariable of the other; otherwise, they are called intersecting variables.

If each of several concurrent processes operates only on private variables and disjoint, common variables, the effect of executing a concurrent statement is the same as the effect of executing the process statements one at a time in any order.

But if concurrent processes operate on intersecting, common variables, the effect of executing a concurrent statement is generally unpredictable since nothing is known about the order in which the processes operate on these variables. However, by restricting the operations on intersecting, common variables to well-defined disciplines under the control of modules (Section 3.4.4), procedures (Section 3.16), and when statements (Section 3.15.6), it is possible to formulate concurrent statements that make predictable use of such variables. The theories used to reason about concurrent statements, when statements, and common variables are beyond the scope of this report.

When concurrent processes terminate, the execution of all procedures called by these processes has also ended. Consequently, the private variables of the processes have disappeared, leaving only the common variables in the context. The execution of the program now continues as a single process in the current context of common variables.

The meaning of variable retrieval (Section 3.13.2) and assignment (Section 3.15.2) defined earlier is valid only if these operations are performed one at a time on a given variable. Concurrent processes can ensure that this assumption is satisfied by performing all operations on intersecting, common variables within when statements. The assumption is always satisfied for operations on private variables since each of these variables can be used only by a single process that performs all its operations (including those on variables) one at a time.

If any of the concurrent processes reaches a concurrent statement, the execution fails.

Examples:
    cobegin 1 **do** print **end**

    cobegin 1 **do** producer
    also 2 **do** consumer **end**

    cobegin 1 **do** node(b[0] , b[1])
    also 2 **do** node (b[1] , b[2])
    also 3 **do** node (b[2] , b[0])
    also 4 **do** send(b[0] , 9999) **end**

3.16 PROCEDURES

Procedure declaration:
    Complete procedure declaration # Split procedure part #
    Library procedure declaration

A procedure declaration describes a named procedure. It is either a complete procedure (Section 3.16.1), a split procedure (Section 3.16.4), or a library procedure (Section 3.16.5).
    A procedure declared in a module can be exported to the immediately surrounding block (Section 3.4.4).

3.16.1 Complete Procedures

Complete procedure declaration:
    Procedure heading Procedure body
Procedure heading:
    'proc' Procedure name ['('Parameter list')']
        [':' Function type]
Procedure name:
    Name
Function type:
    Type name
Procedure body:
    [Declaration] * Statement part

A complete procedure declaration defines a procedure completely. The procedure heading introduces a name, called a procedure name, to denote the procedure and describes the parameters by a parameter list (Section 3.16.2). If the heading includes a known type name, called the function type, the procedure is a function (Section 3.16.3); otherwise, it is a general procedure.

The procedure body consists of declarations (Section 3.4.2) that describe auxiliary entities used by the procedure and a statement part (Section 3.4.4) that describes a sequence of operations on the parameters and auxiliary entities.

A procedure acts as a block (Section 3.4.3). The parameters and auxiliary entities are local to the procedure and can be used only within the procedure body. The procedure name is local to the immediately surrounding block.

The execution of the procedure body is invoked by executing a procedure call (Section 3.15.3).

A procedure may call itself recursively.

Examples:

```
proc init begin full := false end

proc consumer
var y  :  char
begin receive(y);
   while y <> last do
      write(y); receive(y)
   end;
   write(y); write(nl)
end

proc wait(var s  :  semaphore)
begin when s.count > 0 do s.count := s.count - 1 end end

proc push(c  :  int)
begin size := size + 1; lifo[size] := c end

proc gcd(x, y  :  int)  :  int
begin
   while x > y do x := x - y
   else x < y do y := y - x end;
   val gcd := x
end
```

3.16.2 Parameters

Parameter list:
    Parameter group [';' Parameter group] *
Parameter group:
    Value parameter group # Variable parameter group #
    Procedure parameter
Value parameter group:
    Variable group
Variable parameter group:
    'var' Variable group
Procedure parameter:
    Procedure heading

A parameter list describes one or more groups of parameters.

A value parameter group introduces a group of local variables known as value parameters. Each value parameter is assigned the value of an argument before the procedure body is executed.

A variable parameter group introduces a group of local variables known as variable parameters. Each variable parameter denotes a variable argument which is selected before the procedure body is executed.

A procedure parameter introduces a procedure heading to denote a procedure argument and its associated context which are selected before the procedure body is executed.

Examples:
    x, y : int

    var s : semaphore

    id : name; **proc** lookup(x : name; **var** y : attributes)

3.16.3 Functions

A function is a procedure that describes the computation of a single value of a fixed type (the function type). A function call can be used as an operand in an expression. The procedure body of a function assigns the value of the function to a local variable, called the function variable. The last value assigned to this variable during the execution of the procedure body becomes the value of the procedure call that invoked the execution.

Function variable symbol:
    'val' Procedure name

A function variable is denoted by the procedure name of the given function. The function variable is known only in the body of the function.

Example of a function variable symbol:

> **val** gcd

3.16.4   Split Procedures

In a program that contains mutually recursive procedures, some procedure calls must precede the corresponding procedure bodies in the program text. A procedure that is called in this way must have its declaration split into two parts: a predeclaration that precedes these calls and a postdeclaration that follows them.

Split procedure part:
> Procedure predeclaration # Procedure postdeclaration

Procedure predeclaration:
> 'pre' Procedure heading

Procedure postdeclaration:
> 'post' Complete procedure declaration

A procedure predeclaration is a procedure heading that describes how to call a split procedure. The procedure name introduced by the procedure heading can be used in the program text that extends from the predeclaration to the end of the block in which the predeclaration appears.

A procedure postdeclaration is a complete procedure declaration that describes how to call and execute a split procedure. The pre- and postdeclarations must appear in the same block in that order but may be separated by other declarations in the same block. The procedure headings of the pre- and postdeclarations must be identical.

A split procedure declared in a module is exported to the immediately surrounding block (Section 3.4.4) by exporting the corresponding predeclaration.

Example:
> **pre proc** variable_symbol(succ : symbols)
>   ... other declarations ...
> **post proc** variable_symbol(succ : symbols)
> **begin** ... **end**

3.16.5   Library Procedures

A program library is a group of procedures that can be called by a program without being included in the program. The library procedures, which have the form of separate programs (Section 3.17), cannot use global variables or global procedures (Section 3.4.3).

A program may call a library procedure if the program contains a declaration of the procedure heading and a description of where the procedure body is located in the library.

Library procedure declaration:
 'lib' Procedure heading '[' Library key ']'
Library key:
 Expression

A library procedure declaration describes a library procedure by means of a procedure heading and a library key. The library key is an expression that indicates the location of the procedure body in the library. The type of the expression is system dependent.

When the library procedure is called, the library key is evaluated and used to locate the procedure body in the library. The execution of the body then proceeds as described earlier (Section 3.15.3).

The procedure heading used in the program and the procedure heading used in the library to describe the procedure must be the same.

Example:
 lib proc edit(source, dest : name) [name('edit')]

3.17 PROGRAMS

Program:
 [Constant declaration list # Type declaration] *
  Complete procedure declaration

A program consists of declarations of constants, types, and a single, complete procedure (Sections 3.6.1, 3.5.1, and 3.16.1).

A program acts as a block (Section 3.4.3). The declared entities can be used throughout the program.

The execution of the program consists of executing a call of the procedure in a system-dependent context. Initially, the program is executed as a single process in the given context.

Example:

"This program defines two processes connected by a buffer module. A producer process reads a sequence of characters terminated by a period and sends them through the buffer to a consumer process that receives the characters and writes them. The procedures for reading and writing characters are system-dependent parameters of the program."

const last = '.'; nl = char(10)

proc copier(**proc** read(**var** c: char); **proc** write(c : char))

　module
　　var slot : char; full : bool

　　*proc** send(c : char)
　　begin when not full **do** slot := c; full := true **end end**

　　*proc** receive(**var** c : char)
　　begin when full **do** c := slot; full := false **end end**

　begin full := false **end**

　proc producer
　var x : char
　begin read(x);
　　while x <> last **do**
　　　send(x); read(x)
　　end;
　　send(x)
　end

　proc consumer
　var y : char
　begin receive(y);
　　while y <> last **do**
　　　write(y); receive(y)
　　end;
　　write(y); write(nl)
　end

begin
　cobegin 1 **do** producer
　also 2 **do** consumer **end**
end

3.18 SYNTAX SUMMARY

The following is a list of the syntactic rules of the language. Trivial syntactic rules have been omitted. Some rules have been eliminated by replacing all references to their names with the corresponding syntax expressions. Other rules that were defined recursively earlier have been replaced by equivalent ones that are defined iteratively. Separators and character strings, which are alternative representations of other syntactic forms, are defined elsewhere (Sections 3.2.4 and 3.2.5).

Name:
      Letter [Letter # Digit # '_'] *
Numeral:
      Digit [Digit] *
Character symbol:
      '"' Graphic character '"' # 'char' '(' Numeral ')'
Constant symbol:
      Constant name # Numeral # Character symbol
Constant declaration:
      Constant name '=' Constant symbol
Constant declaration list:
      'const' Constant declaration
         [';' Constant declaration] *
Enumeration symbol list:
      Constant name [',' Constant name] *
Enumeration type declaration:
      'enum' Type name '(' Enumeration symbol list')'
Field group:
      Field name [',' Field name] * ':' Type name
Field list:
      Field group [';' Field group] *
Record type declaration:
      'record' Type name '(' Field list ')'
Range symbol:
      Constant symbol ':' Constant symbol
Array type declaration:
      'array' Type name '[' Range symbol ']' '(' Type name ')'
Set type declaration:
      'set' Type name '(' Type name ')'
Type declaration:
      Enumeration type declaration # Record type declaration #
      Array type declaration # Set type declaration
Variable group:
      Variable name [',' Variable name] * ':' Type name
Variable declaration list:
      'var' Variable group [';' Variable group] *
Parameter group:
      ['var'] Variable group # Procedure heading
Parameter list:
      Parameter group [';' Parameter group] *

Procedure heading:
>   'proc' Procedure name ['(' Parameter list ')']
>   [':' Type name]

Complete procedure declaration:
>   Procedure heading [Declaration] * Statement part

Procedure declaration:
>   'pre' Procedure heading #
>   ['post'] Complete procedure declaration #
>   'lib' Procedure heading '[' Expression ']'

Module declaration:
>   'module' [Declaration # Exported declaration] *
>   Statement part

Declaration:
>   Constant declaration list # Type declaration #
>   Variable declaration list # Procedure declaration #
>   Module declaration

Exported declaration:
>   '*' Declaration

Variable symbol:
>   Variable name # 'val' Procedure name #
>   Variable symbol '.' Field name #
>   Variable symbol '[' Expression ']' #
>   Variable symbol ':' Type name

Expression list:
>   Expression [',' Expression] *

Constructor:
>   Type name ['(' Expression list ')']

Factor:
>   Constant symbol # Constructor # Variable symbol #
>   Procedure call # '(' Expression ')' #
>   'not' Factor # Factor ':' Type name

Multiplying operator:
>   '*' # 'div' # 'mod' # 'and'

Term:
>   Factor [Multiplying operator Factor] *

Adding operator:
>   '+' # '-' # 'or'

Simple expression:
>   ['+' # '-'] Term [Adding operator Term] *

Relational operator:
>   '=' # '<>' # '<' # '<=' # '>' # '>=' # 'in'

Expression:
>   Simple expression
>   [Relational operator Simple expression]

Argument:
    Expression # Variable symbol # Procedure name
Argument list:
    Argument [',' Argument] *
Procedure call:
    Procedure name ['(' Argument list ')']
Conditional statement:
    Expression **'do'** Statement list
Conditional statement list:
    Conditional statement [**'else'** Conditional statement] *
Process statement:
    Constant symbol **'do'** Statement list
Process statement list:
    Process statement [**'also'** Process statement] *
Statement:
    'skip' # Variable symbol **':='** Expression #
    Procedure call #
    'if' Conditional statement list **'end'** #
    'while' Conditional statement list **'end'** #
    'when' Conditional statement list **'end'** #
    'cobegin' Process statement list **'end'**
Statement list:
    Statement [';' Statement] *
Statement part:
    'begin' Statement list **'end'**
Program:
    [Constant declaration list # Type declaration] *
       Complete procedure declaration

3.19 EDISON-11

This section describes the version of the programming language Edison which has been implemented for the PDP 11 computers. This language, known as Edison-11, extends standard Edison with octal numerals and standard procedures for manipulating device registers.

3.19.1 Characters

Edison-11 programs are written in the ASCII character set (Section 3.19.11). A program text is a sequence of characters with the following structure:

Program text:

 [Line] *

Line:

 [Graphic character] * Newline character

A new line character (character number 10) marks the end of each line of text. All other control characters are ignored by the compiler.

3.19.2 Standard Names

Standard name:

 'bool' # 'char' # 'false' # 'int' # 'true' #

 'addr' # 'halt' # 'obtain' # 'place' # 'sense'

The new standard names addr, halt, obtain, place, and sense denote standard procedures that can be called throughout a program without being declared (Section 3.19.7).

3.19.3 Type Integer

The range of integers extends from –32768 to 32767 (both values included).

Numeral:

 Decimal numeral # Octal numeral

Decimal numeral:

 Digit [Digit] *

Octal numeral:

 '#' Octal digit [Octal digit] *

Octal digit:

 '0' # '1' # '2' # '3' # '4' # '5' # '6' # '7'

A numeral is a conventional decimal or octal notation for an integer value.

An octal numeral #d5d4 . . . d0 consisting of the six octal digits d5, d4, . . . , d0 denotes an integer value

$$- (8**5)\, d5 + (8**4)\, d4 + \ldots + (8**0)\, d0$$

The digit d5 must be either 0 or 1. An octal number with fewer than six digits, say #602, stands for the given digits extended with leading zeros, say #000602.

Examples of octal numerals:
    #0
    #200
    #177564

3.19.4 Set Types

A set member must have an ordinal value in the range 0:127.

3.19.5 Stored Values

The computer store is divided into a fixed number of units called words. Each word can store a binary numeral of 16 bits. The value of each bit is either zero or one. A binary numeral b15b14 . . . b0 consisting of the bits b15, b14, . . . , b0 denotes an integer value

$$- (2**15)\ b15 + (2**14)\ b14 + . . . + (2**0)\ b0$$

Each word is associated with an even number called its address. A group of words with successive addresses is called a block. The address of a block is the address of its first word. The addresses define an ordering of the words and blocks within the store.

The stored value of an elementary value x is held in a single word. The stored value is the ordinal value of x.

The stored value of a record value is held in a block. The stored value is a sequence consisting of the stored values of its fields. The fields are stored in their order of declaration within the record value.

The stored value of an array value is held in a block. The stored value is a sequence consisting of the stored values of its elements. The elements are stored in the order of their index values within the array value.

The stored value of a set value is held in a block of 8 words. The stored value is a sequence consisting of the stored values of its 128 possible members. Each possible member x is represented by a single bit which has the value one if x is a member of the set value, and zero if it is not. Within the set value the bits are numbered as follows:

            word0: bit15   . . . bit0
            word1: bit31   . . . bit16
                  . . .
            word7: bit127 . . . bit112

The bits are assigned to the possible members in the order of their ordinal value; that is, bit number int(x) represents the possible member x.

3.19.6　Procedure Calls

The standard procedures cannot be used as procedure arguments in a procedure call (Section 3.19.7).

The compiler does not check whether a procedure used as an argument in a procedure call has the same heading as the corresponding parameter. Nor does it check whether the pre- and postheadings of split procedures are identical.

During the execution of a concurrent statement, library procedures cannot be called.

3.19.7　Standard Procedures

The standard procedures addr, halt, obtain, place, and sense can be called throughout a program without being declared.

The operation addr(x) yields an integer value which is the address of a variable x of any type.

The operation halt terminates the execution of the program.

The operation obtain(x, y) assigns the value of a device register with an integer address x to an integer variable y.

The operation place(x, y) assigns an integer value y to a device register with an integer address x.

The operation sense(x, y) compares an integer value y to the value of a device register with an integer address x. If some of the corresponding bits of the two values both are equal to one, the operation yields the value true; otherwise, it yields the value false.

Examples of standard calls:
    addr(data)
    halt
    obtain(buffer, c:int)
    place(#177566, int(c))
    sense(status, ready)

3.19.8　Program Execution

When the execution of an Edison program fails, a message of the form

Program name 'line' Line number Reason

is displayed on the system terminal and the operating system is restarted.

The reason for the program failure is one of the following:

Halt:
    The standard procedure halt was executed.

Invalid program call:
The program attempted to call a library procedure during the execution of a concurrent statement.

Process limit exceeded:
The number of process statements in a concurrent statement exceeds the limit defined by the constant named maxproc in the Edison kernel.

Range limit exceeded:
A range limit is exceeded by an arithmetic operation, an index expression, or a set member expression.

Variable limit exceeded:
The storage limit is exceeded during the execution of a procedure call or a process statement.

If the processor performs an unexpected transfer to a trap procedure within the kernel, one of the following messages is printed:

> processor trap
> instruction trap
> power trap

The meaning of these traps is explained in the PDP 11 Processor Handbook [Digital, 1975].
If a disk error is detected during program loading, the message

> disk error
> push return to continue

is displayed. When the operator types a carriage return, the disk transfer is repeated.

3.19.9 Store Allocation

A PDP 11 store of 32 K words is used as follows:

Edison kernel	2 K words
Variable stack(s)	
+ Free space	26 K words
+ Program stack	
Device registers	4 K words
Store capacity	32 K words

The Edison programs being executed form a program stack, while their variables are stored in a variable stack. The two stacks grow toward one another in the free space between them.

When a procedure is called, an instance of each of its parameters and variables is pushed on the variable stack. They are removed from the stack when the execution of the procedure terminates.

When a program is called, its code is retrieved from a disk and placed on top of the program stack. The code is removed again when the program has been executed.

Initially, an Edison program is executed as a sequential process with a single variable stack. When a concurrent statement is executed, the free space between the variable and program stacks is divided evenly among the processes. The variable stack is now tree structured, with the original stack being used as the trunk of the tree while the branches of the tree are being used by concurrent processes for temporaries. When the processes terminate, their storage space becomes free again and the program execution continues as a sequential process using the original stack of variables. Since concurrent processes cannot call programs, the program stack does not change during the execution of a concurrent statement.

3.19.10 Execution Times

The execution times of Edison-11 programs shown below are measured in units known as average operation times. For a PDP 11/23 microcomputer the average operation time is about 20 μsec.

	Elementary operands	Set operands (n members)	Record or array operands (n words)
Constant c	1	4 + 2n	1 + 0.4n
Whole variable v	1	4	2 + 0.4n
:=	1	4	1 + 0.4n
= <>	2	5	1 + 0.4n
< <= > >=	1		
in		3	
and or not	1		
+ -	1	4	
*	2	6	
div mod	3		

Other execution times are shown below:

field variable v.f	v + 2
indexed variable v[e]	v + e + 4
procedure call (no parameters)	7

if B do S end	B + S + 1
while B do S end	(B + S + 2)n
when B do S end	(B + 6) n + S
cobegin 1 do S1	S1 + . . . + Sn
. . .	+ 8 + 13n
also n do Sn end	

A conditional statement of the form

$$v = c \ do \ S$$

where v is a whole variable and c is a constant of the same elementary type has the execution time S + 1.

3.19.11 ASCII Character Set

0	nul	32		64	@	96	
1	soh	33	!	65	A	97	a
2	stx	34	"	66	B	98	b
3	etx	35	#	67	C	99	c
4	eot	36	$	68	D	100	d
5	enq	37	%	69	E	101	e
6	ack	38	&	70	F	102	f
7	bel	39	'	71	G	103	g
8	bs	40	(	72	H	104	h
9	ht	41	)	73	I	105	i
10	lf	42	*	74	J	106	j
11	vt	43	+	75	K	107	k
12	ff	44	,	76	L	108	l
13	cr	45	–	77	M	109	m
14	so	46	.	78	N	110	n
15	si	47	/	79	O	111	o
16	dle	48	0	80	P	112	p
17	dc1	49	1	81	Q	113	q
18	dc2	50	2	82	R	114	r
19	dc3	51	3	83	S	115	s
20	dc4	52	4	84	T	116	t
21	nak	53	5	85	U	117	u
22	syn	54	6	86	V	118	v
23	etb	55	7	87	W	119	w
24	can	56	8	88	X	120	x
25	em	57	9	89	Y	121	y
26	sub	58	:	90	Z	122	z
27	esc	59	;	91	[	123	{
28	fs	60	<	92	\	124		
29	gs	61	=	93	]	125	}
30	rs	62	>	94	^	126	
31	us	63	?	95	_	127	del

The ASCII characters have the ordinal values shown in the range 0:127.

4

OPERATING SYSTEM DESIGN

The Edison system was designed under the following constraints:

(1) The system must initially run on a PDP 11/23 microcomputer with 28K words of store, a dual disk drive for 8-inch floppy disks, an ASCII display terminal, and a small printer.

(2) Apart from a small kernel written in assembly language, the entire system must be written in the programming language Edison.

(3) The existing kernel and compiler for Edison must be moved from the PDP 11/55 minicomputer with minimal changes.

(4) The system must be able to assemble the kernel and compile any of the Edison programs (including the compiler itself).

(5) It must be possible to move the system to other 16-bit microcomputers with a similar configuration by rewriting the kernel.

The following explains the main design decisions behind the Edison operating system.

4.1 COMMAND LANGUAGE

The Edison system has benefited from six years of experience with the operating systems Solo, Trio, and Mono [Brinch Hansen, 1977, 1980, and 1981]. These systems, which were developed for the PDP 11/55 minicomputer, are very similar. They enable a user to build gradually a library of compiled programs and invoke the execution of these programs by typing commands that are similar to procedure calls, for example:

> print(systemtext, true)

This command specifies the execution of a program named print using the name systemtext and the boolean value true as arguments.

Although commands of this form are readable, they also have some disadvantages:

A user cannot always remember the number and types of arguments required to call a given program. This problem is solved by enabling a user to ask for help by typing

> print(help)

When a program is called like that, it displays its parameter list and terminates, for example:

> Try again:
> print(source: name; linenumbers: boolean)

Each command is input and checked syntactically by a command interpreter which then calls the given program with the given arguments. But since the command interpreter does not know the parameter lists of all programs, it is forced to use a fixed number of arguments of fixed types in all program calls. If the user types a command with fewer arguments, the remaining ones are assigned default values by the command interpreter. This convention is both inflexible and cumbersome to use at the programming level.

To avoid these problems, the Edison system uses a different command language:

(1) Since the command interpreter does not know the parameters of a program, it only inputs the program name.

(2) Since the user cannot always remember the arguments, the program always describes and inputs them one at a time.

The following example shows a typical user command:

> Command = *print*
> File name = *systemtext*
> Print all pages? *yes*
> Print line numbers? *yes*

The Edison operating system displays the message

> Command =

and accepts the program name *print* typed by the user. The rest of the command is displayed and input by the print program. The characters typed by the user are shown in italics.

To avoid a duplication of code in the programs, the operating system implements a set of procedures that enables programs to input and output booleans, integers, names, and lines of text. The following Edison statements taken from the print program illustrate the use of these procedures to input a file name:

> writeline(display, line(' File name = .'));
> readname(accept, title)

Since a program inputs its own arguments, it is possible to use different numbers of arguments in different calls of the same program as shown in the following example:

> Command = *print*
> File name = *systemtext*
> Print all pages? *no*
> First printed page = *22*
> Last printed page = *23*
> Print line numbers? *no*

A user of the Mono system can correct minor mistakes while typing a command by using two control characters to erase either the last character typed or the whole line. Unfortunately, the screen editor uses a different set of conventions for line editing.

The Edison system uses the same conventions for line editing throughout the system. The user can therefore make changes, insertions, and deletions anywhere on a line while it is being typed or edited.

4.2 BACKING STORE

The most crucial design decisions are those that determine how the backing store is used. The backing store is a dual drive for 8-inch floppy disks. Each disk has 77 tracks, each of which is divided into 26 sectors of 64 words each. This gives a total capacity of 125 K words per disk.

4.2.1 Disk Files

In the earlier systems (Solo, Trio, and Mono), a disk file is initially created with a fixed (maximum) length and is then reduced to its actual length when data have been output to the file. The creation and reduction of files are performed by a program that is loaded from the disk whenever it is executed.

These systems use three different kinds of data files:

(1) Text files, which are terminated by an end-of-medium character

(2) Code files, which begin with a word that defines the length of the file

(3) Temporary files, which are interleaved on the disk to reduce head movement during compilation.

The minor differences between these kinds of files lead to a duplication of system programs and operating system procedures which perform similar operations according to slightly different conventions.

For the Edison system, I decided to use files of uniform structure for all purposes. A disk file is simply a named sequence of elementary values stored in 16-bit words held on a single disk. The necessity of grouping the words into disk sectors is hidden from the programmer by the operating system.

When a new file is created, it is empty to begin with. A program can output values at the end of a file (which may or may not be empty). The only limit on the length of a file is the available space on the disk.

A file is normally input word by word from the beginning. Several of the programs do, however, use a more flexible method of text processing:

The screen editor allows the user to go back and forth across a whole text file and make corrections on the screen. The user may move the cursor to any given line by typing a line number. Before the editing begins, the editor scans the whole text and uses an operating system procedure, called *mark*, to determine the disk address of the first character of every line of text. When the user types a line number, the number is used to look up the disk address of the line in a table declared within the editor. Another operating system procedure named *move* enables the editor to continue the text input from that location on the disk.

This mechanism is also used by the text formatting program to scan every line of text twice: once to determine how many words will fit on a printed line and once again to output these words with enough spaces to make the printed line of a fixed length.

Finally, the code generator of the Edison compiler scans its input twice to generate code addresses of forward jumps. So the use of multiple scanning of parts of a sequential file is a fairly common occurrence that is not supported by most operating systems.

4.2.2 Disk Catalogs

The files stored on a single disk are described in a catalog held on the disk. Each file is described by its name and attributes:

Name	12 words
Address	1 word
Length	2 words
Protection	1 word
Catalog entry	16 words

A *file name* of 12 characters has been used for years in the earlier systems and seems to be sufficient. A *disk address* of 16 bits is sufficient to identify any one of the 2002 sectors on a disk. But since a disk can hold more than 64 K words, two words are required to define the *file length* (in words). The *protection status* is a boolean value that indicates whether or not the file may be changed, renamed, or deleted.

A disk that is used to store program texts or compiled programs will typically hold only 5 to 20 files. But a disk used for other purposes (such as correspondence) may hold as many as 50 small files. A catalog of 50 entries will occupy 50 * 16 = 800 words.

In the following, we will assume that a disk catalog occupies about 1 K words. Such a catalog is small enough to be kept in the main store of a computer while a disk is being used. So when a disk is inserted in one of the drives, its catalog is input from the disk and stored by the operating system. When the system has executed a user command, it will output the catalog on the disk if it has been changed during the execution of the command.

Since there are two disk drives, the operating system uses 2 K words of main storage for catalogs.

The use of two disk drives raises several design issues that have obvious solutions if you are guided by simplicity:

(1) Since each drive can be either empty or hold a disk, the entire backing store can be in four different states. Instead of dealing with this complexity, we will require that each of the drives must contain a disk at all times.

(2) If a disk is replaced by another one during the execution of a program, a stored description of an open file might still be referring to the previous disk. This problem is avoided by insisting that disks be replaced only *before* or *after* the execution of a program. More precisely, there is no operating system procedure that can be called by a program to enable the user to change disks during the execution of the program. The user can insert disks only after typing a command which is interpreted by the operating system itself.

(3) If the same file name occurs in both catalogs, the ambiguity is resolved by searching the catalogs in a fixed order starting with the one input from drive number 0.

(4) If the same convention was used for the creation of new files, they would all end up on disk number 0. In practice, the user would then have to switch disks from time to time. It seems much more practical to ask the user to select the disk on which a new file is to be stored. For example:

> Command = *format*
> Input name = *netconcepts*
> Output name = *printable*
> Output drive = *1*

4.2.3 Disk Allocation

The floppy disk drives are very slow [Digital, 1976]:

Track search	0–760 msec
Sector search	0–166 msec
Head settling	20 msec
Sector transfer	6 msec

A backing store with access times varying from 26 msec to 1 sec can severely limit the performance of the system if it is not used wisely. This is the most difficult engineering challenge of the design.

The seriousness of the problem becomes obvious when you consider the use of the system to *edit* the largest part of the Edison compiler—a program text of 1500 lines (or 42,000 characters). During the prescan of the text, the editor executes the following loop for every line of text:

$$\textbf{while } c <> nl \textbf{ do } read(file, c) \textbf{ end}$$

looking for the newline character (nl) at the end of the line.

For every character of the file, the editor calls an operating system procedure named read to unpack the next character from a disk buffer:

```
proc read(var file: stream;   var value: char)
var x:  int
begin x := file.head.words;
   if x = pagelength do "input data from disk"
   else true do file.head.words := x + 1 end;
   value := file.block[x]
end
```

The processor time used is 0.7 msec/character on a PDP 11/23 computer (Section 3.19.10). So before the user can edit a text file of 42,000 characters, he must wait 29 sec. And that does not even take the disk transfer time into consideration! This shows that the processor is a bit too slow even for a personal computer.

Now, let us look at the disk and assume that it is half full. In that case, an average track search moves the disk head across one-fourth of the disk. If the sectors of a disk are scattered randomly across the first 40 tracks, we obtain the following average access time:

Track search (average)	200 msec
Sector search (average)	83 msec
Head settling	20 msec
Sector transfer	6 msec
1 sector	309 msec

or about 5 msec/word. In that case, the prescan of the large text file will take 42,000 * 5.7 msec = 239 sec(!).

The longest delay is caused by the track search, that is, by *disk head movement*. This can be almost completely eliminated by placing a file on neighboring tracks (or at least on tracks that are as close together as possible).

The second largest contribution is the sector search, that is, the *disk rotation*. This can be reduced (but not eliminated) by grouping sectors into larger blocks, called *disk pages*, which can be input during a single disk revolution.

The larger the *page size* is, the more the effect of disk rotation is reduced. The disk pages must, however, be small enough to enable the operating system to store at least one page for every open file. The most demanding programs are the editor and the compiler, which use three open files each.

The Mono system, which was written in Edison for a PDP 11/55 computer with the same amount of store (28 K words), uses about 3 K words of storage for catalogs and disk pages and leaves 2 K words unused [Brinch Hansen, 1981].

If we choose a page size of 512 words for the Edison system, we are using 3.5 K words of this storage space and are leaving 1.5 K words for unanticipated storage requirements:

2 catalogs	2 K words
3 open files	1.5 K words
	3.5 K words

The simplest idea is to store each disk page on eight consecutive sectors. Unfortunately, the short gap between two neighboring sectors does not give the slow processor enough time to finish the input of one sector and start the input of the next one. If this method is used, the disk must complete another revolution before the input of the next sector. So nothing is gained.

The solution is to place a disk page on eight sectors in such a way that each sector belonging to the page is followed by a *gap* of two sectors which can be allocated to other pages.

In this way it is possible to input every third sector of a track during a single disk revolution:

Track search (minimum)	10 msec
Sector search (average)	83 msec
Head settling	20 msec
Page transfer	$3 * 8 * 6$ msec
1 page	257 msec

or about 0.5 msec/char. This is 10 times faster than the worst case considered earlier!

The prescan of a large text file now takes $42,000 * 1.2$ msec = 50 sec. (This is a predicted figure. The actual time is 57 sec.) This is much too long to wait. The combination of a slow microprocessor and a very slow disk drive poses an insurmountable conflict between the convenience of screen editing and the patience of a human being.

Another crucial performance figure is the *loading time* of the largest program. This is the Edison compiler which consists of 5 programs occupying a total of 18 K words (or 288 sectors).

If disk sectors are scattered randomly, the compiler will be loaded in

288 * 0.3 = 86 sec(!). But, as we have already seen, this is the worst possible situation.

In contrast to a data file, a program file is loaded into the main store as a whole. When the sectors are interleaved as described earlier, an entire track can be loaded in three disk revolutions:

Track search (minimum)	10 msec
Sector search (average)	83 msec
Head settling	20 msec
Track transfer	3 * 166 msec
1 track	611 msec

or 24 msec/sector. The compiler can therefore be loaded in 288 * 24 msec = 7 sec, which is 12 times faster than the worst case.

Now although the operating system should *try* to keep the pages of a file close together, it should not be *required* to allocate them consecutively (on every third sector). For in that case, the deletion of files would eventually create holes on the disk which could only be combined by moving all the files to the beginning of the disk. Such an operation is intolerable since it would take several minutes to perform and would be required at unpredictable times.

The solution is to *chain* the pages of a file together, so that the operating system may attempt to keep the pages close together, but is not forced to do so. The worst possible implementation of this idea is to let each page hold the address of its successor. For this makes it necessary to input every page of a file in order to delete it.

In the Solo system, each file begins with a mapping page that describes where the data pages are stored on the disk. But the main store of the microcomputer used here is not large enough to hold additional pages during the processing of open files.

Instead, each disk is described by a single *disk map* which contains a disk address for each of the 250 disk pages. This map is input together with the catalog when a disk is inserted in a drive. By limiting the disk catalog to 47 files (instead of 50), it is possible to store the map and catalog of a single disk on two pages (1 K words).

A file is opened by using its name to look up a set of attributes in one of the disk catalogs. The file attributes include the number of the first page of the file. The rest of the pages are located by following a chain of page numbers stored in the disk map starting with the first page number. To put it differently, the entry for a given page in the disk map contains either (1) the page number of its successor, or (2) a fixed value indicating that the page is the last one in a file, or (3) a fixed value indicating that the page is unused.

As a measure of the success of this file system, it should be mentioned that the standard programs use only the file procedures implemented by the operating system. None of them perform direct disk input/output.

4.3 SIZE AND PERFORMANCE

The final system consists of about 10,000 lines of program text:

Operating system	1200 lines
Compiler	4200 lines
Editor	500 lines
Formatting program	400 lines
PDP 11 assembler	1600 lines
Other programs	400 lines
Edison programs	8300 lines
Kernel	1800 lines
Edison system	10100 lines

The main store of 28 K words is used as follows:

Kernel	1800 words
Operating system code	7200 words
Operating system variables	2400 words
System size	11400 words
User space	17300 words
Storage space	28700 words

When the largest subprogram of the Edison compiler, known as pass 3, compiles itself, the store is filled to the brim:

Compiler code	8600 words
Compiler variables	8500 words
Compiler space	17100 words
Unused space	200 words
User space	17300 words

The following execution times of some of the operating system procedures were measured on a PDP 11/23 microcomputer. They include disk access times.

Create + delete	30 msec/file
Open + close	10 msec/file
More	0.5 msec/word
Read	1.4 msec/word
Write	0.9 msec/word

The benefits of keeping the disk catalogs in the main store are evident.

Let me finally make the following observations about the operating system design:

(1) The system was designed to use 99.2% of the available store during the execution of its most demanding task (the compilation of pass 3).

(2) The original estimate and the final measurement of the most important performance figure (a read operation) differ only by 15%.

This shows that it is possible to develop software products with predictable performance provided that the designer has modest (but achievable) goals.

You may wish to compare the Edison system with the UCSD Pascal system [Bowles, 1980] and CP/M [Zaks, 1980]. The latter system is, however, not written in a high-level programming language.

5

THE EDISON SYSTEM REPORT

This report describes the operating procedures and programming conventions of the Edison system—a portable software system that supports the development of Edison programs on a personal computer. The system includes the following programs written in Edison:

> Operating system
> Edison compiler
> Screen editor
> Text formatter
> Print program
> PDP 11 assembler

These programs can all be edited and recompiled on the system.

The Edison compiler produces abstract (machine-independent) code which is interpreted by an assembly language program, called the kernel.

5.1 MACHINE CONFIGURATION

The system was developed on a PDP 11 microcomputer with the following capabilities:

28 K word store
Extended instruction set
   (ASH, ASHC, DIV, MUL, SOB, SXT, XOR)
Dual floppy disk drive (RX01 or RX02)
ASCII terminal (VT52 or VT100)
ASCII printer (Diablo 1610 or Xerox 1740)

The PDP 11 kernel (of 1800 words) is written in the assembly language Alva. The system includes an Alva assembler written in Edison.

The RX01 and RX02 disk drives require separate versions of the kernel.

A VT100 terminal can be used only if it operates in the VT52 mode.

The system has been used on the LSI 11, PDP 11/23, and PDP 11/55 computers. It can be moved to other 16-bit computers with similar configurations by rewriting the kernel (Section 5.17).

The operating procedures and performance figures described in this report refer to a PDP 11/23 computer with an RX02 disk drive and a VT100 terminal.

5.2 TERMINAL INPUT

The system accepts one command at a time from the terminal and performs the operation denoted by the command.

Example:

> Command = *delete*
> Drive no = *1*
> File name = *printable*

This operation deletes a file named printable from the disk in drive 1. The characters you type are shown in italics in this report.

5.2.1 Line Editing

All standard programs use the same conventions for typed input. You must type a whole line of text before the characters are processed by the system. Using the syntax notation of the Edison report, the structure of a typed line can be defined as follows:

Typed line:
   [Graphic character # Edit character] * Return
Graphic character:
   Letter # Digit # Special character # Space
Edit character:
   Backspace # Delete # Tabulate

Initially, a typed line is empty. The typed characters have the following effect on the screen:

Graphic character: The typed characters displayed from the cursor to the end of the cursor line move one position to the right, and the graphic character is displayed above the cursor. The cursor then moves one position to the right (if possible).

Backspace: The cursor moves one position to the left (if possible).

Tabulate: The cursor moves five positions to the right (if possible).

Delete: The typed character displayed above the cursor disappears from the screen, and the typed characters displayed after it on the cursor line move one position to the left.

Return: The typed characters displayed on the cursor line are ready to be processed by the system, and the cursor moves to the beginning of the next screen line. The cursor may be anywhere on the typed line when the return character is typed.

5.3 DISKS

The system uses 8-inch floppy disks which are compatible with the IBM 3740 system. All new disks must be preformatted for single-density data recording.

5.3.1 Standard Disks

A standard disk is a floppy disk that holds the following data:

(1) A copy of the kernel code (Section 5.9.1)

(2) A copy of the operating system code (Section 5.9.2)

(3) A set of files

(4) A catalog describing the files stored on the disk

A disk catalog can describe up to 47 files.

The disk space for files is divided into blocks of 512 words, called disk pages. The combined size of the files stored on a disk cannot exceed 223 pages (or 114,176 words).

The system is distributed on six standard disks labeled

Edison system
Edison document
Edison programs 1
Edison programs 2
Edison programs 3
Edison kernel

The system and document disks are used to develop programs and documents, respectively (Sections 5.5 and 5.10). The other disks contain the texts of the standard programs.

5.3.2 Disk Drives

The computer has two disk drives labeled 0 (on the left) and 1 (on the right).

The Edison system assumes that both drives always contain a disk. These disks are called disk 0 and disk 1.

The kernel and the operating system are loaded into the store from disk 0.

To improve the efficiency of the system, copies of the two disk catalogs are kept in the store. When a disk is inserted in a drive, its catalog is input. After each command, the system checks whether any of the catalogs have been changed. In that case, they are output to the disks before the next command is typed.

Disks can be inserted in the drives only before a system start and can be replaced by other disks only during an insert or backup operation; otherwise, their contents may be destroyed (Sections 5.3.3, 5.3.4, and 5.3.6).

5.3.3 System Start

On a PDP 11/23 computer, you start the system as follows:

(1) Turn the power on at the computer, the terminal, and the printer.

(2) Insert a standard disk in drive 0 and a standard (or blank) disk in drive 1. (To insert a disk, you remove it from the envelope, open the door of the drive, insert the disk with the labeled side up and the label toward you, and close the door.)

(3) Flip the restart switch on the computer.

(4) When the message "28, START?" is displayed, you type

dy

followed by return.

(5) After 8 sec, the system responds with the message

The Edison system
insert two disks and type
s if both disks are standard
0 if only disk 0 is standard
1 if only disk 1 is standard
b if both disks are blank

In the normal case, when you have inserted two standard disks, you type the character *s* (without a return). The other options are described in Section 5.3.4.

(6) When the message

Command =

appears, the system is ready to accept a command.

If you type an undefined command, such as

Command = *delete*
Drive no = *2*
File name = *printable*

the system displays an error message, in this case

drive no invalid
system line 306 halt

and halts. This is called a *command failure*.
A command that fails does not change the catalogs stored on the disks.
After a failure, the system automatically *restarts* and displays the message of step (5) after 5 sec. You must then type the character *s* as described earlier.

5.3.4 Insert Command

An insert operation

Command = *insert*

displays the message

insert two disks and type
s if both disks are standard
0 if only disk 0 is standard
1 if only disk 1 is standard
b if both disks are blank

You can now remove the disks from the drives and replace them by other disks. Afterward, you must type one of the characters s, 0, 1, or b (without return). These options have the following effects:

s: The system reads a catalog from both disks.

0:   The system reads a catalog from disk 0 and writes an empty catalog on disk 1.

1:   The system reads a catalog from disk 1 and writes an empty catalog on disk 0.

b: The system writes an empty catalog on both disks.

The options 0, 1, and b destroy the existing catalog and files (if any) on one or both disks.

5.3.5 List Command

A list operation displays a list of all the files stored on a given disk. Example:

Command = *list*
Drive no = *0*

Each file is described by its name, protection status, and length (in pages and words), for example:

prefix   protected   4 pages   1947 words

If a file exceeds 63 pages, the length will only be displayed in pages.

The listing includes the number of files on the disk, the number of pages occupied by the files, and the number of unused pages, for example:

13 entries
74 pages used
149 pages available

5.3.6 Backup Command

A backup operation copies the contents of one disk onto another disk in 97 sec.
Example:

> Command = *backup*
> Drive no = *0*
> insert blank disk in drive 1
> push RETURN to continue

After a backup, the system continues its operation using the two identical disks. The original disk (or its copy) can be safely removed from its drive only if it is replaced by another disk during an insert operation (Section 5.3.4).

5.4 FILES

A disk file is a data structure with the following attributes:

(1) A name

(2) A drive number

(3) A protection status

(4) A (possibly empty) sequence of words

Name:
Letter [Letter # Digit # '—']*

A name consists of up to 12 characters. Any capital letter occurring in a name typed on the terminal is equivalent to the corresponding small letter.

The names *notes*, *temp1*, and *temp2* denote temporary files created by some of the standard programs and should not be used for other files (Sections 5.6.5, 5.7, and 5.8).

Each file is stored on a single disk with a drive number that is either 0 or 1. If a file is used for input (or execution) only, the file name is first looked up in the catalog of disk 0, and, if that fails, it is then looked up in the catalog of disk 1. However, if a file is created, changed, or deleted, the user (or the program invoked by the user) must select the disk on which the file is to be stored.

The protection status is a boolean value that indicates whether or not a file is protected against accidental change or deletion.

Each word of a file holds an elementary value, that is, an integer, boolean, character, or enumeration value. A file is generally input word by word from the beginning. A program may, however, record the disk location of a word before it is read and may later return to that location and reread the file from that point. It is possible to output words both to empty and nonempty files. Words are always output at the end of a file.

5.4.1 Text Files

Text file:
    [Line] *
Line:
    [Graphic character] * Newline character

A text file is a sequence of ASCII characters. Each character occupies a single word on a disk.

On the terminal, a newline character (character number 10) is typed as a carriage return and displayed as a carriage return followed by a line feed. The same output convention is followed by the print program (Section 5.14).

The lines of a text file are numbered 1, 2, 3, ... Line numbers are not stored on the disk, but may be displayed or printed together with the text to facilitate text editing (Section 5.6.1).

5.4.2 Create Command

A create operation creates an empty, unprotected file with a given name on a given disk.
    Example:

> Command = *create*
> Drive no = *1*
> File name = *test*

If the disk already holds an unprotected file of the same name, that file is deleted.

5.4.3 Protect Command

A protect operation protects a given file on a given disk.
    Example:

> Command = *protect*
> Drive no = *1*
> File name = *edison3text*

5.4.4 Unprotect Command

An unprotect operation unprotects a given file on a given disk.
Example:

$$Command = unprotect$$
$$Drive\ no = 0$$
$$File\ name = subtitle$$

5.4.5 Rename Command

A rename operation changes the name of an unprotected file on a given disk.
Example:

$$Command = rename$$
$$Drive\ no = 1$$
$$Old\ name = layout$$
$$New\ name = format$$

5.4.6 Delete Command

A delete operation removes an unprotected (possibly empty) file from a given disk.
Example:

$$Command = delete$$
$$Drive\ no = 0$$
$$File\ name = subtitle$$

If the disk does not hold a file of that name, the operation has no effect.

5.4.7 Copy Command

A copy operation copies the contents of an existing file into a new, protected file with a given name on a given disk.
Example:

$$Command = copy$$
$$Input\ name = prefix$$
$$Output\ name = gametext$$
$$Output\ drive = 1$$

The two files may have the same name if they are stored on different disks.

5.5 PROGRAM DEVELOPMENT

An Edison program is a separately compiled procedure stored as a disk file. When you type the name of a program file, such as

$$Command = edit$$

the file is loaded from a disk and executed.

The operating system includes a set of procedures that serve as parameters of other programs. These programs must be prefixed by declarations of the procedure parameters. The declarations are stored on the system disk as a file named *prefix* (Section 5.15).

The development of a new program takes place in several steps:

(1) The system is started with the system disk in drive 0 and another disk in drive 1 (Section 5.3.3).

(2) A copy of the prefix is created on disk 1 using the copy command (Section 5.4.7).

(3) The rest of the program text is typed after the prefix copy using the insert command of the editor (Section 5.6.3).

(4) The program text is compiled (Section 5.7).

(5) If the compiler finds any errors, the program text is edited, and step (4) is repeated.

(6) When the program has been compiled successfully, it can be called from the terminal.

(7) When the program works, the program text can be printed (Section 5.14).

5.6 EDITING

An edit operation enables you to change an existing text file with a given name and store the resulting file under its original name on one of the disks. You may go back and forth across the text and make corrections, insertions, and deletions on the screen. The most recent error messages from the compiler may also be displayed during the editing.

Example:

> Command = *edit*
> File name = *subtitletext*
> Is this a new file? *no*

First, the editor scans the original text at the rate of 27 lines/sec to determine where each line begins on the disk. Then it fills the screen with the first lines of text and is ready to accept editing commands:

Edit session:
    [Edit command] * Finish
Edit command:
    Select line # Change lines # Insert lines #
    Delete lines # Show notes # Help user

The edit commands you type are not displayed, because their effects are both visible and correctable on the screen. The editor responds to an undefined command by ringing the bell.

5.6.1 Cursor Movement

The text is displayed with line numbers. All editing takes place on the current *cursor line* of the screen.The following commands are used to select a cursor line:

Select line:
    Simple jump # Conditional jump # Space #
    Backspace # Line increment
Simple jump:
    Line number Space
Conditional jump:
    Line number '?'
Line number:
    Numeral
Line increment:
    '+' Numeral

Simple jump: The cursor moves to a line given by a line number (if it exists); otherwise, the cursor moves to the last line of the file.

Conditional jump: The cursor moves to a line given by an original line number (that is, a line number in the original, unedited file). If the line no longer exists, the bell rings. (Original line numbers occur in the error messages from the compiler and assembler.)

Space: The cursor moves n lines ahead (if possible).

Backspace: The cursor moves n lines back (if possible).

Line increment: The line increment n is assigned a given value. (Initially, n is 1.)

5.6.2 Changes

Change lines:

'c' [Typed line] * Escape

After typing the character *c*, you can change a sequence of lines starting with the cursor line. The changes are made according to the line editing conventions described earlier (Section 5.2.1). After each return, the cursor moves to the beginning of the next line, which can then be edited. When the last line in the sequence has been edited, you must type an escape character.

5.6.3 Insertions

Insert lines:

'i' [Typed line] * Escape

After typing the character *i*, you can insert a sequence of typed lines after the cursor line. When the last line in the sequence has been typed, you must type an escape character. The screen is now refilled with edited text, and the cursor is positioned after the inserted text.

5.6.4 Deletions

Delete lines:

'd' [Delete] * Escape

After typing the character *d*, you can delete a sequence of lines starting with the cursor line. Each time a delete character is typed, the text on the cursor line is replaced by the word *Deleted*, and the cursor moves to the next line. When the last line in the sequence has been deleted, you must type an escape character. The screen is now refilled with edited text, and the cursor is positioned after the deleted text.

5.6.5 Disk Notes

Show notes:

's'

When you type the character *s*, the text of a disk file named *notes* is shown on the screen, where it remains until you type a return. The screen is then refilled with edited text, and the cursor returns to its previous position. This feature enables you to examine the most recent messages from the compiler and assembler during the editing of a program text.

5.6.6 Command Summary

Help user:
  'h'

When you type the character *h*, a summary of the editing commands is shown on the screen, where it remains until you type a return. The screen is then refilled with edited text, and the cursor returns to its previous position.

5.6.7 Finish

Finish:
  Bell

When you type a bell character, the editor responds with the question

Replace old file by edited file?

If you type *no* (followed by return), the original file is left unedited on the disk, and the edit operation has no effect.

If you type *yes* (followed by return), the editor asks you to type a drive number. The edited text is then stored as a protected file on the given disk under its original name, and the original text file is deleted.

The editor ignores the protection status of the original file.

The final copying of the edited file proceeds at 13 lines/sec. During this operation, the disks must hold both the original and the edited files. If the available disk space is exceeded, the system displays the message *disk limit* and restarts (Section 5.3.3). In that case, the original file is preserved, but the edited file is lost.

To avoid editing failure, you may list the catalog of the output disk before editing to make sure that the number of available pages exceeds the size of the original file (Section 5.3.5).

If the edited file must be placed on the same disk as the original file, it may be necessary to copy the original to the other disk and delete it from the given disk before editing (Sections 5.4.6 and 5.4.7).

Editing also fails if a file exceeds 3500 lines. But a file of that size will normally exceed the capacity of a disk anyhow.

5.6.8 New Files

The previous rules apply to the editing of existing files. The editor can also be used to input the text of a new file. If you answer *yes* to the initial question

Is this a new file?

a new empty file is created, and the message

Type i to insert lines in empty file

is displayed to remind you that insertion is the only possible operation on an empty file. When a sequence of lines has been inserted, all the editing commands apply to the new file. When you type a bell character, the editor asks the question

Save file?

If you answer *yes*, the editor asks for a drive number and stores the new file on the given disk.
If you answer *no*, the new file is lost.

5.7 COMPILATION

A compile operation translates an Edison program text into abstract code and stores it in a new, unprotected file on a given disk.
Example:

Command = *compile*
Text name = *systemtext*
Code name = *system*
Code drive = *0*
Compute check sums? *yes*

The Edison compiler consists of a program named compile, which calls four subprograms named edison1, edison2, edison3, and edison4. (The subprograms are also known as pass 1, pass 2, pass 3, and pass 4.) The compiler requires a code space of 8600 words and a data space of 8500 words in the store. After an initial time of 14 sec, the compilation speed is about 4 lines/sec.
The compiler creates a temporary file on each disk (named temp1 and temp2). Each of these files occupies about 40% of the disk space of the text file. The temporary files are deleted after the compilation.

The check sums (if any) produced by the compiler are first and second order sums of the intermediate and final code output by the passes. They can be used to determine whether a previously compiled program has been changed. The first-order check sum changes if any characters are inserted, deleted, or changed. The second-order check sum changes if any characters are exchanged. The first three passes each generate a single pair of check sums, for example:

systemtext check sums = 3325 4368

The last pass scans its input twice and generates two pairs of check sums. All the sums are stored in a disk file named *notes* created by the compiler. After a successful compilation with check sums, the following message is displayed:

check sums ready (see notes on disk)

If the compiler detects errors in a program text, they are reported in the notes file, and no code file is generated. Instead, the following message is displayed after the compilation:

compilation errors (see notes on disk)

The notes (if any) produced by the compiler are left on the disk after a compilation and may be used during the editing of an incorrect program text (Section 5.6.5).

5.7.1 Compilation Errors

An error message from the compiler is of the form

'**line**' Line number Message

where the message is one of the following:

Ambiguous name:
   The same name is declared more than once in the same block, or a name is exported from a module to a surrounding block in which the same name is declared with another meaning.

Invalid concurrent statement:
   The ordinal number of a process constant is not in the range 0:127, or several process statements have the same process constant.

Invalid constructor:
>   The number of expressions in a record (or array) constructor is not equal to the required number of fields (or elements).

Invalid procedure call:
>   The number of arguments in a procedure call is not equal to the number of parameters described by the procedure declaration.

Invalid range:
>   The lower bound of a range symbol exceeds the upper bound.

Invalid recursive use of name:
>   A name introduced by a constant declaration or a type declaration is being used within the declaration to define itself.

Invalid split procedure:
>   A block contains a pre- or postdeclaration of a split procedure but not both.

Invalid syntax:
>   The syntax of a sentence is invalid.

Invalid type:
>   The kind or type of an operand is invalid in the context in which it is used.

Invalid use of function variable:
>   A function variable is used outside the corresponding function body.

Numeral out of range:
>   A numeral is outside the range of integer values.

Undeclared name:
>   A name is being used without being declared.

5.7.2 Compilation Failure

When the compiler reaches the limit of one of its tables, the system displays one of the following messages and restarts (Section 5.3.3):

Block limit:
>   The depth of block nesting exceeds the limit defined by a constant named maxblock in pass 4.

Char limit:
> The total number of characters in the word symbols and names exceeds the limit defined by the constant named maxchar in pass 1.

Input limit:
> The compiler reaches the end of a temporary input file without recognizing an end symbol. This indicates an error in the compiler itself.

Label limit:
> The number of anonymous labels used to compile jump instructions exceeds the limit defined by the constant named maxlabel in passes 3 and 4.

Name limit:
> The number of named entities exceeds the limit defined by the constant named maxname in passes 1, 2, and 3.

Process limit:
> The number of process statements in a concurrent statement exceeds the limit defined by the constant named maxprocess in pass 3.

Word limit:
> The total number of word symbols and distinct names exceeds the limit defined by the constant named maxword in pass 1.

The standard values of the compiler constants are:

maxblock = 10	maxchar = 6500	maxlabel = 1000
maxname = 750	maxprocess = 20	maxword = 809

Using these limits, any one of the standard programs can be compiled on the system. When the largest pass of the compiler (pass 3) is compiled, the system uses nearly all the available store space (28 K words minus 200 words).

5.8 ASSEMBLING

An assemble operation translates an Alva program text into PDP 11 machine code and stores it in a new, unprotected file on a given disk.

Example:

Command = *assemble*
Text name = *kernel2text*
Code name = *kernel2*
Code drive = *1*
Compute check sums? *no*

The Alva assembler consists of a program named assemble, which calls two subprograms named alva1 and alva2. (The subprograms are also known as pass 1 and pass 2.) After an initial time of 7 sec, the assembling speed is about 10 lines/sec.

The assembler creates a temporary file on each disk. These files are deleted after the assembling (Section 5.7).

Like the compiler, the assembler produces check sums and error messages in a disk file named *notes* (Section 5.7).

5.8.1 Assembly Errors

An error message from the assembler is of the form

'line' Line number Message

where the message is one of the following:

Ambiguous name:
The same name is declared more than once.

Constant out of range:
The value 32768 is used as an operand, or the address used in a branch or repeat instruction is too far away from a given instruction to be reached [Digital, 1975].

Invalid declaration:
The register number used in a register declaration is outside the range 0:7, or the number of words in an array declaration is less than 1.

Invalid name kind:
A declared name is invalid in the context in which it is used.

Invalid padding:
The address given in a padding sentence is not even or is less than the current length of the stored entities.

Invalid syntax:
> The syntax of a sentence is invalid.

Invalid trap:
> The address given in a trap sentence is not a multiple of four or is less than the current length of the stored entities.

Undeclared name:
> A name is being used without being declared.

5.8.2 Assembly Failure

When the assembler reaches the limit of one of its tables, the system displays one of the following messages and restarts (Section 5.3.3):

Char limit:
> The total number of characters in the word symbols and names exceeds the limit defined by the constant named maxchar in pass 1.

Name limit:
> The number of named entities exceeds the limit defined by the constant named maxname in passes 1 and 2.

Word limit:
> The total number of word symbols and names exceeds the limit defined by the constant named maxword in pass 1.

The standard values of the assembler constants are:

$$maxchar = 3500 \qquad maxname = 400 \qquad maxword = 503$$

Using these limits, the system kernel for the PDP 11 computers can be assembled.

5.9 SYSTEM CHANGES

Each of the standard disks holds a copy of the kernel and the operating system (Sections 5.3.1 and 5.16.1). The following explains how the kernel and operating system are placed on a new disk that has been initialized as described in Section 5.3.4. The same operations can be used to put new versions of the kernel and operating system on all disks.

5.9.1 Newkernel Command

A newkernel operation copies an assembled kernel from a given file to a fixed set of pages on a given disk.
Example:

Command = *newkernel*
Drive no = *0*
File name = *kernel2*

The kernel code can occupy at most 4096 words on the disk. (The PDP 11 kernel occupies about 1800 words.)

5.9.2 Newsystem Command

A newsystem operation copies a compiled operating system from a given file to a fixed set of pages on a given disk.
Example:

Command = *newsystem*
Drive no = *1*
File name = *system*

The copy written on the disk consists of the given file name, which occupies 12 words, followed by the given file, which occupies at most 8180 words. (The Edison operating system occupies about 7200 words.) The file name is displayed by the kernel when the operating system fails or halts.

5.10 DOCUMENT PREPARATION

The system includes six standard programs for text processing, called cut, edit, format, paste, print, and underline. These programs are kept on the document disk (Section 5.3.1). The edit and print programs are also stored on the system disk.

A printed document is developed in several steps:

(1) A copy of the document disk is made by means of a backup operation (Section 5.3.6).

(2) A new text file is typed and stored on the disk copy by means of the editor (Section 5.6).

(3) The text file is then formatted and printed (Sections 5.13 and 5.14).

5.11 CUT AND PASTE

A cut operation copies a sequence of lines from an existing text file into a new, unprotected file on a given disk.

Example:

> Command = *cut*
> Input name = *systemtext*
> Output name = *piece*
> Output drive = *1*
> First line = *77*
> Last line = *105*

A paste operation writes the contents of a given text file at the end of another file and protects the latter.

Example:

> Command = *paste*
> Input name = *piece*
> Output name = *whole*

5.12 PROGRAM UNDERLINING

An underline operation makes a copy of a text file in which the lines are indented by a given number of spaces and in which the word symbols of the Edison language are enclosed in bars, for example |begin|, unless they occur within comments or character strings (Sections 3.2.3 and 3.2.4).

Example:

> Command = *underline*
> Input name = *edison3text*
> Output name = *printable*
> Output drive = *0*
> Indent text? *yes*
> Number of spaces = *2*

When the resulting file is printed, each line will be indented as requested and the word symbols will be underlined (i.e., begin) (Section 5.14).

5.13 TEXT FORMATTING

A format operation makes a copy of a text file in which the paragraphs are either flushed, centered, or balanced, as explained in the following. The formatting rate is 4 lines/sec.

Example:

$$Command = \mathit{format}$$
$$Input\ name = \mathit{netconcepts}$$
$$Output\ name = \mathit{printable}$$
$$Output\ drive = \mathit{0}$$

The input file must be a document with the following structure:

Document:
[Blank line # Paragraph # Format line] *
Paragraph:
Flushed paragraph # Centered paragraph #
Balanced paragraph
Blank line:
[Space] * Newline character

The following describes how a document will look when it is printed (Section 5.14).
Blank lines are printed as they stand.

5.13.1   Flushed Paragraphs

Flushed paragraph:
'{' Simple line ['/' Simple line] *
Simple line:
[Marked symbol # Space] * Newline character
Marked symbol:
['^'] Graphic character # Underlined symbol
Underlined symbol:
'|' Graphic sequence '|'
Graphic sequence:
Graphic character [Graphic character] *

A flushed paragraph is a sequence of simple lines that will be printed on the same page according to the following rules:

(1) The graphic characters {, }, ^, |, and \ will be printed only if they are preceded by a *stet* mark ^ .

(2) Each graphic character in an underlined symbol will be printed with an underscore.

(3) Any other graphic or newline character will be printed as it stands.

(4) If a printed page is too short to hold the whole paragraph, it will be printed at the beginning of the next page.

As an example, the paragraph

{   This paragraph consists of an |underlined| word and two /delimiters ^| and ^ ^.

will be printed as follows:

This paragraph consists of an <u>underlined</u> word and two delimiters | and ^ .

5.13.2 Centered Paragraphs

Centered paragraph:
        '}' Simple line ['/' Simple line] *

A centered paragraph is a sequence of simple lines that will be printed on the same page according to rules (1) to (4) for flushed paragraphs (Section 5.13.1) with the following rule added:

(5) The longest line of the paragraph will be centered on a printed page, and the rest of the lines will be indented accordingly.

As an example, the paragraph

}|if| sym = name1 |do| oldname
/|else| true |do| syntax(succ) |end|

will be printed as follows:

$$\text{if sym = name1 } \underline{\text{do}} \text{ oldname}$$
$$\underline{\text{else}} \text{ true } \underline{\text{do}} \text{ syntax(succ) } \underline{\text{end}}$$

5.13.3 Balanced Paragraphs

Balanced paragraph:
        [Space] * Balanced line [Balanced line] *
Balanced line:
        Phrase [Phrase] *

Phrase:
    Marked symbol [Marked symbol] * Separator
Separator:
    Space [Space] * [Newline character] #
    Newline character

A balanced paragraph is printed as follows:

(1) The initial spaces (if any) are printed as they stand.

(2) Each balanced line is printed on a single line. With the exception of the last line of the paragraph, all the balanced lines will be of the same length when they are printed. This is achieved by separating the phrases printed on a given line by one or more spaces.

(3) The phrases printed on the last line of a balanced paragraph will be separated only by single spaces.

(4) The marked symbols are printed according to rules (1), (2), and (3) for flushed paragraphs (Section 5.13.1).

As an example, the paragraph

This is a balanced paragraph that will look very
nice when it is printed on lines of the same
length. (The last
line will, however, be shorter.)

will be printed as follows:

This is a balanced paragraph that will look very nice
when it is printed on lines of the same length. (The last
line will, however, be shorter.)

The number of graphic characters printed on a balanced line is called the line size. The standard line size of 59 can be changed as described in Section 5.13.4.

5.13.4 Line Size

Format line:
    '\' 'linesize' Numeral Newline character

A line size instruction in a document is not printed but defines the number of graphic characters that will be printed on each line of a balanced paragraph (Section 5.13.3).

Example:

$$\text{\textbackslash linesize } 50$$

A document may include other kinds of format lines that influence the printing (Section 5.14.1). These lines have no effect on the text formatting described here but are merely copied into the output file.

5.14 PRINTING

A *program text* is stored as a text file without formatting instructions (Section 5.4.1). It can be printed by typing a command, such as the following:

> Command = *print*
> File name = *systemtext*
> Print all pages? *yes*
> Print line numbers? *yes*

The lines will be numbered consecutively from 1. Each printed page will hold 51 single-spaced lines with a left margin of 13 spaces.

A *formatted document* is a text file produced by the formatting program (Section 5.13). It may include instructions that define the format of the printed pages (Section 5.14.1). Such a document may be printed piecemeal or as a whole (with or without line numbers) by typing a command of the form

> Command = *print*
> File name = *printable*
> Print all pages? *no*
> First printed page = *8*
> Last printed page = *10*
> Print line numbers? *no*

In general, a printed file must have the following structure:

Printed file:
   [Format line # Text line] *

5.14.1 Page Format

Pages are printed according to the following rules:

(1) The pages are numbered consecutively.

(2) A running *header* and a *page number* are printed at the beginning of every page that has a page number > 1.

(3) The header line is followed by a fixed number of (single spaced) blank lines, called the *page top*.

(4) The page top is followed by a number of text lines. The maximum number of text lines printed on a single page is called the *page size*.

(5) Each line consists of a number of graphic characters preceded by a *margin* of fixed length. The maximum number of graphic characters printed on a single line is called the *line size*. Line numbers beginning with 1 may be printed in the margin.

(6) The text lines may be printed either *single spaced* or *double spaced*.

The default values of the printing parameters are the following:

```
First page no = 1
Header        = blank
Page top      = 3 blank lines
Page size     = 51 text lines
Spacing       = single spaced
Margin        = 13 spaces
Line size     = 59 graphic characters
```

The page format can, however, be changed by including format lines in the text:

Format line:
    '\' Instruction Newline character
Instruction:
    'doublespaced' # **'header'** Graphic sequence #
    'linegroup' Numeral # **'linesize'** Numeral #
    'margin' Numeral # **'newpage'** #
    'pageno' Numeral # **'pagesize'** Numeral
    'pagetop' Numeral # **'singlespaced'**

A format line is not printed but serves to redefine the page format:

A running header is centered in accordance with the current line size. The graphic sequence cannot contain any periods.

A *line group* instruction makes the printer skip the rest of the current page if it is too short to hold a given number of lines. (The formatting program outputs line group instructions to ensure that flushed and centered paragraphs are not split across pages. See Sections 5.13.1 and 5.13.2.)

A *new page* instruction makes the printer skip the rest of the current page.

The remaining instructions assign new values to the printing parameters defined earlier.

5.14.2 Line Printing

Text line:
    [Marked symbol # Space] * Newline character
Marked symbol:
    ['^ '] Graphic character # Underlined symbol
Underlined symbol:
    '|' Graphic sequence '|'
Graphic sequence:
    Graphic character [Graphic character] *

A text line is printed according to the following rules:

(1) The graphic characters | and ^ will be printed only if they are preceded by a *stet* mark ^.

(2) Each graphic character in an underlined symbol will be printed with an underscore.

(3) Any other graphic character will be printed as it stands.

(4) A newline character will be printed as a carriage return followed by a single line feed if the printing is single spaced, and by a double line feed if the printing is double spaced.

5.15 PROGRAM PARAMETERS

An Edison program invoked from the terminal must be prefixed by declarations of a set of standard parameters. A file named *prefix* contains a copy of these declarations, which are explained in the following.

5.15.1 Terminal Procedures

proc select(normal: bool)

This operation selects the *terminal mode*, which is either *normal* or *direct*. Before a user command is input, the system always selects the normal mode.

proc display(value: char)

This operation displays a given character on the screen. In the normal mode, a newline character (nl) is displayed as a carriage return (cr) followed by a line feed (lf). In the direct mode, a newline character is displayed as a line feed only.

proc accept(**var** value: char)

This operation accepts a character from the keyboard. In the normal mode, the following rules apply to typed input:

(1) A whole line must be typed before any of its characters can be accepted by a program. The characters are displayed as they are typed and may be edited as described in Section 5.2.1.

(2) A carriage return is converted to a newline character (nl).

In the direct mode, a single character is input directly from the keyboard and is neither displayed nor converted.

proc cursor(row, column: int)

This operation moves the cursor to a given row and column on the screen. The *rows* are numbered 1, 2, . . . , maxrow from top to bottom. The *columns* are numbered 1, 2, . . . , maxcolumn from left to right. The screen dimensions are given by two program parameters named *maxrow* and *max-column*.

proc erase

This operation erases all characters displayed from the cursor to the end of the screen.

proc pause

This operation displays the message

> push RETURN to continue

and waits until a carriage return is typed.

5.15.2 Print Procedure

> **proc** print(value: char)

This operation prints a given character on the printer. A newline character (nl) is printed as a line feed (lf).

5.15.3 File Procedures

> **proc** create(drive: int; title: name)
> **proc** delete(drive: int; title: name)
> **proc** rename(drive: int; old, new: name)

These operations have the same effect as the corresponding user commands (Sections 5.4.2, 5.4.5, and 5.4.6).

> **proc** protect(drive: int; title: name; value: bool)

This operation assigns a protection status to a file on a given disk.

> **proc** locate(**var** drive: int; title: name)

This operation locates the drive on which a given file is stored.

5.15.4 Stream Procedures

An open file is described by a variable of type *stream* which occupies 536 words of storage. A stream can either be open for input or output (but not both at the same time).

Although the values in a stream are declared to be of type character, they can be retyped before output and after input as explained in the Edison language report (Sections 3.13.5 and 3.14.1).

> **proc** openread(**var** file: stream; title: name)

This operation opens a given file as an input stream. Values can now be read from the beginning of the stream.

proc more(**var** file: stream): bool

This operation ascertains whether or not more values can be read from an input stream.

proc read(**var** file: stream; **var** value: char)

This operation reads the next value of an input stream.

proc mark(**var** file: stream): position

This operation records the disk location of the next value in an input or output stream. The location is defined by a value of type *position* (Section 5.16.2).

proc move(**var** file: stream; place: position)

This operation selects a disk location from which the next value of an input stream will be read.

proc endread(**var** file: stream)

This operation closes a given input stream.

proc openwrite(**var** file: stream; title: name)

This operation opens a given file as an output stream. Values can now be written at the end of the stream.

proc write(**var** file: stream; value: char)

This operation writes a given value at the end of an output stream.

proc endwrite(**var** file: stream)

This operation closes a given output stream.
The contents of the disks may be destroyed if a program terminates without closing its output streams.

5.15.5 Load Procedure

An Edison program P may include a declaration of another program Q:

lib proc Q (Parameter list)
[load (Program name)]

When P calls Q, a function named load is evaluated:

proc load(title: name): program

This operation loads a given program file into the store and executes it. The program code is described as a value of type *program* which occupies 12,300 words during the loading. When the program has been loaded, the storage space occupied by the code is determined by its actual length (in words).

5.15.6 Disk Procedures

At the hardware level, a disk is divided into 77 tracks (numbered 0 to 76). Each track consists of 26 sectors (numbered 1 to 26). A *sector* consists of 64 words:

const sectorlength = 64
array sector [1:sectorlength] (int)

The kernel treats a disk as an array of sectors with *sector numbers* in the range 0:2001. Sectors with consecutive numbers are separated by a physical gap of two sectors to reduce rotational delays during data transfers. The kernel uses the following algorithm to convert a sector number to a *disk address:*

track address := sectorno **div** 26
sector address := 3 * sectorno **mod** 26 + 1

The operating system provides two procedures for direct disk access:

proc readsector(drive, sectorno: int; **var** value: sector)
proc writesector(drive, sectorno: int; value: sector)

These operations read and write the contents of a given sector stored on a given disk drive. The use of these procedures requires detailed knowledge of the format of standard disks (Section 5.16).

5.15.7 Boolean Procedures

Boolean symbol:
    [Separator] * Truth symbol
Separator:
    Space # Newline character

Truth symbol:
    'false' # 'true' # 'no' # 'yes'

A capital letter used in a boolean symbol is equivalent to the corresponding small letter. A boolean symbol denotes a boolean value. The symbols *no* and *yes* are equivalent to *false* and *true*, respectively.

proc readbool(**proc** read(**var** c: char);   **var** value: bool)

This operation reads a boolean symbol and yields the corresponding boolean value. Each character is read by a procedure named read.

proc writebool(**proc** write(c: char);   value: bool)

This operation writes a boolean value as a boolean symbol of 5 characters (either *false* or *true*). Each character is written by a procedure named write.

5.15.8 Integer Procedures

Integer symbol:
    [Separator] * ['+' # '–'] Digit [Digit] *

An integer symbol denotes an integer value.

proc readint(**proc** read(**var** c: char);   **var** value: int)

This operation reads an integer symbol and yields the corresponding integer value. Each character is read by a procedure named read.

proc writeint(**proc** write(c: char);   value, length: int)

This operation writes an integer value as an integer symbol possibly preceded by spaces. Each character is written by a procedure named write. The number of characters written is given by a value named length.

5.15.9 Name Procedures

A name is a string type:

                const namelength = 12
                array name [1:namelength] (char)

Name symbol:
    [Separator] * Letter [Letter # Digit # '_'] *

A capital letter used in a name symbol is equivalent to the corresponding
small letter. A name symbol denotes a value of type name.

    proc readname(**proc** read(**var** c: char);   **var** value: name)

This operation reads a name symbol and yields the corresponding name.
Each character is read by a procedure named **read**.

    proc writename(**proc** write(c: char);   value: name)

This operation writes a name possibly followed by spaces. Each character is written by a procedure named **write**. A written name occupies 12
characters.

5.15.10   Line Procedures

A line is a string type:

> **const** linelength = 80
> **array** line [1:linelength] (char)

A *phrase* is a line that contains at least one period or newline character.

    proc writeline(**proc** write(c: char);   value: line)

This operation writes a phrase up to (but not including) the first period,
or up to (and including) the first newline character, whichever occurs first.
Each character is written by a procedure named **write**.

    proc assume(condition: bool;   text: line)

This operation displays a given phrase on the terminal as described
above and restarts the system (Section 5.3.3) if a boolean condition is false.
The operation has no effect if the condition is true.

5.15.11   Subset Procedure

A character set is a set type:

> **set** charset (char)

    proc subset(first, last: char): charset

This operation yields a set consisting of all the characters in a given range first:last.

5.15.12 PDP 11 Programs

An Edison program that uses the standard procedures obtain, place, and sense can be executed only on a PDP 11 computer (Section 3.19.7). Such a program should begin with the statement

assume(pdp11, line('PDP 11 program.'))

to ensure that it will halt immediately on another computer (Section 5.15.10).

The boolean parameter named *pdp11* defines whether or not a program is being executed on a PDP 11 computer.

The standard programs of the Edison system do not use the procedures obtain, place, and sense.

5.16 DISK FORMAT

The following is important only to programmers who wish to move the system to another computer that uses 8-inch floppy disks.

5.16.1 Disk Pages

A disk contains 2002 sectors numbered from 0 to 2001. Two sectors with consecutive numbers are separated by a physical gap of two sectors (Section 5.15.6). The operating system ignores the first 10 sectors and treats the rest of the disk as an array of pages with page numbers in the range 1:249. Each disk page consists of 8 sectors with consecutive sector numbers. The conversion of a page number to a sector number is defined as follows:

sectorno := 8 * pageno + 2

The use of the disk pages is shown below:

Pages	K words	Contents
1-2	1	Disk map and catalog
3-10	4	Kernel code
11-26	8	Operating system code
27-249	111.5	Files

Pages 1 and 2 hold the following data structures:

Disk map   4 sectors
Disk catalog   12 sectors

When the system is started, the first sector of the kernel code (sector 1 on track 1) is automatically loaded from disk 0 into the store at address 0 and is executed. This sector then loads the rest of the kernel code, which in turn loads the operating system code.

5.16.2 Disk Catalogs

A disk catalog is a record

record diskcatalog (size: int; contents: table)

The number of files described in a catalog are given by a size field ($0 \leqslant$ size $\leqslant 47$). The contents of a catalog is an array of items:

array table [1:47] (item)

Each item describes a single file by its name and attributes:

record item (title: name; attr: attributes)

where

record attributes (address: int; length: position;
protected: bool)

The address of a nonempty file is the page number of its first page. The other page numbers are found in the disk map (Section 5.16.3).
The length of a file is defined in terms of the number of pages occupied by the file, and by the number of data words stored on the last page of the file:

record position (pages, words: int)

5.16.3 Disk Maps

A disk map is a record that defines the number of free pages on a disk ($0 \leqslant$ free $\leqslant 223$) and a page number called next ($1 \leqslant$ next $\leqslant 249$):

record diskmap (free, next: int; contents: table)

A disk map includes an array that holds an integer value for every disk page:

array table [1:249] (int)

(1) If contents[m] = 32767, then page number m is free.

(2) If contents[m] = n (where $27 \leqslant n \leqslant 249$), then page number m is part of a file, and is followed by page number n in the file.

(3) If contents[m] = 0, then page number m is either the last page of a file or one of the reserved pages (if $1 \leqslant m \leqslant 26$).

5.17 PORTABILITY

The Edison system was designed to be portable to other microcomputers under the following assumptions:

The *computer* must be a 16-bit processor with a store of 32 K words. Store management facilities for addressing portions of a larger store are unnecessary.

The *display* must have the following properties:

(1) Screen dimensions: 20 lines (or more) of 64 to 80 characters each.

(2) Graphic characters: The full ASCII set. A graphic character is displayed at the cursor position, and the cursor moves one position to the right (if possible).

(3) Backspace character: The cursor moves one position to the left (if possible).

(4) Bell character: The bell rings.

(5) Line feed: If the cursor is above the bottom line of the screen, it moves one position down. If the cursor is on the bottom line, it stays there. In that case, the text shown on the top line disappears, and the remaining text shown moves up one line.

(6) Carriage return: The cursor remains on the same line and moves to the beginning of the line.

(7) Screen erasure: It must be possible to erase all characters shown from the cursor position to the end of the screen (both positions included).

(8) Cursor positioning: It must be possible to move the cursor directly to any position on the screen given by a column and a row number.

The *keyboard* must be able to input all the graphic ASCII characters plus the control characters backspace, bell, delete, escape, line feed, carriage return, and tabulate. A character input from the keyboard must not automatically be displayed on the screen.

The *printer* must be able to print all the graphic ASCII characters plus the control characters form feed, line feed, and carriage return.

The *disk drive* must be a dual drive for 8-inch IBM-compatible disks from which a system kernel (or part of it) can be loaded automatically.

The *system kernel* must be rewritten in the assembler language of the given computer and placed on the standard disks from which it is to be loaded (Section 5.16.1).

The kernel must load the Edison operating system from a disk and supply it with a set of parameters that enable the system to perform input/output operations on the terminal, the disk drives, and the printer. These parameters are declared at the beginning of the operating system.

6

ABSTRACT CODE

This chapter describes an instruction set for an ideal computer tailored to the programming language Edison. The compiler translates an Edison program into *Edison code* consisting of a sequence of these instructions.

On existing computers with different instruction sets the Edison code can be interpreted by a *kernel* written in microcode or assembly language. The kernel contains a small code piece for every Edison instruction.

This approach to code generation and execution has several advantages:

(1) It enables compiler writers to ignore the strange properties of existing computers and make code generation simple and systematic.

(2) It enables programmers to move Edison software to different computers by rewriting the kernel.

(3) It provides hardware designers with a precise specification of a new computer that can execute Edison code efficiently.

The usefulness of *portable code* has been demonstrated successfully by earlier software systems written in the languages Pascal and Concurrent Pascal.

In the following the Edison code is explained in detail.

6.1 VARIABLES

During the execution of an Edison program the code and variables used are kept in a store. The *store* named *st* is an array of words with consecutive addresses. In addition, a set of *index registers* called *b*, *s*, *t*, and *p* are used. These entities can be declared as follows in Edison:

array store [. . .] (int)

var st: store;   b, s, t, p: int

During the execution of a procedure, a block of storage known as a *call instance* of the procedure is used to hold the following local entities (Fig. 6.1):

(1) A function variable (if the procedure is a function)

(2) The parameters of the procedure (if any)

(3) A context link described below

(4) A set of values to be assigned to the index registers when the procedure has been executed

(5) The variables of the procedure and of all modules declared within it

(6) Temporary results used during the execution of the procedure

The address of the context link is called the *base address* of the call instance.

In this figure (and in the subsequent ones) low and high addresses are at the top and bottom of the figure, respectively.

Within a call instance the parameters and variables of the procedure are

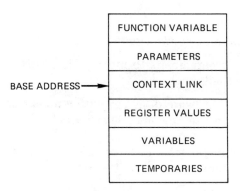

Fig. 6.1 Call instance

assigned store locations in their order of declaration from low toward high addresses.

With the exception of variable parameters, every *variable* occupies a fixed block of words that holds the current value of the variable. The address of the variable is the address of its first word.

A *variable parameter* occupies a single word that holds the address of the variable argument to which it is bound.

The store holds a *variable stack* for every process that is currently being executed. When a process calls a procedure, a call instance of that procedure is added on top of the variable stack of the process. And when the process has executed the procedure, the call instance is removed from the variable stack.

Consider, for example, a process described by the following program:

proc P1
var x1
  proc P2
  var x2
    proc P3
    var x3
    begin . . . **end**

    proc P4
    begin . . . P3 . . . **end**
  begin . . . P4 . . . **end**
begin . . . P2 . . . **end**

When the process has called the procedures P1, P2, P4, and P3 in that order and is executing P3, its variable stack contains a corresponding sequence of call instances (Fig. 6.2).

The *base address* of the most recent call instance created by a process (in this case, an instance of procedure P3) is kept in an index register named *b*.

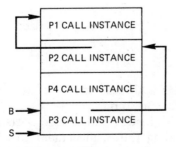

Fig. 6.2 Variable stack

The current top address of the variable stack of the process is held in another register named s (the *stack top*).

At any given moment a process can operate only on a subset of the call instances in its variable stack. This subset is called the *current context* of the process.

When a process is executing the procedure P3 in the example above, its context consists of a call instance of P3 and a call instance of each of the procedures P2 and P1 which surround P3 in the program text.

The call instance of the procedure P3 that is currently being executed is addressed by the base register b. This register points to a word, called the *context link*, which holds the base address of the call instance of the immediately surrounding procedure P2, which in turn points to the call instance of the next enclosing procedure P1.

In short, the call instances that form the current context of a process are linked together in their order of nesting from the currently executed procedure toward the procedures that surround it in the program text.

The dynamic creation and deletion of call instances (and the context links contained in them) are explained in Section 6.5. In the following we discuss the addressing of variables within a given context such as the one shown in Fig. 6.2.

A process selects a *whole variable* in the current context by executing two instructions named instance and variable:

instance(steps)
variable(displ)

Each *instruction* consists of an operation code followed by a single argument.

The execution of the instance instruction locates the call instance that includes the given variable by following the chain of context links a certain number of steps.

During the execution of procedure P3 in the previous example, a process would execute the instruction

instance(0)

to select a local variable x3, whereas the instruction

instance(1)

would be needed to locate a global variable x2 declared in the immediately surrounding procedure P2, and so on.

The execution of the instruction named variable completes the selection of a variable by adding the displacement of the variable to the base address of the call instance.

The operation codes and their arguments occupy one word each. This code representation is well suited to efficient interpretation by means of threaded code [Bell, 1973].

The address of the operation code that is currently being executed by a process is kept in a register named *p* (the *program index*) (Fig. 6.3).

The effect of executing an instruction will be described by an Edison procedure that has one parameter for each argument of the instruction, for example:

```
proc instance(steps: int)
var link, m: int
begin link := b;  m := steps;
    while m > 0 do
        link := st[link];  m := m - 1
    end;
    s := s + 1;  st[s] := link;  p := p + 2
end
```

An instance instruction computes the base address of a call instance in the current context and pushes it on the variable stack.

To obtain the address of a whole variable the instruction named variable adds a displacement to the base address on top of the stack:

```
proc variable(displ: int)
begin st[s] := st[s] + displ;  p := p + 2 end
```

A whole variable may be declared as a variable parameter. In that case, the execution of the instance and variable instructions will only compute the address of the parameter location. To obtain the address of the corresponding variable argument, an instruction named value is executed to replace the address of the parameter location by its value in the top of the stack. The algorithm for the value instruction will be described later.

This discussion of variable selection shows that the compiler may generate different instruction sequences for different instances of the same syntactic form of the Edison language.

The class of instruction sequences that corresponds to a syntactic form of the Edison language will be described by syntactic rules called *code rules*. The code rules are very similar to the syntactic rules of the language itself.

Fig. 6.3 An instruction

The basic symbols of the code rules are *instruction names* printed in bold-face type.

The following rule describes the code generated for the selection of a whole variable discussed above:

Whole variable symbol:
   instance variable [value]

This rule is to be understood as follows:

The code for a whole variable symbol consists of an instance instruction followed by a variable instruction and (possibly) followed by a value instruction.

The code that selects a whole variable may be followed by instructions that either select field variables or execute expressions and select indexed variables within the whole variable:

Variable symbol:
   Whole variable symbol [**field** # Expression **index**] *

A field instruction adds the displacement of a field to the address of a record variable held on top of the variable stack:

```
proc field(displ: int)
begin st[s] := st[s] + displ;   p := p + 2 end
```

An index instruction removes the value of an index expression from the top of the variable stack and computes the displacement of an element with a given length within an array value. The displacement is then added to the address of an array variable selected prior to the indexing:

```
proc index(lower, upper, length, lineno: int)
var i: int
begin i := st[s];   s := s - 1;
   if (i < lower) or (i > upper) do
      rangeerror(lineno)
   end;
   st[s] := st[s] + (i - lower) * length;
   p := p + 5
end
```

(Throughout this chapter the lengths of variables and temporaries are given in words.)

If the index value is outside the index range lower:upper, the program execution fails after reporting a range error.

The value of a selected variable is retrieved by executing an instruction named value:

Variable retrieval:
　　Variable symbol **value**

```
proc value(length: int)
var y, i: int
begin y := st[s]; i := 0;
   while i < length do
      st[s + i] := st[y + i]; i := i + 1
   end;
   s := s + length - 1; p := p + 2
end
```

A value instruction removes the address of a variable from the top of the variable stack and replaces it by the value of the variable.

6.2 CONSTANTS AND CONSTRUCTORS

Data values are stored as binary numerals known as stored values.

The stored value of an elementary value x is the ordinal value of x held in a single word.

An instruction named constant pushes a fixed elementary value on the variable stack:

```
proc constant(value: int)
begin s := s + 1; st[s] := value; p := p + 2 end
```

The evaluation of an elementary constructor involves evaluating an expression that leaves an elementary value on top of the variable stack:

Elementary constructor:
　　Expression

A stored record value is held in a block of words. The value consists of the fields stored in their order of declaration.

Record constructor:
　　Expression list

Expression list:
    Expression [Expression] *

The evaluation of a record constructor involves evaluating a list of expressions to obtain the fields and leave a record value on the variable stack.

A stored array value is held in a block of words. The value consists of the elements stored in their order of indexing.

Array constructor:
    Expression list [**blank**]

The evaluation of an array constructor involves evaluating a list of expressions to obtain the elements and leave an array value on the variable stack.

An abbreviated constructor for a string value includes an instruction named blank which adds the necessary number of spaces to the string value:

```
proc blank(number: int)
var i: int
begin i := 0;
   while i < number do
      i := i + 1;  st[s + i] := int(' ')
   end;
   s := s + number;  p := p + 2
end
```

A stored set value is held in a block of fixed length (called the set length). Within this block the bits are numbered from 0 to an upper bound called the set limit. (The present compiler assumes a set length of 8 words and a set limit of 127.)

Each possible member x of a set value is represented by a single bit: bit number int (x). The bit has the value one if x is a member of the set value, and zero if it is not.

Set constructor:
    [Expression list] **construct**

The evaluation of a set constructor involves evaluating a (possibly empty) list of expressions to obtain the members and then executing an instruction named construct to obtain a set value with the given members (if any).

```
set settype (int)

proc construct(number, lineno: int)
var member, i: int;  new: settype
begin i := 0;  new := settype;
   while i < number do
      member := st[s];  s := s - 1;
      if (member < 0) or (member > setlimit) do
        rangeerror(lineno)
      end;
      new := new + settype(member);  i := i + 1
   end;
   storeset(s + 1, new);
   s := s + setlength;  p := p + 3
end
```

The new set value is initially empty. The number of members given by the instruction are removed one at a time from the variable stack and are included in the set value, which is then finally pushed on the variable stack.

The copying of the new set value from a variable named new to a temporary location on top of the variable stack is performed by calling a procedure named storeset.

If a member is outside the base range 0:setlimit, the program execution fails after calling a procedure named range error that reports the failure and halts.

The following code rule summarizes the possible forms of constructors:

Constructor:
    Elementary constructor # Record constructor #
    Array constructor # Set constructor

6.3 EXPRESSIONS

The evaluation of an expression leaves a value on top of the variable stack according to the rules described in the following.

Factor:
    constant # Constructor # Variable retrieval #
    Function call # Expression # Factor **not**

A factor is evaluated either by executing a constant instruction, a variable retrieval, or a function call, or by evaluating a constructor, an expression, or another factor followed by a not instruction:

```
proc notx
begin st[s] := int(not bool(st[s])); p := p + 1 end
```

Term:

Factor # Term Factor Multiplying instruction

Multiplying instruction:

multiply # divide # modulo # and # intersection

A term is evaluated either by evaluating a factor or by applying a multiplying instruction to the values of another term and a factor:

```
proc multiply(lineno: int)
begin s := s - 1; st[s] := st[s] * st[s + 1];
    if overflow do rangeerror(lineno) end;
    p := p + 2
end
```

A boolean function named overflow determines whether the result of an arithmetic operation is within the range of integers; if not, the program execution fails after reporting a range error.

The divide and modulo instructions are similar to the multiply instruction, but use the operators **div** and **mod** instead of *.

```
proc andx
begin s := s - 1;
    st[s] := int(bool(st[s]) and bool(st[s + 1]));
    p := p + 1
end
```

The intersection instruction uses two operations named loadset and storeset to copy a set value from the stack to a local variable (and vice versa).

```
proc intersection
var x, y: settype
begin s := s - setlength; loadset(s + 1, y);
    loadset(s - setlength + 1, x);
    x := x * y;
    storeset(s - setlength + 1, x); p := p + 1
end
```

Simple expression:

Term [**minus**] #

Simple expression Term Adding instruction

Adding instruction:
    add # **subtract** # **or** # **union** # **difference**

A simple expression is evaluated either by evaluating a term possibly followed by a minus instruction or by applying an adding instruction to the values of another simple expression and a term.

```
proc minus(lineno: int)
begin st[s] := - st[s];
    if overflow do rangeerror(lineno) end;
    p := p + 2
end
```

The add and subtract instructions are similar to the multiply instruction, but use the arithmetic operators + and - instead of *.

The or instruction is similar to the and instruction, but uses the operator or instead of **and.**

The union and difference instructions are similar to the intersection instruction, but use the set operators + and - instead of *.

Expression:
    Simple expression
        [Simple expression Relational instruction]
Relational instruction:
    equal # **notequal** # **less** # **notless** #
    greater # **notgreater** # **in**

An expression is evaluated either by evaluating a simple expression or by applying a relational instruction to the values of two simple expressions.

```
proc equal(length: int)
var y, i:  int
begin y := s - length + 1;
    s := y - length;  i := 0;
    while (i < length - 1) and
        (st[s + i] = st[y + i]) do
            i := i + 1
    end;
    st[s] := int(st[s + i] = st[y + i]);
    p := p + 2
end
```

The instruction notequal is similar but uses the operator <> instead of = in the assignment to st[s].

```
proc less
begin s := s - 1;   st[s] := int(st[s] < st[s + 1]);
   p := p + 1
end
```

The instructions notless, greater, and notgreater are similar, but use the operators $>=, >$, and $<=$ instead of $<$.

```
proc inx(lineno:  int)
var x:  int;  y:  settype
begin s := s - setlength;   loadset(s + 1, y);
   x := st[s];
   if (x < 0) or (x > setlimit) do
     rangeerror(lineno)
   end;
   st[s] := int(x in y);   p := p + 2
end
```

6.4 SEQUENTIAL STATEMENTS

The code rules for statement lists and statements are:

Statement list:
   Statement [Statement] *
Statement:
   Empty # Assignment statement # Procedure call #
   If statement # While statement # When statement #
   Concurrent statement

An assignment involves the selection of a variable and the evaluation of an expression followed by the execution of an instruction named assign:

Assignment statement:
   Variable symbol Expression assign

```
proc assign(length:  int)
var x, y, i:  int
begin s := s - length - 1;   x := st[s + 1];
   y := s + 2;   i := 0;
   while i < length do
     st[x + i] := st[y + i];   i := i + 1
   end;
   p := p + 2
end
```

If statement:
    Conditional statement list
Conditional statement list:
    Conditional statement [Conditional statement] *
Conditional statement:
    Expression **do** Statement list **else**

The execution of an if statement involves executing a list of one or more conditional statements.

The execution of a conditional statement involves evaluating a boolean expression and executing an instruction named do: If the expression yields the value true, the statement list and an instruction named else are then executed; otherwise, the execution continues after the else instruction.

The do instruction removes a boolean value from the variable stack and jumps to a program address if the value is false. The program address is given by a displacement relative to the do instruction:

```
proc dox(displ: int)
begin
  if bool(st[s]) do p := p + 2
  else true do p := p + displ end;
  s := s - 1
end
```

The else instruction jumps to a program address given by a displacement:

```
proc elsex(displ: int)
begin p := p + displ end
```

The code of an if statement

```
if . . .
else B do SL
    . . .
end
```

includes the following program addresses L and M:

```
    . . .
B do(L) SL else(M) L:
    . . .
M:
```

The execution of a while statement involves executing a conditional statement list:

While statement:
    Conditional statement list

The code of a while statement

> **while** . . .
> **else** B **do** SL
>
>   . . .
>
> **end**

includes the following program addresses L and M:

> M: . . .
>   B do(L) SL else(M) L:
>   . . .

    Procedure calls, when statement, and concurrent statements are described elsewhere in this chapter.

6.5 PROCEDURES AND MODULES

    The addressing of variables in a given context was discussed in Section 6.1. The following describes how the context of a process changes during the execution of procedure calls.

    Consider again the program example used in Section 6.1:

> **proc** P1
> **proc** P2
>   **proc** P3
>   **begin** . . . **end**
>
>   **proc** P4
>   **begin** . . . P3 . . . **end**
> **begin** . . . P4 . . . **end**
> **begin** . . . P2 . . . **end**

When a process has called the procedures P1, P2, and P4 in that order and is executing P4, the variable stack of the process contains a call instance of each of these procedures as shown in Fig. 6.4a.

    The effect of calling procedure P3 within P4 is to add a call instance of P3 on top of the stack and link it to the call instances of the procedures P2 and P1 which surround P3 in the program text (Fig. 6.4b).

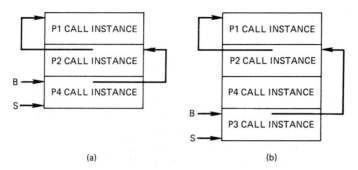

Fig. 6.4 Dynamic context change

When the execution of P3 terminates, the execution of the given process continues in the old context shown in Fig. 6.4a.

We will now describe the sequence of instructions executed when a process calls procedure P3:

(1) If the procedure is a function, its call instance must include a function variable that will hold the result of the call (see Fig. 6.1). The space for this variable is allocated on top of the variable stack by executing an instruction named valspace:

$$\textbf{proc } \text{valspace(length: int)}$$
$$\textbf{begin } s := s + length; \quad p := p + 2 \textbf{ end}$$

(2) The parameters of the procedure called are created by executing the code for the arguments of the procedure call.

The code for an argument is the code for an expression, a variable symbol, or a procedure argument.

The evaluation of an expression allocates space for a value parameter on top of the stack and assigns the given value to it.

The evaluation of a variable symbol allocates space for a variable parameter on top of the stack and assigns the address of the given variable to it.

The evaluation of a procedure argument will be described later.

(3) The procedure P3 must be executed in the context of the procedures P2 and P1 which surround it in the program text. The execution of the instruction

$$\text{instance}(1)$$

locates the call instance of P2 in the old context which is valid before the procedure P3 is called (Fig. 6.4a). This instruction pushes the context link to P2 on top of the parameters in the variable stack.

(4) The jump to the code of the procedure P3 is performed by executing an instruction

$$proccall(displ)$$

When the process returns from the procedure, the index registers b, s, and t must be assigned the values they had prior to the procedure call. Figure 6.4a shows the return values of the registers b and s. The purpose of the t register will be described in Section 6.6. The return value of the program index p is the address of the instruction that follows the procedure call.

The proccall instruction pushes the return values of the index registers b, t, and p (but not s) on top of the stack, and assigns new values to b and s as shown in Fig. 6.5. Following this the program index is assigned the address of the procedure code. The code address is given by its displacement relative to the proccall instruction to make the code relocatable in the store.

```
proc proccall(displ: int)
begin st[s + 1] := b;  st[s + 3] := t;
    st[s + 4] := p + 2;  b := s;
    s := s + 4;  p := p + displ
end
```

(The return value of s is placed in the call instance during the execution of an instruction named procedure which will be described shortly.)

What has been described so far is the code generated for a procedure call (but not for a procedure body). This code is summarized by the fol-

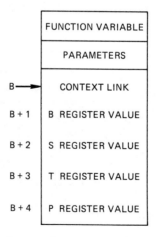

Fig. 6.5 Partial call instance

lowing rules:

Function call:
    valspace Procedure call
Procedure call:
    [Argument list] Procedure jump
Argument list:
    Argument [Argument] *
Argument:
    Expression # Variable symbol # Procedure argument
Procedure jump:
    instance proccall

The execution of the procedure body takes place as follows:
(5) The first instruction executed in the body is named procedure:

```
proc procedure(paramlength, varlength, templength,
    lineno: int)
begin st[b + 2] := b – paramlength – 1;
    s := s + varlength;
    if s + templength > stackmax do
        variablelimit(lineno)
    end;
    p := p + 5
end
```

The procedure instruction completes the call link with a return value of the stack top s that will cause the parameters to be removed from the variable stack when the procedure has been executed. Following this, the call instance is extended with space for the variables of the procedure, and it is checked that there is room in the variable stack for the temporaries used during execution of the procedure body.

The upper limit of the variable stack is given by a global value named stackmax. If this limit is exceeded, the program execution fails after calling a procedure named variable limit that reports the failure and halts.

(6) The modules (if any) declared within the procedure are initialized one at a time by executing the code of their initial operations.

(7) The statements of the procedure itself are executed one at a time.

(8) The last instruction executed in the procedure is named endproc:

```
proc endproc
begin p := st[b + 4]; t := st[b + 3];
    s := st[b + 2]; b := st[b + 1]
end
```

This instruction assigns the return values stored in the call instance of the procedure to the index registers. The effect of this is to remove the call instance (except for a possible function value) from the variable stack and jump to the code that follows the procedure call. This completes the execution of the procedure call.

The procedure code described above is summarized by the following rules:

Complete procedure declaration:
    procedure [Declaration] * Statement list **endproc**
Declaration:
    Procedure declaration # Module declaration # Empty
Module declaration:
    [Declaration] * Statement list

A syntactic form of the language, such as a constant declaration, that is not mentioned in the code rules has an *empty code* sequence.

Several details have been ignored in the general discussion of procedure calls and procedure declarations:

(1) *Standard procedure calls* are compiled into system-dependent instructions that will not be described here. We will merely change the code rule for procedure calls as follows:

Procedure call:
    [Argument list] Procedure jump #
    Standard procedure call

(2) A *procedure parameter* is a parameter that is bound to another procedure, such as Q5 in the following program example:

          proc Q1
            proc Q2
            begin . . . **end**

            proc Q3
              proc Q4(**proc** Q5)
              begin . . . Q5 . . . **end**
             begin . . . Q4(Q2) . . . **end**
           begin . . . Q3 . . . **end**

When a process has called procedures Q1 and Q3 in that order and is executing Q3, its variable stack looks as shown in Fig. 6.6a.

Later, when the process has called procedures Q4 and Q5 (which is bound to procedure Q2), the stack will have changed as shown in Fig. 6.6b.

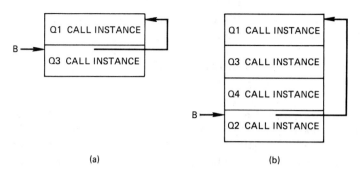

(a)   (b)

Fig. 6.6 Procedure parameter call

The procedure parameter Q5 is now executed in the context of the procedure Q1 which surrounds the argument Q2 in the program text.

This is achieved as follows: When procedure Q4 is called with procedure Q2 as an argument, the following instructions are executed in the old context shown in Fig. 6.6a:

instance(1)
procarg(displ)

The instance instruction computes the base address of the call instance of the procedure Q1 which surrounds the procedure argument Q2 and pushes it on the stack.

The instruction named procarg then pushes the code address of the procedure argument Q2 on top of the base address.

proc procarg(displ: int)
begin s := s + 1; st[s] := p + displ; p := p + 2 **end**

The code address is given by its displacement relative to the procarg instruction.

The execution of these two instructions creates the procedure parameter Q5 in the call instance of procedure Q4. The procedure parameter consists of two words defining the context link and code address to be used when the procedure parameter Q5 is called within Q4 (Fig. 6.7).

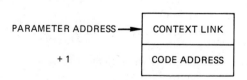

Fig. 6.7 Procedure parameter

When procedure Q4 calls its procedure parameter Q5 (bound to Q2), the following instructions are executed:

instance(0)
paramcall(displ)

The instance instruction locates the call instance of Q4, which includes the procedure parameter Q5. The displacement of the parameter within the call instance is given by the paramcall instruction. The latter pushes the context link held in the procedure parameter on top of the stack and creates a partial call instance of Q2 as shown in Fig. 6.6b. The call then proceeds as described earlier for the proccall instruction except that the code address of the procedure Q2 is also retrieved from the procedure parameter Q5:

```
proc paramcall(displ: int)
var addr: int
begin addr := st[s] + displ;
   st[s] := st[addr];  st[s + 1] := b;
   st[s + 3] := t;  st[s + 4] := p + 2;
   b := s;  s := s + 4;  p := st[addr + 1]
end
```

To summarize the above we need a new rule describing the code for a procedure used as an argument in a procedure call:

Procedure argument:
   instance procarg

and a previous rule must be extended to include the call of a procedure used as a parameter of another procedure:

Procedure jump:
   instance proccall # instance paramcall

As the following example shows, a procedure Q3 may call another procedure Q1 and pass one of its own procedure parameters Q4 as an argument to Q1:

```
proc Q1(proc Q2)
begin . . . Q2 . . . end

proc Q3(proc Q4)
begin . . . Q1(Q4) . . . end
```

This use of a procedure parameter Q4 as a procedure argument in a call causes the following instructions to be executed:

instance(0)

paramarg(displ)

The instance instruction and the displacement of the paramarg instruction serve to locate the procedure parameter Q4 in the call instance of Q3.

The paramarg instruction creates the new procedure parameter Q2 by copying the context link and code address from the original parameter Q4 onto the top of the variable stack.

proc paramarg(displ: int)
var addr: int
begin addr := st[s] + displ;
   st[s] := st[addr];
   st[s + 1] := st[addr + 1];
   s := s + 1; p := p + 2
end

Since a procedure used as an argument in a call can refer to either a procedure declaration or a procedure parameter, the code rule for procedure arguments must be extended as follows:

Procedure argument:
   instance procarg # instance paramarg

(3) When the procedure instruction of a procedure P has been executed, the code of the local declarations of P is executed to initialize the modules declared within P.

During this initialization, the code of the local procedures of P must be bypassed. To achieve this, every procedure in a program (except the outermost one) is preceded by a goto instruction that causes a jump around the entire procedure code.

proc goto(displ: int)
begin p := p + displ **end**

Like all other jumps, this one is relative to the location of the jump instruction.

The goto instruction makes it necessary to revise the previous code rule for complete procedure declarations:

Complete procedure declaration:
    [goto] **procedure** [Declaration] *
        Statement list **endproc**

(4) The possible code sequences for procedure declarations are summarized as follows:

Procedure declaration:
    Complete procedure declaration #
    Library procedure declaration # Empty

Library procedure declarations are described in Section 6.6. Predeclarations of *split procedures* generate no code. The corresponding post declarations are compiled as complete procedure declarations.

6.6 PROGRAMS

In addition to the variable stack, the store holds a *program stack* for each process that is currently being executed.

Initially, the program stack contains the code of a single Edison program (called the operating system). When a process calls a library procedure, the code of the procedure is retrieved from a program library and is added to the program stack. And when the process has executed the procedure body, the corresponding library code is removed from the program stack (Fig. 6.8).

An index register named t holds the address of the current top of the program stack.

The code of an Edison program consists of a single word that defines the length of the compiled program followed by the code of a complete procedure plus a final instruction named endcode:

Program:
    Program length Complete procedure declaration **endcode**

The execution of the program normally consists of executing the code of the procedure declaration. (The endcode instruction will be described later.)

When a program calls a library procedure declaration of the form

        lib proc Procedure name (Parameter list)
        [Expression]

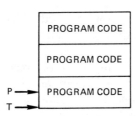

Fig. 6.8 Program stack

an expression is evaluated and used to locate a compiled program in a library and execute it.

The conventions for program loading are system dependent. The following assumes that a software system written in Edison includes a function named load that uses the name of a program to retrieve its code:

proc load(title: name): program

The data types used are declared as follows:

array name [1:namelength] (char)
array code [1:maxcode] (int)
record program (progname: name; progcode: code)

The program name is stored together with the code so that it can be displayed if the execution fails.

Using this convention, the expression in a library procedure declaration is simply a call of the load function, for example:

load(name('edit'))

The advantage of programming the load function in Edison is that the kernel only needs to know the structure of the program code but makes no assumption about the structure of the program library.

A library procedure declaration generates code of the following form:

Library procedure declaration:
goto libproc Expression **endlib**

The purpose of the goto instruction is to skip the library procedure declaration initially as explained earlier (Section 6.5).

When a program calls a library procedure, an instruction named libproc is executed immediately after the procedure jump:

```
proc libproc(paramlength, templength, lineno:  int)
begin st[b + 2]  := b – paramlength – 1;
  if s + templength > stackmax do
    variablelimit(lineno)
  end;
  p := p + 4
end
```

The instruction checks that there is sufficient space in the variable stack for the temporaries needed to evaluate the expression and completes a call link in the top of the variable stack with a return value of the stack top s.

The expression (assumed now to be a call of the load function) is then evaluated to place the name and code of a library procedure on top of the variable stack.

The instruction named endlib moves the library procedure from the variable stack to the program stack and changes the stack top s and the program top t accordingly:

```
proc endlib
begin move_program;  p := start_address end
```

Following this, the execution continues with the first instruction of the program.

As described earlier, a program is compiled as any other procedure beginning with an instruction named procedure and ending with an instruction named endproc (Section 6.5).

When a program P calls a library procedure, a call instance is created in the variable stack. The return value of the program index p is the address of the instruction that follows the call. The return value of the program top t is the value that this register has when the library procedure is being called but has not yet been loaded on the program stack. Consequently, when the library procedure eventually executes an endproc instruction, and thereby assigns the return values to the index registers, the library procedure is automatically removed from the program stack, and the execution continues in the previous program P following the call.

When the computer is started, a fixed Edison program is placed in the program stack and is executed. As all other programs, this operating system will eventually execute an endproc instruction. Since the operating system is called by the kernel (and not by another program), the following ad hoc rule is used: The variable stack is initialized with a call link that holds a dummy return address named none:

b := stackmin;   s := b + 4;   st[s] := none

The endproc instruction is then modified as follows:

> **proc** endproc
> **begin**
>   **if** st[b + 4] <> none **do** as before
>   **else** true **do** p := p + 1 **end**
> **end**

If the execution of the operating system reaches the final endproc instruction, the execution proceeds with the following instruction, which is named endcode:

> **proc** endcode(lineno: int)

This is a system-dependent instruction that reports the termination of the operating system and halts. Although all programs include this instruction, it can be reached only by the operating system.

6.7 CONCURRENT STATEMENTS

Initially, an Edison program is executed as a single process. When this initial process reaches a concurrent statement, it jumps to an instruction named cobegin:

Concurrent statement:
    goto Process statement list **cobegin**
Process statement list:
    Process statement [Process statement] *
Process statement:
    process Statement list **also**

The cobegin instruction creates a *tree-structured variable stack* with a branch for every process statement. Following this the process statements are executed simultaneously.

The stack of the initial process is the *root* of the stack tree. It holds the *common variables* of the processes. When a process calls one or more procedures, its stack branch is extended with local variables that are inaccessible to other processes. The context of a process consists of those call instances in the stack branch and root that are chained together by context links (Fig. 6.9).

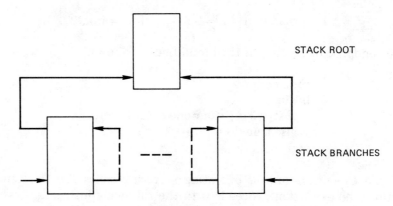

Fig. 6.9 Tree structured variable stack

The execution of a process statement takes place in three steps:

(1) An instruction named process checks that the stack branch of a process has sufficient space for the temporaries needed to execute a statement list.

(2) The statement list is executed.

(3) An instruction named also is executed. This removes a stack branch and terminates the corresponding process with one exception: The last process to reach an also instruction continues the execution after the cobegin instruction in the context of the stack root.

The code of a concurrent statement

> **cobegin** . . .
> **also** ci **do** SLi
>
>   . . .
>
> **end**

includes the following program addresses L1, . . . , Lm, M, N:

>   goto(M) . . .
> Li: process( ) SLi also(N)
>
>   . . .
>
> M: cobegin(m, n, c1, L1, . . , cm, Lm)
> N:

where the constant n is a line number.

A when statement generates the following code:

When statement:

    when Synchronized statement **wait endwhen**

Synchronized statement:

    Conditional statement list

The execution of the instruction named when delays a process until no other process is executing a synchronized statement.

If all the boolean expressions in the synchronized statement yield the value false, the instruction named wait is executed; otherwise, the instruction named endwhen is executed.

The wait instruction enables another process (if any) to execute a synchronized statement and jumps back to the when instruction.

The endwhen instruction enables another process (if any) to execute a synchronized statement.

The code of a when statement

> **when** . . .
> **else** B **do** SL
>   . . .
> **end**

includes the following program addresses L, M, and N:

> M: when . . .
>   B do(L) SL else(N) L:
>   . . .
>   wait(M)
> N: endwhen

The instructions described above are system dependent and are explained further in the following section on Single Processor Systems.

6.8 SINGLE-PROCESSOR SYSTEMS

Initially, an Edison program is executed as a sequential process with a single variable stack and a single program stack.

Figure 6.10 shows the store of a single-processor system which holds a kernel and the two stacks. The stacks grow toward one another in the free space between them.

In this case it is most convenient to let the index register t hold the address of the first free word above the program stack. The value of this register can then also serve as the value *stackmax* that defines the maximum extent of the variable stack.

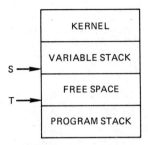

Fig. 6.10 Single-processor store

We will assume that a single-processor system does not permit concurrent processes to call library procedures. Consequently, the program stack does not change during the execution of a concurrent statement.

When a concurrent statement is reached, the free space is divided evenly among the processes. The variable stack is now tree structured as described earlier.

The processor now executes the processes in cyclical order. Each process runs until it reaches an also or a wait instruction. The register values of the other processes are stored in a queue declared as follows:

> **record** procstate (bx, sx, tx, px: int)
> **array** queue [1:maxproc] (procstate)
> **var** q: queue; this, tasks: int

The queue index of the process that is currently being executed is named this, while the number of concurrent processes is named tasks.

The processor preempts and resumes the execution of a process as follows:

> **proc** preempt
> **begin** q[this] := procstate(b, s, t, p) **end**
>
> **proc** resume
> **begin** b := q[this].bx; s := q[this].sx;
>   t := q[this].tx; p := q[this].px
> **end**

When the processor is started, there is only one process:

> this := 1; tasks := 1

A cobegin instruction defines the number of processes to be executed and includes a process constant ci and a program displacement Li for every process:

$$cobegin(m, n, c1, L1, \ldots, cm, Lm)$$

The cobegin instruction saves the current values of the stack top s and the program top t in two kernel variables:

$$\textbf{var } stacktop, progtop: int$$

Following this, the queue is assigned the initial states of the m processes, and the first of these is then executed:

```
proc cobeginx(no, lineno: int;  arg: arglist)
var length, i:  int
begin tasks := no;
   if tasks > maxproc do processlimit(lineno) end;
   stacktop := s;  progtop := t;
   length := (t - s) div tasks;  i := 0;
   while i < tasks do
      i := i + 1;  t := s + length;
      q[i] := procstate(b, s, t, p + arg[i].displ);
      s := t
   end;
   this := 1;  resume
end
```

The first instruction executed by a process checks the size of the local stack space:

```
proc process(templength, lineno:  int)
begin
   if s + templength > t do
      variablelimit(lineno)
   end;
   p := p + 3
end
```

The last instruction executed by a process does one of two things:

(1) If some other processes are not terminated yet, the given process is removed from the queue by compacting the remaining entries and resuming the execution of another process.

(2) If all other processes have terminated, the execution continues after the concurrent statement using the original stack top and program top.

```
proc alsox(displ: int)
begin
  if tasks > 1 do
    while this < tasks do
      q[this] := q[this + 1];  this := this + 1
    end;
    tasks := tasks - 1;  this := 1;  resume
  else true do
    s := stacktop;  t := progtop;  p := p + displ
  end
end
```

Since each process runs to completion or delay, mutual exclusion is automatically ensured during the execution of a synchronized statement. So the instructions named when and endwhen have no effect other than incrementing the program index p by one.

A wait instruction serves to preempt the current process and resume another process (if any). Later, when the preempted process is resumed again, it will jump back to a when instruction given by a program displacement:

```
proc wait(displ: int)
begin p := p + displ;  preempt;
  this := this mod tasks + 1;  resume
end
```

On a PDP 11 computer the Edison kernel occupies 1800 words in a store of 28 K words:

Error reporting	400 words
Program loading	200 words
Code interpreter	1200 words
Kernel	1800 words

The kernel may pass procedures written in assembly language as parameters to the initial Edison program, which may then pass them on to other programs. The reader is referred to the kernel listing for details (Chapter 8).

6.9 CODE SUMMARY

The following is a list of the code rules of the Edison language. Standard procedure calls are not described here since they are system dependent.

Complete procedure declaration:
   [goto] procedure [Declaration] *
      Statement list endproc
Library procedure declaration:
   goto libproc Expression endlib
Procedure declaration:
   Complete procedure declaration #
   Library procedure declaration # Empty
Module declaration:
   [Declaration] * Statement list
Declaration:
   Procedure declaration # Module declaration # Empty
Variable symbol:
   instance variable [value] [field # Expression index] *
Constructor:
   [Expression] * [blank # construct]
Factor:
   constant # Constructor # Variable symbol value #
   valspace Procedure call # Expression # Factor not
Multiplying instruction:
   multiply # divide # modulo # and # intersection
Term:
   Factor [Factor Multiplying instruction] *
Adding instruction:
   add # subtract # or # union # difference
Simple expression:
   Term [minus] [Term Adding instruction] *
Relational instruction:
   equal # notequal # less # notless #
   greater # notgreater # in
Expression:
   Simple expression
      [Simple expression Relational instruction]
Procedure argument:
   instance procarg # instance paramarg
Argument:
   Expression # Variable symbol # Procedure argument

Argument list:
    Argument [Argument] *
Procedure jump:
    instance proccall # **instance paramcall**
Procedure call:
    Standard procedure call #
    [Argument list] Procedure jump
Conditional statement:
    Expression **do** Statement list **else**
Conditional statement list:
    Conditional statement [Conditional statement] *
If statement:
    Conditional statement list
While statement:
    Conditional statement list
When statement:
    when Conditional statement list **wait endwhen**
Process statement:
    process Statement list **also**
Concurrent statement:
    goto Process statement [Process statement] * **cobegin**
Statement:
    Variable symbol Expression **assign** # Procedure call #
    If statement # While statement # When statement #
    Concurrent statement # Empty
Statement list:
    Statement [Statement] *
Program:
    Program length Complete procedure declaration **endcode**

6.10 CODE OPTIMIZATION

The code described so far is called *standard Edison code*. It has the great advantage of corresponding closely to the syntax of the programming language. This makes the code generation simple and systematic.

But in many cases the standard code is too large to fit into microcomputers with limited address spaces. The approximately 50 standard instructions are therefore supplemented with 15 *extra instructions* to reduce the code size.

The choice of extra instructions was guided by a series of experiments using pass 3 of the compiler as an example of a large Edison program.

Initially, the 1500 lines of pass 3 were compiled into 16200 words of standard code. By comparison, an earlier version of pass 3 written in Pascal was compiled into 9000 words of Pascal code.

The standard Edison code of pass 3 was scanned by a program to identify the instruction that made the single largest contribution to the code size.

The code was then studied in detail to find a special case of that instruction which occurred frequently enough to make it worthwhile to replace it with a new, shorter instruction.

After extending the compiler with the new instruction, the process of compilation, and code analysis was repeated to discover another instruction that would reduce the code size significantly.

These experiments were continued until the code reduction became marginal.

Originally, the standard code included a newline instruction of the form

newline(lineno)

to facilitate error reporting.

An initial analysis showed that no less than 17% of the code for pass 3 consisted of newline instructions. On the other hand, the only instructions that needed *line numbers* to report program failure accounted for less than 5% of the code size:

Procedure instructions	2.0%
Index instructions	1.4%
Construct instructions	0.9%
Arithmetic instructions	0.1%
Other instructions	0.2%

The newline instruction was therefore removed from the standard code and instead line numbers were included in the instructions above as described earlier in this chapter.

The encoding of line numbers in instructions eliminated 16% of the original code.

The next step was to replace a pair of instructions

instance(0) variable(displ)

which selects a *local variable* by a single, new instruction

localvar(displ)

Since the new instruction replaces a sequence of other instructions, it can be described by a (parameterized) syntactic rule:

Localvar(displ):
  instance(0) variable(displ)

The extra instructions can therefore be considered as syntactic forms recognized in the standard code.
The instruction named localvar is defined as follows:

> **proc** localvar(displ: int)
> **begin** s := s + 1; st[s] := b + displ; p := p + 2 **end**

Another frequent case is the retrieval of the elementary value of a local variable:

Localvalue(displ):
  Localvar(displ) value(1)

> **proc** localvalue(displ: int)
> **begin** s := s + 1; st[s] := st[b + displ]; p := p + 2 **end**

A conditional statement of the form

$$v = c \ \textbf{do} \ SL$$

where v is a local variable and c is a constant of the same elementary type generates the code

> localcase(v, c, L) SL else( ) L:

The instruction named localcase is defined as follows:

Localcase(vardispl, value, progdispl):
  Localvalue(vardispl) constant(value)
    equal(1) do(progdispl)

> **proc** localcase(vardispl, value, progdispl: int)
> **begin**
>   **if** st[b + vardispl] = value **do** p := p + 4
>   **else** true **do** p := p + progdispl **end**
> **end**

The instructions above refer to variables that are local to the procedure P that is currently being executed. A similar set of instructions are introduced for variables declared in the procedure that immediately surrounds P. These instructions, called outervar, outervalue, and outercase, are obtained from the previous ones by replacing the address expression b + displ by st[b] + displ.

When a procedure contains two local procedures P and Q, then Q may call P by executing an instruction named outercall:

Outercall(displ):
    instance(1) proccall(displ)

> **proc** outercall(displ: int)
> **begin** s := s + 1; st[s] := st[b];
>   st[s + 1] := b; st[s + 3] := t;
>   st[s + 4] := p + 2; b := s;
>   s := s + 4; p := p + displ
> **end**

If a call refers to a procedure parameter declared in the immediately surrounding procedure, it is compiled as a similar instruction named outer-param:

Outerparam(displ):
    instance(1) paramcall(displ)

Some other obvious instructions are:

Elemvalue:
    value(1)
Elemassign:
    assign(1)

The remaining instructions are described below:

Localset(displ):
    Localvar(displ) value(setlength)

> **proc** localset(displ: int)
> **var** x: settype
> **begin** loadset(b + displ, x); storeset(s + 1, x);
>   s := s + setlength; p := p + 2
> **end**

Another instruction named outerset is similar.

Stringconst(n, value1, . . . , valuen):
    constant(value1) . . . constant(valuen)

```
proc stringconst(no: int;  value: valuelist)
var i:  int
begin i := 0;
   while i < no do
      i := i + 1;  st[s + i] := value[i]
   end;
   s := s + no;  p := p + no + 2
end
```

Setconst(n, value1, . . . , valuen):
    Stringconst(n, value1, . . . , valuen)
        construct(n, lineno)

```
proc setconst(no: int;  value: valuelist)
var i: int;  new: settype
begin new := settype;  i := 0;
   while i < no do
      i := i + 1;  new := new + settype(value[i] )
   end;
   storeset(s + 1, new);
   s := s + setlength;  p := p + no + 2
end
```

Singleton(value):
    constant(value) construct(1, lineno)

```
proc singleton(value: int)
var new:  settype
begin new := settype(value);
   storeset(s + 1, new);
   s := s + setlength;  p := p + 2
end
```

In a variable symbol of the form

$$v.f1.f2 \ldots fn$$

the displacements of the fields f1, f2, . . . , fn are added to the displacement of the variable named v during compilation ("field encoding").

A conditional statement of the form

true do SL

generates code only for the statement list SL.

The last statement list of an if statement is not followed by an else instruction ("else elimination").

The combined result of these optimizations was a reduction of the code of pass 3 from 16200 to 6800 words. This makes the Edison code 24% shorter than the corresponding Pascal code.

The reduction of the original Edison code by 58% can be attributed to the various optimizations as follows:

Line number encoding	16%
Localvalue instruction	11%
Localset instruction	6%
Outercall instruction	5%
Outercase instruction	4%
Localvar instruction	3%
Localcase instruction	2%
Outervalue instruction	2%
Outerset instruction	1%
Outervar instruction	1%
Elemassign instruction	1%
Stringconst instruction	1%
Setconst instruction	1%
Else elimination	1%
True do elimination	1%
Field encoding	1%
Singleton instruction	0.5%
Elemvalue instruction	0.5%
Outerparam instruction	0.4%
Code size reduction	58%

In the Edison kernel for the PDP 11 computer, the code pieces that execute the extra instructions occupy only 150 (out of 1800) words.

The generated code consists of 40% standard instructions and 60% extra instructions.

This completes the description of the Edison code.

The process of code generation has been explained as a two-pass algorithm in which both passes are syntax directed:

First the program text is scanned and translated into standard code that corresponds closely to the syntactic rules of the language.

Then the standard code is scanned and some code sequences are replaced by extra instructions described by another set of syntactic rules.

The ability to explain a complicated data transformation as the result of two straightforward transformations is crucial. It would be much harder to explain the final code without using the standard code as a preliminary, pedagogical concept.

7

THE ALVA LANGUAGE REPORT

This report defines the assembly language Alva, a minimal and readable language for the implementation of system kernels to support the programming language Edison on PDP 11 computers.

The readability of Alva is achieved mainly by spelling the names of PDP 11 instructions in full and by allowing operand names to be of arbitrary length, for example:

$$compare(linefeed, st[sp + 2])$$

Store locations are described as indexed variables of the form st[address].

The following describes the Alva language in detail for readers who are familiar with the PDP 11 processor handbook [Digital, 1975].

7.1 SYMBOLS AND SENTENCES

The assembly language Alva is a formal notation in which programs can be written for the PDP 11 computers. The programs are texts composed of symbol sequences known as sentences.

The language is described in terms of syntactic forms as defined in the Edison language report. Syntactic forms that are referred to (but not defined) in this report are defined in the Edison language report.

7.1.1 Basic Symbols

Basic symbol:
    Special symbol # Word symbol # Name #
    Numeral # Character symbol # Text string
Special symbol:
    '+' # '–' # '=' # '(' # ')' # '[' # ']' # ',' # ':'
Word symbol:
    'addr' # 'array' # 'call' # 'const' # 'do' # 'instr' #
    'pad' # 'pop' # 'push' # 'reg' # 'repeat' # 'return' #
    'st' # 'text' # 'trap' # 'word' # Branch operator #
    Dyadic operator # Monadic operator # Register operator

The basic symbols are either special symbols, word symbols, names (Section 7.2), numerals (Section 7.3.1), character symbols (Section 7.3.2), or text strings (Section 7.5).

The word symbols are the ones shown plus the branch operators (Section 7.9.4), dyadic operators (Section 7.9.2), monadic operators (Section 7.9.1), and register operators (Section 7.9.3).

Any capital letter used in a word symbol is considered equivalent to the corresponding small letter.

The special symbols and word symbols have fixed meanings that will be defined later.

7.1.2 Separators

Separator:
    Space # ['$' Comment] New line character
Comment:
    [Graphic character] *

Any basic symbol preceded or followed by one or more separators stands for the basic symbol itself. Two adjacent word symbols or names must be separated by at least one separator.

Example:
    $ This is a comment

7.2 NAMED ENTITIES

Name:
    Letter [Letter # Digit # '_'] *

Any capital letter used in a name is considered equivalent to the corresponding small letter. The word symbols cannot be used as names. Apart from that names may be chosen freely.

A name denotes an entity used in a program. The entity is either a constant (Section 7.3), a register (Section 7.4), a text string (Section 7.5), a word (Section 7.6), an array (Section 7.7), a statement (Section 7.10), or an address list (Section 7.11).

Examples:
    w
    tasks
    status1
    processor_trap

7.2.1 Declarations

Declaration:
    Constant declaration # Register declaration #
    Stored entity declaration

A declaration introduces a name to denote a program entity and describes some of its properties. The entity is either a constant (Section 7.3.3), a register (Section 7.4), or a stored entity (Section 7.2.2).

Every name used to denote an entity must be introduced by a declaration. A given name can be declared only once in a program.

A name is said to be known in that part of the program text in which it can be used with its declared meaning.

The name of a constant or register is known from its declaration to the end of the program text.

The name of a stored entity is known throughout the program text.

7.2.2 Stored Entities

During the execution of a program some of its entities are held in the store. These stored entities occupy a fixed number of words with addresses beginning at zero.

Stored entity declaration:
    Text declaration # Word declaration #
    Array declaration # Statement declaration #
    Address list declaration

The declaration of a stored entity introduces a name, known as an address name, to denote the address of the entity. A stored entity is either a text string (Section 7.5), a word (Section 7.6), an array (Section 7.7), a statement (Section 7.10), or an address list (Section 7.11).

A stored entity described by a given declaration will occupy one or more words with fixed, consecutive addresses. The first of these addresses is known as the address of the entity.

7.3 CONSTANTS

Constant symbol:
    Numeral # Character symbol # Constant name

A constant symbol denotes a fixed integer value and is either a numeral (Section 7.3.1), a character symbol (Section 7.3.2), or a known constant name (Section 7.3.3).

7.3.1 Numerals

Numeral:
    Decimal numeral # Octal numeral
Decimal numeral:
    Digit [Digit] *
Octal numeral:
    '#' Octal digit [Octal digit] *
Octal digit:
    '0' # '1' # '2' # '3' # '4' # '5' # '6' # '7'

A numeral is a conventional decimal or octal notation for an integer value in the range –32768 to 32767 (both values included).

An octal numeral #d5d4 . . . d0 has at most six octal digits d5, d4, . . . , d0 and denotes the integer value

$$- (8**5)\ d5 + (8**4)\ d4 + \ldots + (8**0)\ d0$$

The digit d5 must be either 0 or 1. An octal number with fewer than six digits, say #602, stands for the given digits extended with leading zeros, say # 000602.

Example:
    0
    1351
    #200
    #177564

7.3.2 Character Symbols

Character symbol:
    ''' Ascii character '''
Ascii character:
    Graphic character # Control character
Control character:
    '[' Decimal numeral ']'

A character symbol 'c' denotes the ordinal value of the graphic character c in the ASCII character set. A control character [n] is denoted by the integer value n (where $0 \leqslant n \leqslant 127$).

Examples:
    'a'
    '0'
    '.'
    '[13]'

7.3.3 Constant Declarations

Constant declaration:
    'const' Constant name '=' Constant symbol
Constant name:
    Name

A constant declaration introduces a name, called a constant name, to denote a constant. A constant declaration cannot be of the form

$$const\ c = c$$

where c is the constant name.

Examples:
    const nl = '[10]'
    const status1 = # 177564
    const space = ' '
    const lf = nl

7.4 REGISTER DECLARATIONS

Register declaration:
    'reg' Register name '(' Constant symbol ')'
Register name:
    Name

A register declaration

$$\text{reg r(n)}$$

introduces a name r, called a register name, to denote register number n (where $0 \leqslant n \leqslant 7$).

Examples:
    reg x(1)
    reg s(4)
    reg p(5)
    reg sp(6)
    reg pc(7)

7.5 TEXT DECLARATIONS

Text declaration:
    'text' Address name '=' Text string
Address name:
    Name
Text string:
    ''' Ascii character [Ascii character] * '''

A text declaration introduces an address name to denote the address of a text string consisting of a sequence of ASCII characters. Every character occupies one word of storage.

Example:
    text pausetext = 'push RETURN to continue [10] #'

7.6 WORD DECLARATIONS

Word declaration:
    'word' Address name

A word declaration introduces a name to denote the address of a storage word.

Example:
   word tasks

7.7 ARRAY DECLARATIONS

Array declaration:
   'array' Address name '[' Constant symbol ']'

An array declaration

$$\text{array } A[n]$$

introduces an address name A to denote the address of an array of n storage words (where $n \geqslant 1$).

Example:
   array stack [99]

7.8 OPERANDS

The statements of a program (Section 7.10) describe operations on operands which denote constants, registers, or stored entities.

7.8.1 Constant Operands

Constant operand:
   Constant symbol # Address name

A constant operand denotes a constant or the address of a stored entity (that is, the address of a known text string, word, array, statement, or address list).

Examples:
   1351
   'a'
   status1
   tasks

7.8.2   Variable Symbols

Variable symbol:
    Register name # Location symbol
Location symbol:
    'st' '[' Address symbol ']'
Address symbol:
    Direct address # Indirect address
Direct address:
    Constant operand # Register address
Register address:
    Register name # Composite address
Composite address:
    Incremented address # Decremented address #
    Indexed address
Incremented address:
    Register name '+'
Decremented address:
    Register name '-'
Indexed address:
    Register name Sign Constant operand
Sign:
    '+' # '-'
Indirect address:
    'st' '[' Composite address ']'

A variable symbol denotes a variable used as an operand. The variable is either a named register or a store location.

During program execution, a store location is selected by evaluating an address symbol to obtain an address. The address can either be given directly or indirectly.

A direct address is obtained by evaluating a constant operand or a register address.

A register address is either the value of a named register or a composite address obtained in one of three ways:

(1) By using the value of a named register as an address and then incrementing the value of the register by 1 or 2 (incremented addressing)

(2) By decrementing the value of a named register by 1 or 2 and using the resulting value as an address (decremented addressing)

(3) By adding the values of a named register and a signed constant and using the resulting value as an address (indexed addressing)

During the evaluation of an incremented (or decremented) address, the given register is incremented (or decremented) by 1 for byte instructions and by 2 for word instructions.

An indirect address is obtained by first evaluating a composite address A as described above and then using the value of the store location st[A] as the final address.

Examples:

x	$ register variable
st[tasks]	$ constant address
st[x]	$ register address
st[x+]	$ incremented address
st[x-]	$ decremented address
st[x + 2]	$ indexed address
st[x - 8]	$ indexed address
st[st[x+]]	$ indirect, incremented address
st[st[x-]]	$ indirect, decremented address
st[st[x + 2]]	$ indirect, indexed address
st[st[x - 8]]	$ indirect, indexed address

7.8.3 Value Operands

Value operand:
    [Sign] Constant operand # Variable symbol

A value operand denotes a (possibly signed) constant or the value of a variable (that is, a register or store location) used as an operand.

Examples:
    #177770
    -3
    pausetext
    st[x - setlength]

7.9 INSTRUCTIONS

Instruction:
    Monadic instruction # Dyadic instruction #
    Register instruction # Branch instruction #
    Call instruction # Return instruction #
    Repeat instruction # Push instruction #
    Pop instruction # Encoded instruction

An instruction denotes an operation on one or more operands. It is either a monadic instruction (Section 7.9.1), a dyadic instruction (Section 7.9.2), a register instruction (Section 7.9.3), a branch instruction (Section 7.9.4), a call instruction (Section 7.9.5), a return instruction (Section 7.9.6), a repeat instruction (Section 7.9.7), a push instruction (Section 7.9.8), a pop instruction (Section 7.9.9), or an encoded instruction (Section 7.9.10).

The meaning of the instructions is defined in the PDP 11 processor handbook [Digital, 1975]. The correspondence between the word symbols used in the Alva language and the acronyms used in the PDP 11 handbook to denote instructions is defined in Section 7.15.

7.9.1 Monadic Instructions

Monadic instruction:
    Monadic operator '(' Variable symbol ')'
Monadic operator:
    'addcarry' # 'addcarry_byte' # 'clear' # 'clear_byte' #
    'decrement' # 'decrement_byte' # 'double' #
    'double_byte' # 'extendsign' # 'halve' # 'halve_byte' #
    'increment' # 'increment_byte' # 'negate' #
    'negate_byte' # 'not' # 'not_byte' # 'rotateleft' #
    'rotateleft_byte' # 'rotateright' # 'rotateright_byte' #
    'subtractcarry' # 'subtractcarry_byte' # 'swapbytes' #
    'test' # 'test_byte'

A monadic instruction denotes an operation on a variable.

Examples:
    halve(w)
    test(st[s+])

7.9.2 Dyadic Instructions

Dyadic instruction:
    Dyadic operator '(' Value operand ',' Variable symbol ')'
Dyadic operator:
    'add' # 'andnot' # 'andnot_byte' # 'compare' #
    'compare_byte' # 'move' # 'move_byte' # 'or' #
    'or_byte' # 'subtract' # 'testbit' # 'testbit_byte'

A dyadic instruction denotes an operation on a value operand and a variable.

Examples:
    testbit(st[s], st[st[s-]])
    or_byte(x, st[s - setlength])
    move(1, x)

7.9.3 Register Instructions

Register instruction:
    Register operator '(' Value operand ',' Register name ')'
Register operator:
    'divide' # 'doubleshift' # 'multiply' # 'shift'

A register instruction denotes an operation on a value operand and a named register.

Examples:
    multiply(st[s-], x)
    shift(-3, x)

7.9.4 Branch Instructions

Branch instruction:
    Branch operator '(' Address name ')'
Branch operator:
    'branch' # 'ifcarry' # 'ifequal' # 'ifgreater' #
    'ifhigher' # 'ifless' # 'iflower' # 'ifnotcarry' #
    'ifnotequal' # 'ifnotgreater' # 'ifnothigher' #
    'ifnotless' # 'ifnotlower' # 'ifnotoverflow' #
    'ifoverflow'

A branch instruction denotes an unconditional or conditional jump to a named address.

Examples:
    branch(load2)
    ifnotoverflow(subtract2)

7.9.5 Call Instructions

Call instruction:
    'call' '(' Address name ')'

A call instruction denotes a procedure jump to a named address.

Example:
    call(write)

7.9.6 Return Instructions

Return instruction:
    'return'

A return instruction denotes a return jump from a procedure.

7.9.7 Repeat Instructions

Repeat instruction:
    'repeat' '(' Address name ',' Register name ')'

A repeat instruction denotes the decrementing of a named register by one followed by a jump to a named address, if the resulting register value is nonzero.

Example:
    repeat(instance2, x)

7.9.8 Push Instructions

Push instruction:
    'push' '(' Value operand ')'

A push instruction

$$push(x)$$

is an abbreviation for the dyadic instruction

$$move\ (x, st[sp-])$$

Examples:
    push('H')
    push(st[s + 4])

7.9.9　Pop Instructions

Pop instruction:
　　'pop' '(' Constant symbol ')'

　　A pop instruction

$$pop(n)$$

is an abbreviation for one of the following instructions:

$$
\begin{array}{ll}
\text{test(st[sp+])} & \text{(if } n = 1) \\
\text{add(2n, sp)} & \text{(if } n <> 1)
\end{array}
$$

Examples:
　　pop(1)
　　pop(3)

7.9.10　Encoded Instructions

Encoded instruction:
　　'instr' '(' Constant symbol ')'

　　An encoded instruction denotes an instruction that occupies a single word and has the operation code given by a constant.

Examples:
　　The encoded instruction

$$instr(3)$$

denotes a breakpoint trap instruction.
　　If the following declarations are assumed:

$$
\begin{array}{l}
\text{const next} = \#13507 \\
\text{reg p(5)} \\
\text{reg pc(7)}
\end{array}
$$

then the encoded instruction

$$instr(next)$$

stands for the dyadic instruction

$$move(st[st[p+]], pc)$$

7.10 STATEMENT DECLARATIONS

Statement declaration:
    'do' Address name ':' [Instruction] *

A statement declaration introduces an address name to denote the address of a (possibly empty) sequence of instructions.

Example:

do localvar:	$ proc localvar(displ : int)
test(st[s+])	$ begin s := s + 1;
move(b, st[s])	$ st[s] := b + displ;
add(st[p+], st[s])	$ p := p + 2
instr(next)	$ end

7.11 ADDRESS LIST DECLARATIONS

Address list declaration:
    'addr' Address name '=' Address list
Address list:
    Address name [',' Address name] *

An address list declaration introduces an address name to denote the address of a list of other addresses given by names declared elsewhere. Each address in the address list occupies one word of storage.

Example:
    addr opcode =
        addx, alsox, . . . , stringconst

7.12 SENTENCES

Sentence:
    Declaration # Padding sentence # Trap sentence

A sentence is either a declaration (Section 7.2.1), a padding sentence (Section 7.12.1), or a trap sentence (Sentence 7.12.2).

7.12.1 Padding Sentences

Padding sentence:
    'pad' Constant symbol

A padding sentence

$$pad(n)$$

extends the stored entities of the preceding program text with additional words (if necessary) to make the address of the padding sentence equal to n (bytes), where n must be even.

Example:
    pad #400

7.12.2 Trap Sentences

Trap sentence:
    'trap' Trap address ':' Trap vector
Trap address:
    Constant symbol
Trap vector:
    Address name ',' Constant symbol

A trap sentence denotes a trap vector with an address given by a constant symbol. The trap vector consists of the named address of a statement to be executed when the trap is activated, and a constant to be used as processor status during the execution of the trap statement.

A trap sentence

$$trap\ n:\ a,\ c$$

extends the stored entities of the preceding program text with additional words (if necessary) to make the address of the trap vector equal to n (which must be a multiple of 4). The trap vector is then stored in two words at the given address.

Example:
    trap #4: processor—trap, kernelmode

7.13 PROGRAMS

Program:
  [Sentence] *

A program consists of a possible empty sequence of sentences.

Example:
  (See the Edison-11 kernel listing)

7.14 SYNTAX SUMMARY

Name:
  Letter [Letter # Digit # '_'] *
Decimal numeral:
  Digit [Digit] *
Octal numeral:
  '#' Octal digit [Octal digit] *
Ascii character:
  Graphic character # '[' Decimal numeral ']'
Constant symbol:
  Decimal numeral # Octal numeral #
  ''' Ascii character ''' # Constant name
Constant declaration:
  'const' Constant name '=' Constant symbol
Register declaration:
  'reg' Register name '(' Constant symbol ')'
Text string:
  ''' Ascii character [Ascii character] *'''
Text declaration:
  'text' Address name '=' Text string
Word declaration:
  'word' Address name
Array declaration:
  'array' Address name '[' Constant symbol ']'
Constant operand:
  Constant symbol # Address name
Sign:
  '+' # '-'
Composite address:
  Register name Sign [Constant operand]

Register address:
    Register name # Composite address
Direct address:
    Constant operand # Register address
Indirect address:
    'st' '[' Composite address ']'
Address symbol:
    Direct address # Indirect address
Location symbol:
    'st' '[' Address symbol ']'
Variable symbol:
    Register name # Location symbol
Value operand:
    [Sign] Constant operand # Variable symbol
Instruction:
    Monadic operator '(' Variable symbol ')' #
    Dyadic operator '(' Value operand ','
        Variable symbol ')' #
    Register operator '(' Value operand ','
        Register name ')' #
    Branch operator '(' Address name ')' #
    'call' '(' Address name ')' #
    'return' #
    'repeat' '(' Address name ',' Register name ')' #
    'push' '(' Value operand ')' #
    'pop' '(' Constant symbol ')' #
    'instr' '(' Constant symbol ')'
Statement declaration:
    'do' Address name ':' [Instruction] *
Address list:
    Address name [',' Address name] *
Address list declaration:
    'addr' Address name '=' Address list
Declaration:
    Constant declaration # Register declaration #
    Text declaration # Word declaration #
    Array declaration # Statement declaration #
    Address list declaration
Sentence:
    Declaration # 'pad' Constant symbol #
    'trap' Constant symbol ':' Address name ','
        Constant symbol
Program:
    [Sentence] *

7.15 INSTRUCTION SYMBOLS

The following is an alphabetic list of the instruction symbols used in the Alva language and the corresponding abbreviations used in the PDP 11 processor handbook [Digital, 1975]. The numbers on the right refer to the appropriate sections of this report.

Alva symbol	DEC symbol	Section
add	ADD	7.9.2
addcarry(_byte)	ADC(B)	7.9.1
andnot(_byte)	BIC(B)	7.9.2
branch	BR	7.9.4
call	JSR	7.9.5
clear(_byte)	CLR(B)	7.9.1
compare(_byte)	CMP(B)	7.9.2
decrement(_byte)	DEC(B)	7.9.1
divide	DIV	7.9.3
double(_byte)	ASL(B)	7.9.1
doubleshift	ASHC	7.9.3
extendsign	SXT	7.9.1
halve(_byte)	ASR(B)	7.9.1
ifcarry	BCS	7.9.4
ifequal	BEQ	7.9.4
ifgreater	BGT	7.9.4
ifhigher	BHI	7.9.4
ifless	BLT	7.9.4
iflower	BLO	7.9.4
ifnotcarry	BCC	7.9.4
ifnotequal	BNE	7.9.4
ifnotgreater	BLE	7.9.4
ifnothigher	BLOS	7.9.4
ifnotless	BGE	7.9.4
ifnotlower	BHIS	7.9.4
ifnotoverflow	BVC	7.9.4
ifoverflow	BVS	7.9.4
increment(_byte)	INC(B)	7.9.1
move(_byte)	MOV(B)	7.9.2
multiply	MUL	7.9.3
negate(_byte)	NEG(B)	7.9.1
not(_byte)	COM(B)	7.9.1
or(_byte)	BIS(B)	7.9.2
repeat	SOB	7.9.7
return	RTS	7.9.6
rotateleft(_byte)	ROL(B)	7.9.1
rotateright(_byte)	ROR(B)	7.9.1
shift	ASH	7.9.3
subtract	SUB	7.9.2
subtractcarry(_byte)	SBC(B)	7.9.1
swapbytes	SWAB	7.9.1
test(_byte)	TST(B)	7.9.1
testbit(_byte)	BIT(B)	7.9.2

8

KERNEL

The function of the Edison kernel is described in the chapter on abstract code (Chapter 6). The present chapter contains the complete text of the PDP 11 kernel with some additional comments.

The kernel described here is used on a PDP 11/23 computer with an RX02 floppy disk system. The kernel is written in the assembly language Alva (Chapter 7) and is commented by algorithms written in Edison.

Operating System Parameters

The operating system loaded by the kernel must be an Edison program with the following heading:

```
const sectorlength = 64
array sector [1:sectorlength] (int)

proc progname(
  pdp11: bool;
  maxrow, maxcolumn: int;
  proc cursor(row, column: int);
  proc erase;
  proc display(value: char);
  proc accept(var value: char);
  proc print(value: char);
  proc readsector(drive, sectorno: int;
    var value: sector);
  proc writesector(drive, sectorno: int;
    value: sector))
```

These program parameters denote constants and procedures declared within the kernel:

The boolean named pdp11 is true if the kernel is written for a PDP 11 computer, and is false otherwise (Section 5.15.12).

The integers named maxrow and maxcolumn define the dimensions of the screen (Section 5.15.1).

The procedures named cursor, erase, display, and accept control the terminal in the direct mode (Section 5.15.1).

The procedure print controls the printer (Section 5.15.2).

The procedures readsector and writesector control the disk drives (Section 5.15.6). (They are called "get" and "put" inside the kernel.)

Although these procedures could have been programmed in Edison for the PDP 11 computers, they were placed in the kernel to make the Edison system portable (Section 5.17).

The operating system calls these kernel procedures as if they were Edison procedures. The operating system uses some of them as arguments when it calls other Edison programs (Section 5.15).

Stacks, Variables, and Registers

The variable stack used by Edison programs begins immediately after the kernel (at the "minaddr") and grows from low toward high addresses. It is addressed by means of a base register b and a stack top s (Sections 3.19.9 and 6.1).

The program stack that holds Edison code begins at the highest store address (named "maxaddr," which immediately precedes the device registers) and grows from high toward low addresses. It is addressed by a program index p (held in a register) and a program top t (kept in a store location) (Sections 3.19.9, 6.1, and 6.6).

The register values of concurrent processes are stored in a queue. In addition, four variables named this, tasks, stacktop, and progtop are used to execute concurrent processes (Section 6.8).

A third stack is used by the kernel to call its own procedures. This stack is stored in an array of 100 words (named "stack") and is addressed by means of stack pointer sp. When the kernel calls a procedure, the arguments are pushed on this stack one at a time in the order in which they are described by the parameter list of the procedure. Each call instruction is followed by an instruction that pops the arguments after the call (Sections 7.9.5, 7.9.6, 7.9.8, and 7.9.9).

Three registers, called w, x, and y, are used to hold temporary results during the execution of a single Edison instruction or kernel procedure. The values of these registers are always assumed to be unknown at the beginning of an Edison instruction or kernel procedure and after each procedure call within the kernel.

Disk Addressing

The kernel treats each of the floppy disks as an array of sectors with sector numbers in the range 0:2001. Sectors with consecutive numbers are separated by a physical gap of two sectors (Section 5.15.6).

System Start

When the system is started (Section 5.3.3), sector number 26 (the autoload sector) is automatically loaded from disk number 0 and is executed at store address 0 (Section 5.16.1).

For a PDP 11 computer, the first word of the autoload sector must contain a skip instruction (NOP).

All interrupts are immediately disabled permanently by executing a trap instruction (BPT) that causes a jump to the next instruction (Sections 2.7 and 7.9.10).

The autoload sector, which is the first half of a loader module, now loads sector number 27, which is the second half of the loader module. The complete loader then inputs the rest of the kernel and begins to execute instructions at the very end of the kernel.

While the kernel is being loaded, the kernel stack is temporarily placed at the other end of the store. When the kernel has been loaded, the kernel stack is placed where it is declared within the kernel.

The kernel then creates the program parameters described earlier at the bottom of the variable stack and loads the operating system from disk number 0.

Each procedure parameter is represented by two words defining an (irrelevant) context link and a code address (Section 6.5). The code address of a kernel procedure is an index in the range 0:maxparam-1 (where maxparam = 7).

The operating system is loaded from sector number 90 (Sections 5.9.2 and 5.16.1). Although the operating system code (and its name) cannot exceed 8192 words, the kernel loads 12300 words from the disk in the variable stack. (The 12300 words is the maximum length of an Edison program called by the operating system.) The first word of the code (following the name) defines the actual program length in bytes (Section 6.6). The kernel then moves the program name and the actual amount of code from the variable stack to the program stack and starts the execution of the first instruction of the code.

Code Interpretation

The Edison algorithms used as comments in the kernel assume that the program index p always holds the address of an operation code (Section 6.1). The Alva code uses a slightly different convention that is more efficient on a PDP 11 computer: Whenever the kernel fetches an operation code or an argument from a compiled program, the p register is incremented to make it point to the next word.

The real program counter pc points to a machine instruction in the code piece that is used to interpret an Edison instruction.

A table stored at address #400 contains the addresses of all the code pieces. The operation code of an Edison instruction is represented by the (byte) address of an entry in this table, which in turn contains the address of the corresponding code piece.

Each code piece ends with an encoded instruction, called next, that uses the next operation code st[p] to look up the table and jump to a code piece. At the same time, the program index p is increased by one word (2 bytes) to make it point to the first argument of the instruction (Section 7.9.10). The effect of this jump can be described as follows in Edison:

$$pc := st[st[p]]; \quad p := p + 2$$

This single machine instruction is the only overhead of code interpretation. This efficient method of interpretation is called threaded code [Bell, 1973].

The indirect addressing of code pieces through a table has the advantage that the operation codes generated by the Edison compiler are unaffected by modifications of the kernel (which change the addresses of the code pieces but not the location of the table).

The code pieces are explained in detail in Chapter 6. In the Edison comments, the store is described as an array of words with addresses 0, 1, 2, . . . (as in Chapter 6). In reality, the words of a PDP 11 computer have byte addresses 0, 2, 4, ... An instruction argument that defines the length or displacement of a stored value (or an instruction) is therefore expressed in bytes in the generated code.

Program Failure

After a program failure, the kernel displays an error message and restarts the operating system (Sections 3.19.8 and 5.3.3).

Kernel Text

```
$ "Edison kernel for the PDP 11/23 computer
$        with RX02 floppy disk loader

$   30 October 1981

$   Copyright (c) 1981 Per Brinch Hansen"

reg w(0)
reg x(1)
reg y(2)
reg sp(6)
reg pc(7)

const skip = #240
const kernelmode = #340
do loadpoint:
   instr(skip)
   branch(load2)

trap #4: processor_trap, kernelmode
trap #10: instruction_trap, kernelmode
trap #14: disable_trap, kernelmode
trap #24: power_trap, kernelmode

                              $ proc kernel

const maxaddr = #157776       $ const maxaddr = 9999
                              $ array store [0:maxaddr]
                              $    (int)
                              $ var st: store
```

```
const sectorlength = 128        $ module "RX02 loader"
const disable_interrupts = #3
do load2:
  move(maxaddr, sp)
  instr(disable_interrupts)
do disable_trap:
  push(1)                       $ * const
  push(4)                       $     status = #177170;
  push(sectorlength)            $     buffer = #177172;
  call(readdisk)                $     ready = #200;
  branch(load3)                 $     done = #40;
                                $     error = #100000;
const status0 = #177170         $     read = #7;
const buffer0 = #177172         $     empty = #3;
const ready0 = #200             $     sectorlength = 64;
const done0 = #40               $     kernelsector = 26:
const error0 = #100000          $     minaddr = 999
const read0 = #7
const empty0 = #3
const sector = 64
const kernelsector = 26


do awaitready :                 $ proc awaitready
  testbit(ready0, st[status0])  $ begin
  ifequal(awaitready)           $   while not sense(status,
  return                        $       ready) do skip end
                                $ end


do readdisk:                    $ proc readdisk(trackaddr,
  move(read0, st[status0])      $     sectaddr, addr: int)
  call(awaitready)              $ begin place(status, read);
  move(st[sp+4], st[buffer0])   $   awaitready;
  call(awaitready)              $   place(buffer, sectaddr);
  move(st[sp+6], st[buffer0])   $   awaitready;
do readdisk2:                   $   place(buffer, trackaddr);
  testbit(done0, st[status0])   $   while not sense(status,
  ifequal(readdisk2)            $       done) do skip end;
  move(empty0, st[status0])     $   place(status, empty);
  call(awaitready)              $   awaitready;
  move(sector, st[buffer0])     $   place(buffer,
  call(awaitready)              $       sectorlength);
  move(st[sp+2], st[buffer0])   $   awaitready;
do readdisk3:                   $   place(buffer, addr);
  testbit(done0, st[status0])   $   while not sense(status,
  ifequal(readdisk3)            $       done) do skip end
  return                        $ end


$ "end of autoload sector"
```

```
do readsector:                        $ * proc readsector(
  clear(w)                            $       sectorno, addr: int)
  move(st[sp+4], x)                   $ var trackaddr,
  divide(26, w)                       $     sectaddr: int
  push(w)                             $ begin
  clear(w)                            $     trackaddr :=
  move(3, x)                          $        sectorno div 26;
  multiply(st[sp+6], x)               $     sectaddr :=
  divide(26, w)                       $        3 * sectorno
  increment(x)                        $           mod 26 + 1;
  push(x)                             $     readdisk(sectaddr,
  push(st[sp+6])                      $        trackaddr, addr)
  call(readdisk)                      $ end
  pop(3)
  return

word adr                              $ var addr, sectorno: int
word sectorno                         $ begin

do load3:                             $     readdisk(1, 4,
  move(kernelsector,                  $       sectorlength);
    st[sectorno])                     $     sectorno :=
  increment(st[sectorno])             $       kernelsector + 2;
  move(sectorlength, st[adr])         $     addr := 2 * sectorlength;
do load4:                             $     while addr < minaddr do
  increment(st[sectorno])             $       readsector(sectorno,
  add(sectorlength, st[adr])          $         addr);
  compare(minaddr, st[adr])           $       sectorno :=
  ifnotgreater(restart)               $         sectorno + 1;
  push(st[sectorno])                  $       addr := addr +
  push(st[adr])                       $         sectorlength
  call(readsector)                    $     end
  pop(2)                              $ end "loader"
  branch(load4)

do restart:
  move(stackbottom, sp)
  move(begin, pc)

const none = 0                        $ const none = 0;
const nl = 10                         $   nl = char(10); sp = ' ';
const esc = 27                        $   esc = char(27);
const pdp11 = 1                       $   pdp11 = true;
const maxrow = 24                     $   maxrow = 24;
const maxcolumn = 80                  $   maxcolumn = 80;
const space = ' '                     $   textlength = 80 "char";
const namelength = 24                 $   namelength = 12 "char";
const setlength = 16                  $   setlength = 8;
```

```
const setlimit = 127          $   setlimit = 127;
const cursorno = 0            $   cursorno = 0;
const eraseno = 1             $   eraseno = 1;
const displayno = 2           $   displayno = 2;
const acceptno = 3            $   acceptno = 3;
const printno = 4             $   printno = 4;
const getno = 5               $   getno = 5;
const putno = 6               $   putno = 6;
const paramlength = 34        $   paramlength = 17
const maxparam = 7            $     "words";
const maxproc = 5             $   maxparam = 7
const name = 12               $     "procedures";
const settype = 8             $   maxproc = 5
const statelength = 8         $     "processes";
const queue = 20              $   overflow = false

                              $ array text
                              $   [1:textlength] (char)
                              $ array name
                              $   [1:namelength] (char)
                              $ set settype1 (int)
                              $ array settype2
                              $   [1:setlength] (int)
                              $ record procstate(
                              $   bx, sx, tx, px: int)
                              $ array queue [1:maxproc]
                              $   (procstate)

pad #400
addr opcode =                 $ enum opcode(
  addx,                       $   "standard codes" add4,
  alsox, andx, assign,        $   also4, and4, assign4,
  blank, cobeginx,            $   blank4, cobegin4,
  constant, construct,        $   constant4, construct4,
  difference, dividex,        $   difference4, divide4,
  dox, elsex, endcode,        $   do4, else4, endcode4,
  endlib, endproc,            $   endlib4, endproc4,
  endwhen, equal, field,      $   endwhen4, equal4, field4,
  goto, greater, inx,         $   goto4, greater4, in4,
  index, instance,            $   index4, instance4,
  intersection, less,         $   intersection4, less4,
  libproc, minusx,            $   libproc4, minus4,
  modulo, multiplyx,          $   modulo4, multiply4,
  newline, notx,              $   newline4, not4,
  notequal, notgreater,       $   notequal4, notgreater4,
  notless, orx,               $   notless4, or4,
  paramarg, paramcall,        $   paramarg4, paramcall4,
  procarg, proccall,          $   procarg4, proccall4,
  procedure , process,        $   procedure4, process4,
  subtractx, union,           $   subtract4, union4,
  valspace, value,            $   valspace4, value4,
  variable, wait,             $   variable4, wait4,
```

```
  whenx, addrx, haltx,              $    when4, addr4, halt4,
  obtainx, placex, sensex,          $    obtain4, place4, sense4,
                                    $    "extra codes"
  elemassign, elemvalue,            $    elemassign4, elemvalue4,
  localcase, localset,              $    localcase4, localset4,
  localvalue, localvar,             $    localvalue4, localvar4,
  outercall, outercase,             $    outercall4, outercase4,
  outerparam, outerset,             $    outerparam4, outerset4,
  outervalue, outervar,             $    outervalue4, outervar4,
  setconst, singleton,              $    setconst4, singleton4,
  stringconst                       $    stringconst4)

array stack [99]
word stackbottom

array q [queue]                     $  var q: queue;
word this                           $    this,
word tasks                          $    tasks: int;
word stacktop                       $    stacktop: int;
word progtop                        $    progtop: int;
reg b(3)                            $    b, s, t, p: int
reg s(4)
word t
reg p(5)


                                    $  proc loadset(addr: int;
                                    $    var value: settype1)
                                    $  var i: int
                                    $  begin i := 0;
                                    $    while i < setlength do
                                    $      i := i + 1;
                                    $      value:settype2[i] :=
                                    $        st[addr + i - 1]
                                    $    end
                                    $  end

                                    $  proc storeset(addr: int;
                                    $    var value: settype1)
                                    $  var i: int
                                    $  begin i := 0;
                                    $    while i < setlength do
                                    $      i := i + 1;
                                    $      st[addr + i - 1] :=
                                    $        value:settype2[i]
                                    $    end
                                    $  end

do loadname:                        $  proc loadname(addr: int;
  move(name, w)                     $    var value: name)
  move(st[sp+2], y)                 $  var i: int
  move(st[sp+4], x)                 $  begin i := 0;
```

```
do loadname2:                        $    while i < namelength do
  move(st[x+], st[y+])               $       i := i + 1;
  repeat(loadname2, w)               $       value[i] := char(
  return                             $          st[addr + i - 1])
                                     $    end
                                     $ end


do findname:                         $ proc findname(var id: name)
  move(st[t], x)                     $ var addr: int
  compare(1, st[tasks])              $ begin
  ifequal(findname2)                 $    if tasks = 1 do
  move(st[progtop], x)               $       addr := t + 1
do findname2:                        $    else true do
  test(st[x+])                       $       addr := progtop + 1
do findname3:                        $    end;
  compare(x, p)                      $    while addr < p do
  ifnotlower(findname4)              $       loadname(addr, id);
  push(x)                            $       addr :=
  push(st[sp+4])                     $          addr + namelength;
  call(loadname)                     $       addr :=
  pop(1)                             $          addr + st[addr]
  move(st[sp+], x)                   $    end
  add(namelength, x)                 $ end
  add(st[x], x)
  branch(findname3)
do findname4:
  return


const status1 = #177564             $ proc write(value: char)
const buffer1 = #177566             $ const status = #177564;
const ready1 = #200                 $    buffer = #177566;
do write:                           $    ready = #200
  testbit(ready1, st[status1])$ begin
  ifequal(write)                     $    while not
  move(st[sp+2],                     $       sense(status, ready)
     st[buffer1])                    $       do skip end;
  return                             $    place(buffer, int(value))
                                     $ end


const lf = nl                        $ proc writechar(value: char)
const cr = 13                        $ const lf = nl;
do writechar:                        $    cr = char(13)
  compare(lf, st[sp+2])              $ begin
  ifnotequal(writechar2)             $    if value = lf do
  push(cr)                           $       write(cr)
  call(write)                        $    end;
  pop(1)                             $    write(value)
do writechar2:                       $ end
  push(st[sp+2])
  call(write)
  pop(1)
  return
```

```
do writetext:                          $ proc writetext(value: text)
  move(st[st[sp+2]], w)                 $ var i: int; c: char
  compare('#', w)                       $ begin i := 1;
  ifequal(writetext2)                   $   c := value[1];
  push(w)                               $   while c <> '#' do
  call(writechar)                       $     writechar(c);
  pop(1)                                $     i := i + 1;
  add(2, st[sp+2])                      $     c := value[i]
  branch(writetext)                     $   end
do writetext2:                          $ end
  return

word i1                                 $ proc writeint(value: int)
do writeint:                            $ array table [1:6] (char)
  clear(st[i1])                         $ var no: table; i: int
  move(st[sp+2], w)                     $ begin "value >= 0"
do writeint2:                           $   if value = 0 do
  increment(st[i1])                     $     i := 1; no[1] := '0'
  move(w, x)                            $   else value > 0 do
  extendsign(w)                         $     i := 0;
  divide(10, w)                         $     while value > 0 do
  add('0', x)                           $       i := i + 1;
  push(x)                               $       no[i] := char(
  test(w)                               $         value mod 10
  ifnotequal(writeint2)                 $         + int('0'));
do writeint3:                           $       value :=
  call(writechar)                       $         value div 10
  pop(1)                                $     end
  decrement(st[i1])                     $   end;
  ifnotequal(writeint3)                 $   while i > 0 do
  return                                $     writechar(no[i]);
                                        $     i := i - 1
                                        $   end
                                        $ end

word i2                                 $ proc writename(value: name)
do writename:                           $ var i: int; c: char
  move(name, st[i2])                     $ begin
do writename2:                          $   i := 0;
  move(st[st[sp+2]], w)                 $   while i < namelength do
  compare(space, w)                     $     i := i + 1;
  ifequal(writename3)                   $     c := value[i];
  push(w)                               $     if c <> sp do
  call(writechar)                       $       writechar(c)
  pop(1)                                $     end
do writename3:                          $   end
  add(2, st[sp+2])                      $ end
  decrement(st[i2])
  ifnotequal(writename2)
  return
```

```
const status2 = #177560       $ proc readx(var value: char)
const buffer2 = #177562       $ const status = #177560;
const ready2 = #200           $   buffer = #177562;
do read:                      $   ready = #200
  testbit(ready2, st[status2])$ begin
  ifequal(read)               $   while not
  move(st[sp+2], x)           $     sense(status, ready)
  move(st[buffer2], st[x])    $   do skip end;
  andnot(#177600, st[x])      $   obtain(buffer,
  return                      $     value:int);
                              $   value := char(
                              $     int(value) mod 128)
                              $ end


text pausetext =              $ proc pause
  'push return to continue#'  $ var response: char
word response                 $ begin
do pause:                     $   writetext(text(
  push(pausetext)             $     'push return to',
  call(writetext)             $     ' continue#'));
  push(response)              $   readx(response);
  call(read)                  $   writechar(nl)
  push(nl)                    $ end
  call(writechar)
  pop(3)
  return


text linetext = ' line [7]#'  $ proc stop(lineno: int;
word ln                       $   reason: text)
array id1 [name]              $ var id: name
do stop:                      $ begin
  push(id1)                   $   findname(id);
  call(findname)              $   writechar(nl);
  pop(1)                      $   writename(id);
  push(nl)                    $   writetext(text(
  call(writechar)             $     ' line #'));
  pop(1)                      $   writeint(lineno);
  push(id1)                   $   writechar(sp);
  call(writename)             $   writetext(reason);
  pop(1)                      $   writechar(nl);
  push(linetext)              $   halt
  call(writetext)             $ end
  pop(1)
  push(st[ln])
  call(writeint)
  pop(1)
  push(space)
  call(writechar)
  pop(1)
  push(st[sp+2])
  call(writetext)
  pop(1)
```

```
  push(nl)
  call(writechar)
  pop(1)
  move(restart, pc)

text processortext =           $ proc processor_trap
  'processor trap#'            $ "called by processor only"
do processor_trap:             $ begin stop(1, text(
  move(1, st[ln])              $   'processor trap#'))
  push(processortext)          $ end
  call(stop)

text instructiontext =         $ proc instruction_trap
  'instruction trap#'          $ "called by processor only"
do instruction_trap:           $ begin stop(1, text(
  move(1, st[ln])              $   'instruction trap#'))
  push(instructiontext)        $ end
  call(stop)

text powertext =               $ proc power_trap
  'power trap#'                $ "called by processor only"
do power_trap:                 $ begin stop(1, text(
  move(1, st[ln])              $   'power trap#'))
  push(powertext)              $ end
  call(stop)

text processtext =             $ proc processlimit(
  'process limit exceeded#'    $   lineno: int)
do processlimit:               $ begin stop(lineno, text(
  push(processtext)            $   'process limit',
  call(stop)                   $   ' exceeded#'))
                               $ end

text vartext =                 $ proc variablelimit(
  'variable limit exceeded#'   $   lineno: int)
do variablelimit:              $ begin stop(lineno, text(
  push(vartext)                $   'variable limit',
  call(stop)                   $   ' exceeded#'))
                               $ end

text rangetext =               $ proc rangeerror(
  'range limit exceeded#'      $   lineno: int)
do rangeerror:                 $ begin stop(lineno, text(
  push(rangetext)              $   'range limit exceeded#'))
  call(stop)                   $ end

text calltext =                $ proc callerror(lineno: int)
  'invalid program call#'      $ begin stop(lineno, text(
do callerror:                  $   'invalid program call#'))
  push(calltext)               $ end
  call(stop)
```

```
const maxcode = 24576          $ const maxcode = 12288
do moveprogram:                $ proc moveprogram
  subtract(maxcode, s)         $ var m: int
  move(st[s+2], w)             $ begin
  subtract(namelength, s)      $   m := st[s - maxcode + 1]
  add(namelength, w)           $      + namelength;
  move(s, x)                   $   s := s - maxcode
  add(w, x)                    $      - namelength;
  add(2, x)                    $   t := t - m;
  move(st[t], y)               $   while m > 0 do
  add(2, y)                    $     st[t + m] :=
  subtract(w, st[t])           $        st[s + m];
  halve(w)                     $     m := m - 1
do moveprogram2:               $   end
  move(st[x-], st[y-])         $ end
  repeat(moveprogram2, w)
  return


const progsector = 90          $ proc loadprogram
word sectorno1                 $ const progsector = 90
word addr1                     $ var sectorno, addr: int
do loadprogram:                $ begin addr := s + 1;
  move(s, st[addr1])           $   s := s + namelength +
  add(2, st[addr1])            $     maxcode;
  add(maxcode, s)              $   sectorno := progsector;
  add(namelength, s)           $   while addr < s do
  move(progsector,             $     readsector(sectorno,
    st[sectorno1])             $        addr);
do loadprogram2:               $     sectorno := sectorno
  compare(st[addr1], s)        $       + 1;
  ifnotless(loadprogram3)      $     addr := addr +
  push(st[sectorno1])          $        sectorlength
  push(st[addr1])              $   end;
  call(readsector)             $   moveprogram
  pop(2)                       $ end
  increment(st[sectorno1])
  add(sectorlength, st[addr1])
  branch(loadprogram2)
do loadprogram3:
  call(moveprogram)
  return


do resume:                     $ proc resume
  move(st[this], x)            $ begin
  decrement(x)                 $   b := q[this].bx;
  shift(3, x)                  $   s := q[this].sx;
  add(q, x)                    $   t := q[this].tx;
  move(st[x+], b)              $   p := q[this].px
  move(st[x+], s)              $ end
  move(st[x+], st[t])
  move(st[x+], p)
  return
```

```
do preempt:                        $ proc preempt
  move(st[this], x)                $ begin
  decrement(x)                     $   q[this].bx := b;
  shift(3, x)                      $   q[this].sx := s;
  add(q, x)                        $   q[this].tx := t;
  move(b, st[x+])                  $   q[this].px := p
  move(s, st[x+])                  $ end
  move(st[t], st[x+])
  move(p, st[x+])
  return


do initialize:                     $ proc initialize
  move(1, st[this])                $ begin this := 1;
  move(1, st[tasks])               $   tasks := 1;
  move(minaddr, b)                 $   b := minaddr +
  add(paramlength, b)              $     paramlength;
  move(pdp11, st[b-34])            $   st[b - 17] :=
  move(maxrow, st[b-32])           $     int(pdp11);
  move(maxcolumn, st[b-30])        $   st[b - 16] := maxrow;
  move(cursorno, st[b-26])         $   st[b - 15] := maxcolumn;
  move(eraseno, st[b-22])          $   st[b - 13] := cursorno;
  move(displayno, st[b-18])        $   st[b - 11] := eraseno;
  move(acceptno, st[b-14])         $   st[b - 9] := displayno;
  move(printno, st[b-10])          $   st[b - 7] := acceptno;
  move(getno, st[b-6])             $   st[b - 5] := printno;
  move(putno, st[b-2])             $   st[b - 3] := getno;
  move(b, s)                       $   st[b - 1] := putno;
  add(8, s)                        $   s := b + 4;
  move(none, st[s])                $   st[s] := none
  move(maxaddr, st[t])             $     "dummy return";
  call(loadprogram)                $   t := maxaddr;
  move(st[t], p)                   $   loadprogram;
  add(namelength, p)               $   p := t + namelength
  add(4, p)                        $     + 2
  return                           $ end


$ "procedure parameters"

do cursor:                         $ proc cursor
  subtract(4, s)                   $ var row, column: int
  push(esc)                        $ begin
  call(write)                      $   s := s - 2;
  push('Y')                        $   row := st[s + 1];
  call(write)                      $   column := st[s + 2];
  push(st[s+2])                    $   write(esc);
  add(31, st[sp])                  $   write('Y');
  call(write)                      $   write(char(31 + row));
  push(st[s+4])                    $   write(
  add(31, st[sp])                  $     char(31 + column))
  call(write)                      $ end
  pop(4)
  return
```

```
do erase:                              $ proc erase
  push(esc)                            $ begin
  call(write)                          $   write(esc);
  push('J')                            $   write('J')
  call(write)                          $ end
  pop(2)
  return

do display:                           $ proc display
  push(st[s])                         $ var value: char
  call(write)                         $ begin value := char(st[s]);
  pop(1)                              $   write(value);
  subtract(2, s)                      $   s := s - 1
  return                              $ end

do accept:                            $ proc accept
  push(st[s])                         $ var addr: int
  call(read)                          $ begin addr := st[s];
  pop(1)                              $   readx(st[addr]:char);
  subtract(2, s)                      $   s := s - 1
  return                              $ end

const status3 = #176504               $ proc print
const buffer3 = #176506               $ const status = #176504;
const ready3 = #200                   $   buffer = #176506;
do print:                             $   ready = #200
  testbit(ready3, st[status3])        $ var value: char
  ifequal(print)                      $ begin value := char(st[s]);
  move(st[s], st[buffer3])            $   while not
  subtract(2, s)                      $     sense(status, ready)
  return                              $       do skip end;
                                      $   place(buffer,
                                      $     int(value));
                                      $   s := s - 1
                                      $ end

                                      $ proc diskwait(result: int)
                                      $ begin
                                      $   while not sense(status,
                                      $     result) do skip end
                                      $ end

text disktext =                       $ proc disktransfer(oper,
  '[10]disk error #'                  $   driveno, sectorno: int)
do disktransfer:                      $ var again: bool
  testbit(done0, st[status0])         $ begin again := true;
  ifequal(disktransfer)               $   while again do
  move(st[sp+4], w)                   $     diskwait(done);
  shift(4, w)                         $     place(status, oper
  add(st[sp+6], w)                    $       + 16 * driveno);
  move(w, st[status0])                $     diskwait(ready);
```

```
do disktransfer2:                    $      place(buffer,
   testbit(ready0, st[status0])$              3 * sectorno mod 26
   ifequal(disktransfer2)            $              + 1);
   clear(w)                          $          diskwait(ready);
   move(3, x)                        $          place(buffer,
   multiply(st[sp+2], x)             $              sectorno div 26);
   divide(26, w)                     $          diskwait(done);
   increment(x)                      $          again :=
   move(x, st[buffer0])              $              sense(status, error);
do disktransfer3:                    $          if again do
   testbit(ready0, st[status0])$                  writetext(text(nl,
   ifequal(disktransfer3)           $                  'disk error #'));
   clear(w)                         $              pause
   move(st[sp+2], x)                $          end
   divide(26, w)                    $      end
   move(w, st[buffer0])             $  end
do disktransfer4:
   testbit(done0, st[status0])
   ifequal(disktransfer4)
   testbit(error0, st[status0])
   ifequal(disktransfer5)
   push(disktext)
   call(writetext)
   pop(1)
   call(pause)
   branch(disktransfer)
do disktransfer5:
   return


do get:                              $  proc get
   subtract(6, s)                    $  var driveno, sectorno,
   push(read0)                       $      count, addr: int
   push(st[s+2])                     $  begin s := s - 3;
   push(st[s+4])                     $      driveno := st[s + 1];
   call(disktransfer)                $      sectorno := st[s + 2];
   pop(3)                            $      addr := st[s + 3];
   move(empty0, st[status0])         $      disktransfer(read,
do get2:                             $          driveno, sectorno);
   testbit(ready0, st[status0])$            place(status, empty);
   ifequal(get2)                     $      diskwait(ready);
   move(sector, st[buffer0])         $      place(buffer,
do get3:                             $          sectorlength);
   testbit(ready0, st[status0])$            diskwait(ready);
   ifequal(get3)                     $      place(buffer, addr);
   move(st[s+6], st[buffer0])        $      diskwait(done)
do get4:                             $  end
   testbit(done0, st[status0])
   ifequal(get4)
   return


const write0 = #5                    $  proc put
const fill0 = #1                     $  const write = #5;
```

```
do put:                           $    fill = #1
  subtract(sectorlength, s)       $ var driveno, sectorno,
  subtract(4, s)                  $    count, addr: int
  move(s, x)                      $ begin
  add(6, x)                       $    s := s - sectorlength
  move(fill0, st[status0])        $      - 2;
do put2:                          $    driveno := st[s + 1];
  testbit(ready0, st[status0])$        sectorno := st[s + 2];
  ifequal(put2)                   $    addr:= s + 3;
  move(sector, st[buffer0])       $    place(status, fill);
do put3:                          $    diskwait(ready);
  testbit(ready0, st[status0])$        place(buffer,
  ifequal(put3)                   $      sectorlength);
  move(x, st[buffer0])            $    diskwait(ready);
  push(write0)                    $    place(buffer, addr);
  push(st[s+2])                   $    disktransfer(write,
  push(st[s+4])                   $      driveno, sectorno)
  call(disktransfer)              $ end
  pop(3)
  return

do kernelcall:                    $ proc kernelcall(
  move(st[sp+2], x)               $    procno: int)
  multiply(6, x)                  $ begin
  add(kernelcall2, x)             $    if procno = cursorno
  move(x, pc)                     $      do cursor
do kernelcall2:                   $    else procno = eraseno
  call(cursor)                    $      do erase
  return                          $    else procno = displayno
  call(erase)                     $      do display
  return                          $    else procno = acceptno
  call(display)                   $      do accept
  return                          $    else procno = printno
  call(accept)                    $      do print
  return                          $    else procno = getno
  call(print)                     $      do get
  return                          $    else procno = putno
  call(get)                       $      do put
  return                          $    end
  call(put)                       $ end
  return

$ "standard instructions"

$ "comment:
$    empty # 'newline'"

const next = #13507

do newline:                       $ proc newline(lineno: int)
  instr(next)                     $ begin p := p + 2 end
```

```
$ "library_procedure:
$    'goto' 'libproc' expression 'endlib'"

do goto:                      $ proc goto(displ: int)
  add(st[p], p)               $ begin
  test(st[p-])                $   p := p + displ
  instr(next)                 $ end

do libproc:                   $ proc libproc(paramlength,
  move(st[p+], x)             $   templength, lineno: int)
  move(st[p+], y)             $ begin
  move(st[p+], st[ln])        $   if tasks > 1 do
  compare(1, st[tasks])       $     callerror(lineno)
  ifequal(libproc2)           $   end;
  call(callerror)             $   st[b + 2] :=
do libproc2:                  $     b - paramlength - 1;
  move(b, w)                  $   if s + templength > t do
  subtract(x, w)              $     variablelimit(lineno)
  test(st[w-])                $   end;
  move(w, st[b + 4])          $   p := p + 4
  add(s, y)                   $ end
  compare(st[t], y)
  ifnotlower(libproc3)
  call(variablelimit)
do libproc3:
  instr(next)

array id2 [name]              $ proc endlib(lineno: int)
word length2                  $ begin
do endlib:                    $   moveprogram;
  move(st[p+], st[ln])        $   p := t + namelength + 2
  call(moveprogram)           $ end
  move(st[t], p)
  add(namelength, p)
  add(4, p)
  instr(next)

$ "complete_procedure:
$    [ 'goto' ] 'procedure' [ declaration ]*
$    statement_part 'endproc'"

do procedure:                 $ proc procedure(
  move(b, w)                  $   paramlength, varlength,
  subtract(st[p+], w)         $   templength, lineno: int)
  test(st[w-])                $ begin
  move(w, st[b+4])            $   st[b + 2] :=
  add(st[p+], s)              $     b - paramlength - 1;
  move(st[p+], x)             $   s := s + varlength;
  move(st[p+], st[ln])        $   if s + templength > t do
  add(s, x)                   $     variablelimit(lineno)
  compare(st[t], x)           $   end;
```

```
    ifnotlower(procedure2)        $   p := p + 5
    call(variablelimit)           $ end
do procedure2:
  instr(next)

do endproc:                       $ proc endproc
  test(st[b+8])                   $ begin
  ifequal(endproc2)               $   if st[b + 4] <> none do
  move(b, x)                      $     p := st[b + 4];
  test(st[x+])                    $     t := st[b + 3];
  move(st[x+], b)                 $     s := st[b + 2]:
  move(st[x+], s)                 $     b := st[b + 1]
  move(st[x+], st[t])             $   else true do
  move(st[x], p)                  $     p := p + 1
do endproc2:                      $   end
  instr(next)                     $ end

$ "procedure_declaration:
$    complete_procedure # library_procedure # empty
$  module_declaration:
$    [ declaration ]* statement_part
$  declaration:
$    procedure_declaration # module_declaration # empty"

$ "variable_symbol:
$    whole_variable #
$    variable_symbol [ 'field' ] #
$    variable_symbol expression 'index'
$  whole_variable:
$    'instance' 'variable' [ 'value' ]"

do field:                         $ proc field(displ: int)
  add(st[p+], st[s])              $ begin
  instr(next)                     $   st[s] := st[s] + displ;
                                  $   p := p + 2
                                  $ end

do index:                         $ proc index(lower, upper,
  move(st[p+], w)                 $   length, lineno: int)
  move(st[p+], x)                 $ var i: int
  move(st[p+], y)                 $ begin
  move(st[p+], st[ln])            $   i := st[s];
  compare(st[s], x)               $   s := s - 1;
  ifgreater(index2)               $   if (i < lower) or
  move(st[s], x)                  $     (i > upper) do
  subtract(w, x)                  $       rangeerror(lineno)
  ifnotless(index3)               $   end;
do index2:                        $   st[s] := st[s] +
  call(rangeerror)                $     (i - lower) * length;
do index3:                        $   p := p + 5
  multiply(y, x)                  $ end
  add(x, st[s-])
  instr(next)
```

```
do instance:                        $ proc instance(steps: int)
  move(b, x)                        $ var link, m: int
  move(st[p+], w)                   $ begin link := b;
  ifequal(instance3)                $   m := steps;
do instance2:                       $   while m > 0 do
  move(st[x], x)                    $     link := st[link];
  repeat(instance2, w)              $     m := m - 1
do instance3:                       $   end;
  test(st[s+])                      $   s := s + 1;
  move(x, st[s])                    $   st[s] := link;
  instr(next)                       $   p := p + 2
                                    $ end

do variable:                        $ proc variable(displ: int)
  add(st[p+], st[s])                $ begin
  instr(next)                       $   st[s] := st[s] + displ;
                                    $   p := p + 2
                                    $ end


         $ "constructor:
         $    elementary_constructor # record_constructor #
         $    array_constructor # set_constructor
         $ elementary_constructor:
         $    expression
         $ record_constructor:
         $    expression [ expression ]*
         $ array_constructor:
         $    expression [ expression ]* [ 'blank' ]
         $ set_constructor:
         $    [ expression ]* 'construct'"

do blank:                           $ proc blank(number: int)
  move(st[p+], w)                   $ var i: int
do blank2:                          $ begin i := 0;
  test(st[s+])                      $   while i < number do
  move(space, st[s])                $     i := i + 1;
  repeat(blank2, w)                 $     st[s + i] := int(sp)
  instr(next)                       $   end;
                                    $   s := s + number;
                                    $   p := p + 2
                                    $ end


word m1                             $ proc construct(number,
array new [settype]                 $   lineno: int)
do construct:                       $ var member, i: int;
  move(st[p+], st[m1])              $   new: settype1
  move(st[p+], st[ln])              $ begin
  move(settype, w)                  $   i := 0;
  move(new, x)                      $   new := settype1;
do construct2:                      $   while i < number do
  clear(st[x+])                     $     member := st[s];
  repeat(construct2, w)             $     s := s - 1;
  test(st[s+])                      $     if (member < 0) or
```

```
do construct3:                    $         (member > setlimit)
  test(st[m1])                    $            do rangeerror(
  ifequal(construct6)             $               lineno)
  move(st[s-], w)                 $      end;
  ifless(construct4)              $      new := new +
  compare(setlimit, w)            $        settype1(member);
  ifnotless(construct5)           $      i := i + 1;
do construct4:                    $    end;
  call(rangeerror)                $    storeset(s + 1, new);
do construct5:                    $    s := s + setlength;
  move(w, x)                      $    p := p + 3
  andnot(#177770, w)              $ end
  shift(-3, x)
  move(1, y)
  shift(w, y)
  or_byte(y, st[x+new])
  decrement(st[m1])
  branch(construct3)
do construct6:
  move(settype, w)
  move(new, x)
do construct7:
  move(st[x+], st[s+])
  repeat(construct7, w)
  test(st[s-])
  instr(next)


$ "factor:
$    'constant' # constructor # variable_symbol 'value' #
$    'valspace' procedure_call # expression #
$    factor 'not' # factor"

do constant:                      $ proc constant(value: int)
  test(st[s+])                    $ begin s := s + 1;
  move(st[p+], st[s])             $    st[s] := value;
  instr(next)                     $    p := p + 2
                                  $ end


do value:                         $ proc value(length: int)
  move(st[p+], w)                 $ var y, i: int
  halve(w)                        $ begin y := st[s]; i := 0;
  move(st[s], x)                  $    while i < length do
do value2:                        $      st[s + i] := st[y + i];
  move(st[x+], st[s+])            $      i := i + 1
  repeat(value2, w)               $    end;
  test(st[s-])                    $    s := s + length - 1;
  instr(next)                     $    p := p + 2
                                  $ end


do valspace:                      $ proc valspace(length: int)
  add(st[p+], s)                  $ begin s := s + length;
  instr(next)                     $    p := p + 2
                                  $ end
```

```
do notx:                         $ proc notx
  negate(st[s])                  $ begin st[s] :=
  increment(st[s])               $   int(not bool(st[s]));
  instr(next)                    $     p := p + 1
                                 $ end


$ "term:
$     factor [ factor multiplying_instruction ]*
$   multiplying_instruction:
$     'multiply' # 'divide' # 'modulo' #
$     'and' # 'intersection'"

const clear_carry = #241
do multiplyx:                    $ proc multiply(lineno: int)
  move(st[p+], st[ln])           $ begin
  move(st[s], x)                 $   s := s - 1;
  instr(clear_carry)             $   st[s] :=
  multiply(st[s-], x)            $     st[s] * st[s + 1];
  ifnotcarry(multiply2)          $   if overflow do
  call(rangeerror)               $     rangeerror(lineno)
do multiply2:                    $   end;
  move(x, st[s])                 $   p := p + 2
  instr(next)                    $ end


do dividex:                      $ proc divide(lineno: int)
  move(st[p+], st[ln])           $ begin
  move(st[s-], x)                $   s := s - 1;
  extendsign(w)                  $   st[s] :=
  divide(st[s+2], w)             $     st[s] div st[s + 1];
  ifnotoverflow(divide2)         $   if overflow do
  call(rangeerror)               $     rangeerror(lineno)
do divide2:                      $   end;
  move(w, st[s])                 $   p := p + 2
  instr(next)                    $ end


do modulo:                       $ proc modulo(lineno: int)
  move(st[p+], st[ln])           $ begin
  move(st[s-], x)                $   s := s - 1;
  extendsign(w)                  $   st[s] :=
  divide(st[s+2], w)             $     st[s] mod st[s + 1];
  ifnotoverflow(modulo2)         $   if overflow do
  call(rangeerror)               $     rangeerror(lineno)
do modulo2:                      $   end;
  move(x, st[s])                 $   p := p + 2
  instr(next)                    $ end


do andx:                         $ proc andx
  move(st[s], w)                 $ begin s := s - 1;
  not(w)                         $   st[s] := int(bool(st[s])
  andnot(w, st[s-])              $     and bool(st[s + 1]));
  instr(next)                    $   p := p + 1
                                 $ end
```

```
do intersection:                  $ proc intersection
  move(settype, w)                $ var x, y: settype1
  test(st[s+])                    $ begin
  move(s, x)                      $   s := s - setlength;
  subtract(setlength, x)          $   loadset(s + 1, y);
do intersection2:                 $   loadset(
  not(st[s-])                     $     s - setlength + 1, x);
  andnot(st[s], st[x-])           $   x := x * y;
  repeat(intersection2, w)        $   storeset(
  test(st[s-])                    $     s - setlength + 1, x);
  instr(next)                     $   p := p + 1
                                  $ end


$ "signed_term:
$    term [ empty # 'minus' ]"

do minusx:                        $ proc minus(lineno: int)
  move(st[p+], st[ln])            $ begin
  negate(st[s])                   $   st[s] := - st[s];
  ifnotoverflow(minus2)           $   if overflow do
  call(rangeerror)                $     rangeerror(lineno)
do minus2:                        $   end;
  instr(next)                     $   p := p + 2
                                  $ end


$ "simple_expression:
$    signed_term [ term adding_instruction ]*
$  adding_instruction:
$    'add' # 'subtract' # 'or' # 'union' # 'difference'"

do addx:                          $ proc add(lineno: int)
  move(st[p+], st[ln])            $ begin
  add(st[s], st[s-])              $   s := s - 1;
  ifnotoverflow(add2)             $   st[s] :=
  call(rangeerror)                $     st[s] + st[s + 1];
do add2:                          $   if overflow do
  instr(next)                     $     rangeerror(lineno)
                                  $   end;
                                  $   p := p + 2
                                  $ end


do subtractx:                     $ proc subtract(lineno: int)
  move(st[p+], st[ln])            $ begin
  subtract(st[s], st[s-])         $   s := s - 1;
  ifnotoverflow(subtract2)        $   st[s] :=
  call(rangeerror)                $     st[s] - st[s + 1];
do subtract2:                     $   if overflow do
  instr(next)                     $     rangeerror(lineno)
                                  $   end;
                                  $   p := p + 2
                                  $ end
```

```
do orx:                            $ proc orx
   or(st[s], st[s-])               $ begin s := s - 1;
   instr(next)                     $    st[s] := int(bool(st[s])
                                   $       or bool(st[s + 1]));
                                   $    p := p + 1
                                   $ end


do union:                          $ proc union
   move(settype, w)                $ var x, y: settype1
   test(st[s+])                    $ begin
   move(s, x)                      $    s := s - setlength;
   subtract(setlength, x)          $    loadset(s + 1, y);
do union2:                         $    loadset(
   or(st[s-], st[x-])              $       s - setlength + 1, x);
   repeat(union2, w)               $    x := x + y;
   test(st[s-])                    $    storeset(
   instr(next)                     $       s - setlength + 1, x);
                                   $    p := p + 1
                                   $ end


do difference:                     $ proc difference
   move(settype, w)                $ var x, y: settype1
   test(st[s+])                    $ begin
   move(s, x)                      $    s := s - setlength;
   subtract(setlength, x)          $    loadset(s + 1, y);
do difference2:                    $    loadset(
   andnot(st[s-], st[x-])          $       s - setlength + 1, x);
   repeat(difference2, w)          $    x := x - y;
   test(st[s-])                    $    storeset(
   instr(next)                     $       s - setlength + 1, x);
                                   $    p := p + 1
                                   $ end


$ "expression:
$    simple_expression
$       [ simple_expression relational_instruction ]
$  relational_instruction:
$    'equal' # 'notequal' # 'less' # 'notless' #
$    'greater' # 'notgreater' # 'in'"

do equal:                          $ proc equal(length: int)
   move(st[p+], w)                 $ var y, i: int
   test(st[s+])                    $ begin
   subtract(w, s)                  $    y := s - length + 1;
   move(s, y)                      $    s := y - length;
   subtract(w, s)                  $    i := 0;
   move(s, x)                      $    while (i < length - 1)
   halve(w)                        $       and (st[s + i]
do equal2:                         $          = st[y + i]) do
   compare(st[x+], st[y+])         $             i := i + 1
```

```
  ifnotequal(equal3)
  repeat(equal2, w)
do equal3:
  clear(w)
  compare(st[x-], st[y-])
  ifnotequal(equal4)
  increment(w)
do equal4:
  move(w, st[s])
  instr(next)

do notequal:
  move(st[p+], w)
  test(st[s+])
  subtract(w, s)
  move(s, y)
  subtract(w, s)
  move(s, x)
  halve(w)
do notequal2:
  compare(st[x+], st[y+])
  ifnotequal(notequal3)
  repeat(notequal2, w)
do notequal3:
  clear(w)
  compare(st[x-], st[y-])
  ifequal(notequal4)
  increment(w)
do notequal4:
  move(w, st[s])
  instr(next)

do less:
  clear(w)
  compare(st[s], st[s-])
  ifnotgreater(less2)
  increment(w)
do less2:
  move(w, st[s])
  instr(next)

do notless:
  clear(w)
  compare(st[s], st[s-])
  ifgreater(notless2)
  increment(w)
do notless2:
  move(w, st[s])
  instr(next)
```

```
$   end;
$   st[s] := int(
$     st[s + i] = st[y + i]);
$   p := p + 2
$ end


$ proc notequal(
$   length: int)
$ var y, i: int
$ begin
$   y := s - length + 1;
$   s := y - length;
$   i := 0;
$   while (i < length - 1)
$     and (st[s + i]
$       = st[y + i]) do
$         i := i + 1
$   end;
$   st[s] := int(
$     st[s + i] <>
$       st[y + i]);
$   p := p + 2
$ end


$ proc less
$ begin
$   s := s - 1;
$   st[s] := int(
$     st[s] < st[s + 1]);
$   p := p + 1
$ end


$ proc notless
$ begin
$   s := s - 1;
$   st[s] := int(
$     st[s] >= st[s + 1]);
$   p := p + 1
$ end
```

```
do greater:                          $ proc greater
  clear(w)                           $ begin
  compare(st[s], st[s-])             $   s := s - 1;
  ifnotless(greater2)                $   st[s] := int(
  increment(w)                       $      st[s] > st[s + 1]);
do greater2:                         $   p := p + 1
  move(w, st[s])                     $ end
  instr(next)


do notgreater:                       $ proc notgreater
  clear(w)                           $ begin
  compare(st[s], st[s-])             $   s := s - 1;
  ifless(notgreater2)                $   st[s] := int(
  increment(w)                       $      st[s] <= st[s + 1]);
do notgreater2:                      $   p := p + 1
  move(w, st[s])                     $ end
  instr(next)


do inx:                              $ proc inx(lineno: int)
  move(st[p+], st[ln])               $ var x: int;
  subtract(setlength, s)             $   y: settype1
  move(st[s], w)                     $ begin
  ifless(inx2)                       $   s := s - setlength;
  compare(setlimit, w)               $   loadset(s + 1, y);
  ifnotless(inx3)                    $   x := st[s];
do inx2:                             $   if (x < 0) or
  call(rangeerror)                   $      (x > setlimit) do
do inx3:                             $        rangeerror(lineno)
  move(w, x)                         $   end;
  andnot(#177770, w)                 $   st[s] := int(
  shift(-3, x)                       $     x in y);
  add(s, x)                          $   p := p + 2
  move(1, y)                         $ end
  shift(w, y)
  clear(w)
  testbit byte(y, st[x+2])
  ifequal(inx4)
  increment(w)
do inx4:
  move(w, st[s])
  instr(next)


$ "assignment_statement:
$     variable_symbol expression 'assign'"

do assign:                           $ proc assign(length: int)
  move(st[p+], w)                    $ var x, y, i: int
  test(st[s+])                       $ begin
  subtract(w, s)                     $   s := s - length - 1;
  move(s, y)                         $   x := st[s + 1];
  move(st[s-], x)                    $   y := s + 2;
  test(st[s-])                       $   i := 0;
  halve(w)                           $   while i < length do
```

```
do assign2:                      $      st[x + i] := st[y + i];
  move(st[y+], st[x+])           $      i := i + 1
  repeat(assign2, w)             $    end;
  instr(next)                    $    p := p + 2
                                 $ end


                                 $ "standard_call:
                                 $    variable_symbol 'addr' #
                                 $    'halt' #
                                 $    expression variable_symbol 'obtain' #
                                 $    expression expression 'place' #
                                 $    expression expression 'sense'"

do addrx:                        $ proc addrx
  subtract(2, s)                 $ begin s := s - 1;
  move(st[s+2], st[s])           $    st[s] := st[s + 1];
  instr(next)                    $    p := p + 1
                                 $ end

text halttext = 'halt#'          $ proc haltx(lineno: int)
do haltx:                        $ begin stop(lineno,
  move(st[p+], st[ln])           $    text('halt#'))
  push(halttext)                 $ end
  call(stop)

do obtainx:                      $ proc obtainx
  subtract(4, s)                 $ begin s := s - 2;
  move(st[st[s+2]],              $    obtain(st[s + 1],
    st[st[s+4]])                 $      st[st[s + 2]]);
  instr(next)                    $    p := p + 1
                                 $ end

do placex:                       $ proc placex
  subtract(4, s)                 $ begin s := s - 2;
  move(st[s+4],                  $    place(st[s + 1],
    st[st[s+2]])                 $      st[s + 2]);
  instr(next)                    $    p := p + 1
                                 $ end

do sensex:                       $ proc sensex
  clear(w)                       $ begin
  testbit(st[s], st[st[s-]])     $    s := s - 2;
  ifequal(sense2)                $    st[s] :=
  increment(w)                   $      sense(st[s + 1],
do sense2:                       $        st[s + 2]):int;
  move(w, st[s-])                $    p := p + 1
  instr(next)                    $ end

                                 $ "procedure_argument:
                                 $    'instance' 'procarg' # 'instance' 'paramarg'"
```

```
do procarg:                    $ proc procarg(displ: int)
  test(st[s+])                 $ begin
  move(p, st[s])               $   s := s + 1;
  subtract(2, st[s])           $   st[s] := p + displ;
  add(st[p+], st[s])           $   p := p + 2
  instr(next)                  $ end

do paramarg:                   $ proc paramarg(displ: int)
  move(st[s], x)               $ var addr: int
  add(st[p+], x)               $ begin
  move(st[x+], st[s+])         $   addr := st[s] + displ;
  move(st[x+], st[s])          $   st[s] := st[addr];
  instr(next)                  $   st[s + 1] :=
                               $     st[addr + 1];
                               $   s := s + 1; p := p + 2
                               $ end
```

```
$ "argument:
$     expression # variable_symbol # procedure_argument
$   argument_list:
$     argument [ argument ]*
$   procedure_call:
$     standard_call #
$     [ argument_list ] 'instance' 'proccall' #
$     [ argument_list ] 'instance' 'paramcall'"
```

```
do proccall:                   $ proc proccall(displ: int)
  move(p, x)                   $ begin
  add(st[p+], x)               $   st[s + 1] := b;
  test(st[x-])                 $   st[s + 3] := t;
  move(s, y)                   $   st[s + 4] := p + 2;
  test(st[s+])                 $   b := s;
  move(b, st[s+])              $   s := s + 4;
  test(st[s+])                 $   p := p + displ
  move(st[t], st[s+])          $ end
  move(p, st[s])
  move(y, b)
  move(x, p)
  instr(next)
```

```
do paramcall:                  $ proc paramcall(displ: int)
  move(st[s], x)               $ var addr, dest: int
  add(st[p+], x)               $ begin
  move(st[x+2], w)             $   addr := st[s] + displ;
  compare(maxparam, w)         $   dest := st[addr + 1];
  iflower(paramcall2)          $   if dest <= maxparam do
  test(st[s-])                 $     s := s - 1;
  push(w)                      $     kernelcall(dest);
  call(kernelcall)             $     p := p + 2
  pop(1)                       $   else true do
  branch(paramcall3)           $     st[s] := st[addr];
```

```
do paramcall2:                 $      st[s + 1] := b;
   move(s, y)                  $      st[s + 3] := t;
   move(st[x+], st[s+])        $      st[s + 4] := p + 2;
   move(b, st[s+])             $      b := s;
   test(st[s+])                $      s := s + 4;
   move(st[t], st[s+])         $      p := dest
   move(p, st[s])              $   end
   move(y, b)                  $ end
   move(w, p)
do paramcall3:
   instr(next)


$ "conditional_statement:
$    [ expression 'do' ] statement_list [ 'else' ]
$ conditional_statement_list:
$    conditional_statement [ conditional_statement ]*"


do dox:                        $ proc dox(displ: int)
   move(st[p+], w)             $ begin
   test(st[s])                 $    if bool(st[s]) do
   ifnotequal(do2)             $      p := p + 2
   add(w, p)                   $    else true do
   subtract(4, p)             $      p := p + displ
do do2:                        $    end;
   test(st[s-])                $    s := s - 1
   instr(next)                 $ end


do elsex:                      $ proc elsex(displ: int)
   add(st[p], p)               $ begin
   test(st[p-])                $    p := p + displ
   instr(next)                 $ end


$ "if_statement:
$    conditional_statement_list
$ while_statement:
$    conditional_statement_list
$ when_statement:
$    'when' conditional_statement_list 'wait' 'endwhen'"


do whenx:                      $ proc whenx
   instr(next)                 $ begin p := p + 1 end


do wait:                       $ proc wait(displ: int)
   add(st[p], p)               $ begin p := p + displ;
   test(st[p-])                $    preempt;
   call(preempt)               $    this := this mod tasks
   increment(st[this])         $      + 1;
   compare(st[this], st[tasks])$    resume
   ifnotgreater(wait2)         $ end
   move(1, st[this])
```

```
do wait2:
  call(resume)
  instr(next)

do endwhen:                         $ proc endwhen
  instr(next)                       $ begin p := p + 1 end

$ "process_statement:
$     'process' statement_list 'also'"

do process:                         $ proc process(templength,
  move(st[p+], w)                   $    lineno: int)
  move(st[p+], st[ln])              $ begin
  add(s, w)                         $    if s + templength > t do
  compare(st[t], w)                 $       variablelimit(lineno)
  ifnotlower(process2)              $    end;
  call(variablelimit)               $    p := p + 3
do process2:                        $ end
  instr(next)

do alsox:                           $ proc alsox(displ: int)
  move(st[tasks], w)                $ begin
  compare(1, w)                     $    if tasks > 1 do
  ifequal(also4)                    $       while this < tasks do
  move(st[this], x)                 $          q[this] :=
  subtract(x, w)                    $             q[this + 1];
  shift(2, w)                       $          this := this + 1
  ifequal(also3)                    $       end;
  shift(3, x)                       $       tasks := tasks - 1;
  add(q, x)                         $       this := 1;
  move(x, y)                        $       resume
  subtract(statelength, y)          $    else tasks = 1 do
do also2:                           $       s := stacktop;
  move(st[x+], st[y+])              $       t := progtop;
  repeat(also2, w)                  $       p := p + displ
do also3:                           $    end
  decrement(st[tasks])              $ end
  move(1, st[this])
  call(resume)
  branch(also5)
do also4:
  move(st[stacktop], s)
  move(st[progtop], st[t])
  add(st[p], p)
  test(st[p-])
do also5:
  instr(next)

$ "process_statement_list:
$    process_statement [ process_statement ]*
$ concurrent_statement:
$    'goto' process_statement_list 'cobegin'"
```

```
word base                             $ proc cobeginx(number,
word no                               $   lineno: int)
do cobeginx:                          $ var length, i: int
  move(p, st[base])                   $ begin
  subtract(2, st[base])               $   "(this = 1) and
  move(st[p+], st[no])                $    (tasks = 1)"
  move(st[p+], st[ln])                $   tasks := number;
  compare(maxproc, st[no])            $   if tasks > maxproc do
  ifnotless(cobegin2)                 $     processlimit(lineno)
  call(processlimit)                  $   end;
do cobegin2:                          $   stacktop := s;
  move(s, st[stacktop])               $   progtop := t;
  move(st[t], st[progtop])            $   length :=
  move(st[t], x)                      $     (t - s) div tasks;
  subtract(s, x)                      $   i := 0;
  halve(x)                            $   while i < tasks do
  andnot(#100000, x)                  $     i := i + 1;
  extendsign(w)                       $     t := s + length;
  divide(st[no], w)                   $     q[i].bx := b;
  double(w)                           $     q[i].sx := s;
  move(st[no], x)                     $     q[i].tx := t;
  move(q, y)                          $     q[i].px := p +
  move(x, st[tasks])                  $       st[p + 2 * i + 2];
do cobegin3:                          $     s := t
  move(s, st[t])                      $   end;
  add(w, st[t])                       $   this := 1;
  move(b, st[y+])                     $   resume
  move(s, st[y+])                     $ end
  move(st[t], st[y+])
  test(st[p+])
  move(st[base], st[y])
  add(st[p+], st[y+])
  move(st[t], s)
  repeat(cobegin3, x)
  move(1, st[this])
  call(resume)
  instr(next)
```

```
$ "statement:
$     empty # assignment_statement # procedure_call #
$     if_statement # while_statement #
$     when_statement # concurrent_statement
$   statement_list:
$     statement [ statement ]*
$   statement_part:
$     statement_list
$   program:
$     program_length complete_procedure 'endcode'"
```

```
text endtext = 'terminated#'     $ proc endcode(lineno: int)
do endcode:                      $ begin stop(lineno, text(
  move(st[p], st[ln])            $   'terminated#'))
  push(endtext)                  $ end
  call(stop)

$ "extra instructions"

$ "localvar(displ):
$    'instance(0)' 'variable(displ)'"

do localvar:                     $ proc localvar(displ: int)
  test(st[s+])                   $ begin s := s + 1;
  move(b, st[s])                 $   st[s] := b + displ;
  add(st[p+], st[s])             $   p := p + 2
  instr(next)                    $ end

$ "outervar(displ):
$    'instance(1)' 'variable(displ)'"

do outervar:                     $ proc outervar(displ: int)
  test(st[s+])                   $ begin s := s + 1;
  move(st[b], st[s])             $   st[s] := st[b] + displ;
  add(st[p+], st[s])             $   p := p + 2
  instr(next)                    $ end

$ "localvalue(displ):
$    localvar(displ) 'value(1)'"

do localvalue:                   $ proc localvalue(displ: int)
  test(st[s+])                   $ begin s := s + 1;
  move(b, x)                     $   st[s] := st[b + displ];
  add(st[p+], x)                 $   p := p + 2
  move(st[x], st[s])             $ end
  instr(next)

$ "outervalue(displ);
$    outervar(displ) 'value(1)'"

do outervalue:                   $ proc outervalue(displ: int)
  test(st[s+])                   $ begin s := s + 1;
  move(st[b], x)                 $   st[s] :=
  add(st[p+], x)                 $     st[st[b] + displ];
  move(st[x], st[s])             $   p := p + 2
  instr(next)                    $ end

$ "localset(displ):
$    localvar(displ) 'value(setlength)'"
```

```
do localset:                      $ proc localset(displ: int)
  test(st[s+])                    $ var addr, i: int
  move(settype, w)                $ begin addr := b + displ;
  move(b, x)                      $   i := 0;
  add(st[p+], x)                  $   while i < setlength do
do localset2:                     $     st[s + i + 1] :=
  move(st[x+], st[s+])            $       st[addr + i];
  repeat(localset2, w)            $     i := i + 1
  test(st[s-])                    $   end;
  instr(next)                     $   s := s + setlength;
                                  $   p := p + 2
                                  $ end

$ "outerset(displ):
$     outervar(displ) 'value(setlength)'"

do outerset:                      $ proc outerset(displ: int)
  test(st[s+])                    $ var addr, i: int
  move(settype, w)                $ begin
  move(st[b], x)                  $   addr := st[b] + displ;
  add(st[p+], x)                  $   i := 0;
do outerset2:                     $   while i < setlength do
  move(st[x+], st[s+])            $     st[s + i + 1] :=
  repeat(outerset2, w)            $       st[addr + i];
  test(st[s-])                    $     i := i + 1
  instr(next)                     $   end;
                                  $   s := s + setlength;
                                  $   p := p + 2
                                  $ end

$ "localcase(vardispl, value, progdispl):
$     localvalue(vardispl) 'constant(value)'
$     'equal(1)' 'do(progdispl)'"

do localcase:                     $ proc localcase(vardispl,
  move(st[p+], w)                 $    value, progdispl: int)
  move(st[p+], x)                 $ begin
  move(st[p+], y)                 $   if st[b + vardispl]
  add(b, w)                       $     = value
  compare(st[w], x)               $   do p := p + 4
  ifequal(localcase2)             $   else true do
  add(y, p)                       $     p := p + progdispl
  subtract(8, p)                  $   end
do localcase2:                    $ end
  instr(next)

$ "outercase(vardispl, value, progdispl):
$     outervalue(vardispl) 'constant(value)'
$     'equal(1)' 'do(progdispl)'"

do outercase:                     $ proc outercase(vardispl,
  move(st[p+], w)                 $    value, progdispl: int)
  move(st[p+], x)                 $ begin
```

```
      move(st[p+], y)           $     if st[st[b] + vardispl]
      add(st[b], w)             $        = value
      compare(st[w], x)         $     do p := p + 4
      ifequal(outercase2)       $     else true do
      add(y, p)                 $        p := p + progdispl
      subtract(8, p)            $     end
do outercase2:                  $  end
      instr(next)


$  "stringconst(number, value1, ..., valuen):
$       'constant(value1)' ... 'constant(valuen)'"


do stringconst:                 $  proc stringconst(
   move(st[p+], w)              $     number: int)
   test(st[s+])                 $  var i: int
do stringconst2:                $  begin i := 0;
   move(st[p+], st[s+])         $     while i < number do
   repeat(stringconst2, w)      $        i := i + 1;
   test(st[s-])                 $        st[s + i] :=
   instr(next)                  $           st[p + i + 1]
                                $     end;
                                $     s := s + number;
                                $     p := p + number + 2
                                $  end


$  "setconst(number, value1, ..., valuen):
$     stringconst(number, value1, ..., valuen)
$       'construct(number, lineno)'"


word m2                         $  proc setconst(number: int)
do setconst:                    $  var i: int; new: settype1
   move(st[p+], st[m2])         $  begin
   test(st[s+])                 $     new := settype1;
   move(settype, w)             $     i := 0;
do setconst2:                   $     while i < number do
   clear(st[s+])                $        i := i + 1;
   repeat(setconst2, w)         $        new := new +
do setconst3:                   $           settype1(
   move(st[p+], w)              $              st[p + i + 1])
   move(w, x)                   $     end;
   andnot(#177770, w)           $     storeset(s + 1, new);
   shift(-3, x)                 $     s := s + setlength;
   add(s, x)                    $     p := p + number + 2
   move(1, y)                   $  end
   shift(w, y)
   or_byte(y, st[x-setlength])
   decrement(st[m2])
   ifnotequal(setconst3)
   test(st[s-])
   instr(next)
```

```
$ "singleton(value):
$     'constant(value)' 'construct(1, lineno)'"

do singleton:                        $ proc singleton(value: int)
  test(st[s+])                       $ var new: settype1
  move(settype, w)                   $ begin
do singleton2:                       $   new := settype1(value);
  clear(st[s+])                      $   storeset(s + 1, new);
  repeat(singleton2, w)              $   s := s + setlength;
  move(st[p+], w)                    $   p := p + 2
  move(w, x)                         $ end
  andnot(#177770, w)
  shift(-3, x)
  add(s, x)
  move(1, y)
  shift(w, y)
  or_byte(y, st[x-setlength])
  test(st[s-])
  instr(next)


$ "elemvalue:
$     'value(1)'"

do elemvalue:                        $ proc elemvalue
  move(st[st[s+0]], st[s])           $ begin st[s] := st[st[s]];
  instr(next)                        $   p := p + 1
                                     $ end


$ "elemassign:
$     'assign(1)'"

do elemassign:                       $ proc elemassign
  move(st[s], st[st[s-]])            $ begin
  test(st[s-])                       $   st[st[s - 1]] := st[s];
  instr(next)                        $   s := s - 2; p := p + 1
                                     $ end


$ "outercall(displ):
$     'instance(1)' 'proccall(displ)'"

do outercall:                        $ proc outercall(displ: int)
  move(p, x)                         $ begin
  add(st[p+], x)                     $   s := s + 1;
  test(st[x-])                       $   st[s] := st[b];
  test(st[s+])                       $   st[s + 1] := b;
  move(s, y)                         $   st[s + 3] := t;
  move(st[b], st[s+])                $   st[s + 4] := p + 2;
  move(b, st[s+])                    $   b := s;
  test(st[s+])                       $   s := s + 4;
  move(st[t], st[s+])                $   p := p + displ
  move(p, st[s])                     $ end
```

```
  move(y, b)
  move(x, p)
  instr(next)

$ "outerparam(displ):
$     'instance(1)' 'paramcall(displ)'"

do outerparam:                      $ proc outerparam(displ: int)
  move(st[b], x)                    $ var addr, dest: int
  add(st[p+], x)                    $ begin
  move(st[x+2], w)                  $     addr := st[b] + displ;
  compare(maxparam, w)              $     dest := st[addr + 1];
  iflower(outerparam2)              $     if dest <= maxparam do
  push(w)                           $        kernelcall(dest);
  call(kernelcall)                  $        p := p + 2
  pop(1)                            $     else true do
  branch(outerparam3)               $        s := s + 1;
do outerparam2:                     $        st[s] := st[addr];
  test(st[s+])                      $        st[s + 1] := b;
  move(s, y)                        $        st[s + 3] := t;
  move(st[x+], st[s+])              $        st[s + 4] := p + 2;
  move(b, st[s+])                   $        b := s;
  test(st[s+])                      $        s := s + 4;
  move(st[t], st[s+])               $        p := dest
  move(p, st[s])                    $     end
  move(y, b)                        $ end
  move(w, p)
do outerparam3:
  instr(next)

$ proc execute_instruction
$ var op: opcode
$ begin
$     op := opcode(st[p]);
$     if op = add4 do add(st[p + 1])
$     else op = also4 do alsox(st[p + 1])
$     else op = and4 do andx
$     else op = assign4 do assign(st[p + 1])
$     else op = blank4 do blank(st[p + 1])
$     else op = cobegin4 do cobeginx(st[p + 1], st[p + 2])
$     else op = constant4 do constant(st[p + 1])
$     else op = construct4 do
$        construct(st[p + 1], st[p + 2])
$     else op = difference4 do difference
$     else op = divide4 do divide(st[p + 1])
$     else op = do4 do dox(st[p + 1])
$     else op = else4 do elsex(st[p + 1])
$     else op = endcode4 do endcode(st[p + 1])
$     else op = endlib4 do endlib(st[p + 1])
$     else op = endproc4 do endproc
$     else op = endwhen4 do endwhen
```

```
$    else op = equal4 do equal(st[p + 1])
$    else op = field4 do field(st[p + 1])
$    else op = goto4 do goto(st[p + 1])
$    else op = greater4 do greater
$    else op = in4 do inx(st[p + 1])
$    else op = index4 do
$      index(st[p + 1], st[p + 2], st[p + 3], st[p + 4])
$    else op = instance4 do instance(st[p + 1])
$    else op = intersection4 do intersection
$    else op = less4 do less
$    else op = libproc4 do
$      libproc(st[p + 1], st[p + 2], st[p + 3])
$    else op = minus4 do minus(st[p + 1])
$    else op = modulo4 do modulo(st[p + 1])
$    else op = multiply4 do multiply(st[p + 1])
$    else op = newline4 do newline(st[p + 1])
$    else op = not4 do notx
$    else op = notequal4 do notequal(st[p + 1])
$    else op = notgreater4 do notgreater
$    else op = notless4 do notless
$    else op = or4 do orx
$    else op = paramarg4 do paramarg(st[p + 1])
$    else op = paramcall4 do paramcall(st[p + 1])
$    else op = procarg4 do procarg(st[p + 1])
$    else op = proccall4 do proccall(st[p + 1])
$    else op = procedure4 do
$      procedure(st[p + 1], st[p + 2], st[p + 3], st[p + 4])
$    else op = process4 do process(st[p + 1], st[p + 2])
$    else op = subtract4 do subtract(st[p + 1])
$    else op = union4 do union
$    else op = valspace4 do valspace(st[p + 1])
$    else op = value4 do value(st[p + 1])
$    else op = variable4 do variable(st[p + 1])
$    else op = wait4 do wait(st[p + 1])
$    else op = when4 do whenx
$    else op = addr4 do addrx
$    else op = halt4 do haltx(st[p + 1])
$    else op = obtain4 do obtainx
$    else op = place4 do placex
$    else op = sense4 do sensex
$    else op = elemassign4 do elemassign
$    else op = elemvalue4 do elemvalue
$    else op = localcase4 do
$      localcase(st[p + 1], st[p + 2], st[p + 3])
$    else op = localset4 do localset(st[p + 1])
$    else op = localvalue4 do localvalue(st[p + 1])
$    else op = localvar4 do localvar(st[p + 1])
$    else op = outercall4 do outercall(st[p + 1])
$    else op = outercase4 do
$      outercase(st[p + 1], st[p + 2], st[p + 3])
$    else op = outerparam4 do outerparam(st[p + 1])
```

```
$    else op = outerset4 do outerset(st[p + 1])
$    else op = outervalue4 do outervalue(st[p + 1])
$    else op = outervar4 do outervar(st[p + 1])
$    else op = setconst4 do setconst(st[p + 1])
$    else op = singleton4 do singleton(st[p + 1])
$    else op = stringconst4 do stringconst(st[p + 1])
$    end
$ end

do begin:                        $ begin
  call(initialize)               $    initialize;
  instr(next)                    $    while true do
                                 $       execute_instruction
                                 $    end
                                 $ end "kernel"


word minaddr
```

9

OPERATING SYSTEM

The function of the Edison operating system is described in Chapters 4 and 5. This chapter contains the complete text of the operating system with some additional comments.

Operating System Parameters

The parameters of the operating system denote constants and procedures declared within the kernel (Chapter 8).

Modules

The following is a list of the modules in the operating system and the sections in which their functions are defined.

Character sets (Section 5.15.11)
Integers (Section 5.15.8)

Names (Section 5.15.9)
Lines (Section 5.15.10)
Booleans (Section 5.15.7)
Terminal (Sections 5.2.1 and 5.15.1)
Failures (Section 5.15.10)
Disk tracks (Section 5.15.6)
Disk pages (Section 5.16.1)
Disk maps (Sections 5.16.1 and 5.16.3)
Disk catalogs (Sections 4.2.2, 5.3.5, and 5.16.2)
Disk library (Sections 5.3 and 5.4)
Disk files (Section 5.4)
Data streams (Section 5.15.4)
Standard commands (Sections 5.3, 5.4, and 5.9)
Library commands (Section 5.15)

Names

The less function determines whether or not a name x precedes another name y in the alphabetic order determined by the character set.

Terminal

The operating system halts if the maximum length of a program line is less than the length of a screen line (that is, if linelength < maxcolumn).

Disk Maps

The extend procedure finds an available page in a given disk map and appends it at the end of a given chain of page numbers. The first page number in the chain is called its (start) address. An empty chain has a dummy start address called endlist.

The discard procedure follows a chain of page numbers with a given start address in a page map and makes the pages available for future files.

The address function follows a chain of page numbers with a given start address and converts a relative page number (1, 2, 3, . . .) within a file to an absolute page number on a disk.

Disk Catalogs

The entries of a disk catalog are stored at the beginning of a table of fixed length. The entries are kept in the alphabetic order of their names.

The search procedure performs a linear search of a disk catalog and retrieves the attributes of an entry with a given name (if it exists).

The include procedure inserts a new entry with a given name and attributes in a disk catalog.

The change procedure assigns a set of attributes to an existing entry with a given name in a disk catalog.

The exclude procedure removes an existing entry with a given name from a disk catalog.

Disk Library

This module describes operations on a pair of disks. It uses a pair of booleans to determine whether any of the disks have been changed during the execution of the most recent user command (Section 4.2.2).

Disk Files

This module describes operations on a disk file viewed as a sequence of disk pages with (relative) page numbers 1, 2, 3, ...

The open procedure initializes a record that describes a file with a given name as being open, possibly protected ("safe"), and of unchanged length. In addition, the drive number, start address, and size of the file are retrieved from a disk catalog.

The read procedure inputs a page with a given page number from a given file.

The write procedure outputs a page with a given page number to a given file.

The extend procedure changes the length of a given file. If the boolean parameter named newpage is true, another page is appended at the end of the file. The integer parameter named newwords defines the number of words stored on the last page of the file.

The end procedure marks a file as being closed. If the length of the file has been changed, its description is changed in the relevant disk catalog.

Data Streams

This module describes operations on a disk file viewed as a sequence of elementary values. A stream is described by its length and by the position of the next value to be input (or output). This position is called the head of the stream. A block is used to hold the values of a single disk page.

The openread procedure opens an input stream and positions the head at the first word of the first page.

The more function determines whether or not the head of a stream has passed the end of the stream.

The read procedure retrieves a value from the head position and moves the head to the next position in a stream.

The value of the mark function is the current head position of a stream.

The move procedure moves the head to a given position within a stream.

The endread procedure closes an input stream.

When a data value is output at the end of an existing, nonempty file, there are two possibilities: (1) Either the value must be stored on the last page of the already existing part of the file, or (2) it must be stored on a new page to be appended to the file. These two cases are distinguished by means of a boolean named newpage.

The openwrite procedure opens an output stream and positions the head immediately after the last value (if any) stored in the existing file.

The write procedure places a given value at the head position and moves the head to the next position in a stream.

The endwrite procedure closes an output stream.

Operating System Text

```
"The Edison operating system
            14 July 1981
 Copyright (c) 1981 Per Brinch Hansen"

array sector [1:64] (int)

proc system(
    pdp11: bool;
    maxrow, maxcolumn: int;
    proc cursor(row, column: int);
    proc erase;
    proc display(value: char);
    proc accept(var value: char);
    proc print(value: char);
    proc read_sector(drive, sectorno: int;
        var value: sector);
    proc write_sector(drive, sectorno: int;
        value: sector))

const nl = char(10); sp = ' '


module "character sets"

*  set charset (char)

*  var capitals, comment: charset
```

```
*   proc subset(first, last: char): charset
    var c: char; value: charset
    begin c := first; value := charset;
       while c <= last do
          value := value + charset(c);
          c :=·char(int(c) + 1)
       end;
       val subset := value
    end

*   proc lowercase(c: char): char
    begin
       if c in capitals do
          c := char(int(c) + 32)
       end;
       val lowercase := c
    end

begin capitals := subset('A', 'Z');
   comment := charset(nl, sp)
end
```

module "integers"

```
*   const minint = #100000; maxint = 32767

    var signs, digits, numeric: charset

*   proc read_int(proc read(var c: char);
       var value: int)
    var c: char; plus: bool; digit: int
    begin value := 0; read(c);
       while c in comment do read(c) end;
       if c in signs do plus := c = '+'; read(c)
       else true do plus := true end;
       while c in digits do
          digit := int(c) - int('0');
          if value >= (minint + digit) div 10 do
             value := 10 * value - digit
          end;
          read(c)
       end;
       if plus and (value > minint) do
          value := - value
       end
    end

*   proc write_int(proc write(c: char); value, length: int)
    const max = 6
    array numeral [1:max] (char)
    var no: numeral; min, i: int; negative: bool
```

```
begin
  if value = minint do
    no := numeral('-32768'); min := max
  else value = 0 do
    no[max] := '0'; min := 1
  else true do
    if value < 0 do
      negative := true; value := - value
    else true do negative := false end;
    min := 0;
    while value > 0 do
      no[max - min] := char(value mod 10 + int('0'));
      min := min + 1; value := value div 10
    end;
    if negative do
      no[max - min] := '-'; min := min + 1
    end
  end;
  while length > min do
    write(sp); length := length - 1
  end;
  while min > 0 do
    min := min - 1; write(no[max - min])
  end
end

begin signs := charset('+-');
  digits := subset('0', '9')
end


module "names"

* const namelength = 12
* array name [1:namelength] (char)

  var alphanum, letters: charset

* proc read_name(proc read(var c: char);
    var value: name)
  var i: int; c: char
  begin value := name(sp); read(c);
    while c in comment do read(c) end;
    if c in letters do
      i := 1;
      while (c in alphanum) and (i <= namelength) do
        c := lowercase(c); value[i] := c;
        read(c); i := i + 1
      end
    end
  end
```

```
* proc write_name(proc write(c: char); value: name)
  var i: int
  begin i := 1;
    while i <= namelength do
      write(value[i]); i := i + 1
    end
  end

* proc less_name(x, y: name): bool
  var i: int
  begin i := 1;
    while (i < namelength) and (x[i] = y[i]) do
      i := i + 1
    end;
    val less_name := x[i] < y[i]
  end

begin letters := capitals + subset('a', 'z');
  alphanum := letters + subset('0', '9') + charset('_')
end


module "lines"

* const linelength = 80
* array line [1:linelength] (char)

  var endline: charset

* proc write_line(proc write(c: char); text: line)
  var i: int; c: char
  begin i := 1; c := text[1];
    while not (c in endline) and (i < linelength) do
      write(c); i := i + 1; c := text[i]
    end;
    if c = nl do write(nl) end
  end

begin endline := charset(nl, '.') end


module "booleans"

* proc read_bool(proc read(var c: char); var value: bool)
  var word: name
  begin read_name(read, word);
    value := (word = name('true')) or
      (word = name('yes'))
  end
```

```
* proc write_bool(proc write(c: char); value: bool)
  begin
    if value do write_line(write, line('true .'))
    else true do write_line(write, line('false.')) end
  end

begin skip end


module "terminal"

* const bel = char(7); bs = char(8); ht = char(9);
    lf = char(10); cr = char(13); esc = char(27);
    del = char(127); right = ht; left = bs;
    tab = 5 "char"

* array sentence [1:150] (char)


  var normal: bool; graphic: charset;
    text: line; typed, used: int

* proc write_terminal(value: char)
  begin
    if normal and (value = lf) do display(cr) end;
    display(value)
  end

* proc writename_terminal(value: name)
  begin write_name(write_terminal, value) end

* proc writeline_terminal(value: line)
  begin write_line(write_terminal, value) end

* proc writeint_terminal(value, length: int)
  begin write_int(write_terminal, value, length) end

* proc writebool_terminal(value: bool)
  begin write_bool(write_terminal, value) end

* proc writesentence_terminal(value: sentence)
  var i: int; c: char
  begin i := 1; c := value[1];
    while c <> '.' do
      write_terminal(c); i := i + 1; c := value[i]
    end
  end

  proc typeline
  var i, x, n: int; c: char
  begin text[1] := nl; n := 1; x := 1; accept(c);
    while c <> cr do
      if (c = left) and (x > 1) do
        display(bs); x := x - 1
```

```
      else c = right do
        i := x;
        if x + tab < n do x := x + tab
        else x < n do x := n end;
        while i < x do display(text[i]); i := i + 1 end
      else (c = del) and (x < n) do
        n := n - 1; i := x;
        while i < n do
          text[i] := text[i + 1]; display(text[i]);
          i := i + 1
        end;
        text[n] := nl; display(sp); i := n + 1;
        while i > x do display(bs); i := i - 1 end
      else (c in graphic) and (n < linelength - 1) do
        n := n + 1; i := n;
        while i > x do
          text[i] := text[i - 1]; i := i - 1
        end;
        text[x] := c; x := x + 1;
        while i < n do
          display(text[i]); i := i + 1
        end;
        while i > x do display(bs); i := i - 1 end
      end;
      accept(c)
    end;
    write_terminal(nl); typed := n; used := 0
  end

* proc read_terminal(var value: char)
  begin
    if normal do
      if used = typed do typeline end;
      used := used + 1; value := text[used]
    else true do accept(value) end
  end

* proc readname_terminal(var value: name)
  begin read_name(read_terminal, value) end

* proc readint_terminal(var value: int)
  begin read_int(read_terminal, value) end

* proc select_terminal(standard: bool)
  begin normal := standard; used := typed; display(nl) end

* proc pause_terminal
  var value: char
  begin
```

```
      writeline_terminal(
        line('push RETURN to continue', nl));
      accept(value)
    end

begin
    if linelength < maxcolumn do
      writeline_terminal(line('line limit.')); halt
    end;
    graphic := subset(char(32), char(126));
    select_terminal(true);
    writeline_terminal(line('The Edison system', nl))
end


module "failures"

* proc assume1(condition: bool; text: line)
    begin
      if not condition do
        writeline_terminal(text); halt
      end
    end

* proc assume2(condition: bool; title: name;
    text: line)
    begin
      if not condition do
        writename_terminal(title);
        write_terminal(sp);
        writeline_terminal(text); halt
      end
    end

begin skip end


module "disk tracks"

* const tracksectors = 26; firsttrack = 0; lasttrack = 76
* array track [1:tracksectors] (sector)

* proc read_track(drive, trackno: int; var block: track)
    var i: int
    begin i := 1;
      while i <= tracksectors do
        read_sector(drive, tracksectors * trackno + i - 1,
          block[i]);
        i := i + 1
      end
    end
```

```
* proc write_track(drive, trackno: int; var block: track)
  var i: int
  begin i :=.1;
    while i <= tracksectors do
      write_sector(drive, tracksectors * trackno + i - 1,
        block[i]);
      i := i + 1
    end
  end

begin skip end


module "disk pages"

* const pagelength = 512; pagesectors = 8
* array page [1:pagelength] (char)
  array overlay [1:pagesectors] (sector)

* proc read_page(drive, pageno: int; var block: page)
  var i: int
  begin i := 1;
    while i <= pagesectors do
      read_sector(drive, pagesectors * pageno + i + 1,
        block:overlay[i]);
      i := i + 1
    end
  end

* proc write_page(drive, pageno: int; var block: page)
  var i: int
  begin i := 1;
    while i <= pagesectors do
      write_sector(drive, pagesectors * pageno + i + 1,
        block:overlay[i]);
      i := i + 1
    end
  end

begin skip end


module "disk maps"

  const diskaddr = "sectorno" 10; disksectors = 4;
    firstpage = 27; lastpage = 249;
    available = maxint; endlist = 0

  array table [1:lastpage] (int)
  array filler [1:5] (int)
```

```
* record diskmap (free, next: int; contents: table;
    unused: filler)

  array overlay [1:disksectors] (sector)

* var allpages: int

* proc new_diskmap(var map: diskmap)
  var i: int
  begin i := 1;
    while i < firstpage do
      map.contents[i] := endlist; i := i + 1
    else i <= lastpage do
      map.contents[i] := available; i := i + 1
    end;
    map.free := allpages; map.next := firstpage
  end

* proc read_diskmap(var map: diskmap; drive: int)
  var i: int
  begin i := 1;
    while i <= disksectors do
      read_sector(drive, diskaddr + i - 1,
        map:overlay[i]);
      i := i + 1
    end
  end

* proc write_diskmap(var map: diskmap; drive: int)
  var i: int
  begin i := 1;
    while i <= disksectors do
      write_sector(drive, diskaddr + i - 1,
        map:overlay[i]);
      i := i + 1
    end
  end

* proc empty_diskmap(var map: diskmap): int
  begin val empty_diskmap := endlist end

* proc extend_diskmap(var map: diskmap;
    var address: int)
  var elem, succ: int
  begin assume1(map.free > 0, line('disk limit.'));
    while map.contents[map.next] <> available do
      map.next := map.next mod lastpage + 1
    end;
    if address = endlist do address := map.next
    else true do
      elem := address; succ := map.contents[elem];
      while succ <> endlist do
```

```
          elem := succ; succ := map.contents[elem]
        end;
        map.contents[elem] := map.next
      end;
      map.contents[map.next] := endlist;
      map.free := map.free - 1
    end

*  proc discard_diskmap(var map: diskmap;
      address: int)
    var succ: int
    begin
      if address <> endlist do
        while address <> endlist do
          succ := map.contents[address];
          map.contents[address] := available;
          map.free := map.free + 1;
          address := succ
        end;
        map.next := firstpage
      end
    end

*  proc address_diskmap(var map: diskmap;
      address, pageno: int): int
    var succ, p: int
    begin assume1(address <> endlist, line('file limit.'));
      succ := map.contents[address]; p := 1;
      while (p < pageno) and (succ <> endlist) do
        address := succ; succ := map.contents[address];
        p := p + 1
      end;
      assume1(p = pageno, line(' file limit.'));
      val address_diskmap := address
    end

begin allpages := lastpage - firstpage + 1 end


record position (pages, words: int)

record attributes (address: int; length: position;
  protected: bool)


module "disk catalogs"

  const diskaddr = "sectorno" 14; disksectors = 12;
    maxitem = 47

  record item (title: name; attr: attributes)
  array table [1:maxitem] (item)
  array filler [1:15] (int)
```

```
* record diskcatalog (size: int; contents: table;
    unused: filler)

  array overlay [1:disksectors] (sector)

  proc locate(var catalog: diskcatalog; key: name;
    var index: int; var found: bool)
  begin
    if catalog.size = 0 do found := false
    else true do
      index := 1;
      while (catalog.contents[index].title <> key) and
        (index < catalog.size) do index := index + 1
      end;
      found := catalog.contents[index].title = key
    end
  end

* proc new_diskcatalog(var catalog: diskcatalog)
  begin catalog.size := 0 end

* proc read_diskcatalog(var catalog: diskcatalog;
    drive: int)
  var i: int
  begin i := 1;
    while i <= disksectors do
      read_sector(drive, diskaddr + i - 1,
        catalog:overlay[i]);
      i := i + 1
    end
  end

* proc write_diskcatalog(var catalog: diskcatalog;
    drive: int)
  var i: int
  begin i := 1;
    while i <= disksectors do
      write_sector(drive, diskaddr + i - 1,
        catalog:overlay[i]);
      i := i + 1
    end
  end

* proc list_diskcatalog(var catalog: diskcatalog;
    proc write(c: char))
  var index: int; entry: item; lengthx: position;
    used: int
  begin index := 1; used := 0; write(nl);
    while index <= catalog.size do
      entry := catalog.contents[index];
      lengthx := entry.attr.length;
      write_name(write, entry.title);
```

```
    if entry.attr.protected do
      write_line(write, line(' protected   .'))
    else true do
      write_line(write, line(' unprotected.'))
    end;
    write_int(write, lengthx.pages, 4);
    write_line(write, line(' pages.'));
    if (0 < lengthx.pages) and
      (lengthx.pages < 64) do
        write_int(write, pagelength *
          (lengthx.pages - 1) + lengthx.words, 7);
        write_line(write, line(' words.'))
    end;
    write(nl); used := used + lengthx.pages;
    if index mod (maxrow - 5) = 0 do
      pause_terminal
    end;
    index := index + 1
  end;
  write(nl); write_int(write, catalog.size, 5);
  write_line(write, line(' entries', nl));
  write_int(write, used, 5);
  write_line(write, line(' pages used', nl));
  write_int(write, allpages - used, 5);
  write_line(write, line(' pages available', nl))
end

* proc include_diskcatalog(var catalog: diskcatalog;
    key: name; attr: attributes)
  var x, y: item; index: int
  begin
    assume1(catalog.size < maxitem,
      line('catalog full.'));
    x := item(key, attr); index := 1;
    while index <= catalog.size do
      y := catalog.contents[index];
      assume2(x.title <> y.title, key,
        line(' ambiguous.'));
      if less_name(x.title, y.title) do
        catalog.contents[index] := x; x := y
      end;
      index := index + 1
    end;
    catalog.size := catalog.size + 1;
    catalog.contents[catalog.size] := x
  end

* proc search_diskcatalog(var catalog: diskcatalog;
    key: name; var value: attributes; var found: bool)
  var index: int
  begin locate(catalog, key, index, found);
    if found do value := catalog.contents[index].attr end
  end
```

```
* proc change_diskcatalog(var catalog: diskcatalog;
     key: name; value: attributes)
  var index: int; found: bool
  begin locate(catalog, key, index, found);
     assume2(found, key, line(' unknown.'));
     catalog.contents[index].attr := value
  end

* proc exclude_diskcatalog(var catalog: diskcatalog;
     key: name)
  var index: int; found: bool
  begin locate(catalog, key, index, found);
     assume2(found, key, line(' unknown.'));
     while index < catalog.size do
        catalog.contents[index] :=
           catalog.contents[index + 1];
        index := index + 1
     end;
     catalog.size := catalog.size - 1
  end

begin skip end

module "disk library"

   array boolpair [0:1] (bool)
   array mappair [0:1] (diskmap)
   array catalogpair [0:1] (diskcatalog)

   var original: boolpair; maps: mappair;
      catalogs: catalogpair

   proc check(drive: int)
   begin
      assume1((drive = 0) or (drive = 1),
         line('drive no invalid.'))
   end

   proc flushdisk_library(drive: int)
   begin
      if original[drive] do
         write_diskmap(maps[drive], drive);
         write_diskcatalog(catalogs[drive], drive);
         original[drive] := false
      end
   end

   proc insertnew_library(drive: int)
   begin
      new_diskmap(maps[drive]);
      new_diskcatalog(catalogs[drive]);
      original[drive] := true
   end
```

```
  proc insertold_library(drive: int)
  begin
    read_diskmap(maps[drive], drive);
    read_diskcatalog(catalogs[drive], drive);
    original[drive] := false
  end

* proc flush_library
  begin flushdisk_library(0);
    flushdisk_library(1)
  end

* proc insert_library
  var c: char
  begin
    writesentence_terminal(sentence(nl,
      'insert two disks and type', nl, nl,
      's if both disks are standard', nl,
      '0 if only disk 0 is standard', nl,
      '1 if only disk 1 is standard', nl,
      'b if both disks are blank', nl, '.'));
    accept(c);
    while not (c in charset('sS01bB')) do
      accept(c)
    end;
    c := lowercase(c);
    writeline_terminal(line(c, nl));
    if c = 's' do
      insertold_library(0); insertold_library(1)
    else true do
      pause_terminal;
      if c = '0' do
        insertold_library(0); insertnew_library(1)
      else c = '1' do
        insertnew_library(0); insertold_library(1)
      else c = 'b' do
        insertnew_library(0); insertnew_library(1)
      end
    end
  end

* proc list_library(drive: int; proc write(c: char))
  begin check(drive);
    list_diskcatalog(catalogs[drive], write)
  end

* proc backup_library(drive: int)
  var block: track; i: int
  begin check(drive); i := firsttrack;
    while i <= lasttrack do
      read_track(drive, i, block);
```

```
      write_track(1 - drive, i, block);
      i := i + 1
    end;
    insertold_library(1 - drive)
  end

* proc delete_library(drive: int; title: name)
  var attr: attributes; found: bool
  begin check(drive);
    search_diskcatalog(catalogs[drive], title,
      attr, found);
    if found do
      assume2(not attr.protected, title,
        line(' protected.'));
      discard_diskmap(maps[drive], attr.address);
      exclude_diskcatalog(catalogs[drive], title);
      original[drive] := true
    end
  end

* proc create_library(drive: int; title: name)
  begin check(drive);
    delete_library(drive, title);
    include_diskcatalog(catalogs[drive], title,
      attributes(empty_diskmap(maps[drive]),
        position(0, 0), false));
    original[drive] := true
  end

* proc protect_library(drive: int; title: name;
    value: bool)
  var attr: attributes; found: bool
  begin check(drive);
    search_diskcatalog(catalogs[drive], title,
      attr, found);
    assume2(found, title, line(' unknown.'));
    attr.protected := value;
    change_diskcatalog(catalogs[drive], title, attr);
    original[drive] := true
  end

* proc rename_library(drive: int; old, new: name)
  var attr: attributes; found: bool
  begin check(drive);
    search_diskcatalog(catalogs[drive], new, attr, found);
    assume2(not found, new, line(' ambiguous.'));
    search_diskcatalog(catalogs[drive], old, attr, found);
    assume2(found, old, line(' unknown.'));
    assume2(not attr.protected, old, line(' protected.'));
    exclude_diskcatalog(catalogs[drive], old);
    include_diskcatalog(catalogs[drive], new, attr);
    original[drive] := true
  end
```

```
* proc change_library(drive: int; title: name;
     new: attributes)
  var old: attributes; found: bool
  begin check(drive);
     search_diskcatalog(catalogs[drive], title, old, found);
     assume2(found, title, line(' unknown.'));
     assume2(not old.protected, title, line(' protected.'));
     change_diskcatalog(catalogs[drive], title, new);
     original[drive] := true
  end

* proc search_library(var drive: int; title: name;
     var attr: attributes)
  var found: bool
  begin drive := 0;
     search_diskcatalog(catalogs[0], title, attr, found);
     if not found do
        drive := 1;
        search_diskcatalog(catalogs[1], title, attr, found)
     end;
     assume2(found, title, line(' unknown.'))
  end

* proc locate_library(var drive: int; title: name)
  var attr: attributes
  begin search_library(drive, title, attr) end

* proc address_library(drive, start, pageno: int): int
  begin check(drive);
     val address_library :=
        address_diskmap(maps[drive], start, pageno)
  end

* proc extend_library(drive: int; var start: int)
  begin check(drive); extend_diskmap(maps[drive], start);
     original[drive] := true
  end

begin original := boolpair(false, false);
  insert_library "both drives contain disks"
end


module "disk files"

* record diskfile (title: name; open, safe, changed: bool;
     drive, start: int; size: position)

* proc open_file(var file: diskfile; title: name;
     var size: position)
  var drive: int; attr: attributes
  begin search_library(drive, title, attr);
```

```
      size := attr.length;
      file := diskfile(title, true, attr.protected, false,
        drive, attr.address, size)
   end

* proc read_file(var file: diskfile; pageno: int;
      var block: page)
   begin assume1(file.open, line('file closed.'));
      assume2((1 <= pageno) and
        (pageno <= file.size.pages),
        file.title, line(' limit.'));
      read_page(file.drive, address_library(file.drive,
        file.start, pageno), block)
   end

* proc write_file(var file: diskfile; pageno: int;
      var block: page)
   begin assume1(file.open, line('file closed.'));
      assume2(not file.safe, file.title,
        line(' protected.'));
      assume2((1 <= pageno) and
        (pageno <= file.size.pages),
        file.title, line(' limit.'));
      write_page(file.drive, address_library(file.drive,
        file.start, pageno), block)
   end

* proc extend_file(var file: diskfile;
      newpage: bool; newwords: int)
   begin assume1(file.open, line('file closed.'));
      assume2(not file.safe, file.title,
        line(' protected.'));
      if newpage do
        extend_library(file.drive, file.start);
        file.size.pages := file.size.pages + 1
      end;
      file.size.words := newwords; file.changed := true
   end

* proc end_file(var file: diskfile)
   begin assume1(file.open, line('file closed.'));
      if file.changed do
        change_library(file.drive, file.title,
          attributes(file.start, file.size, file.safe))
      end;
      file.open := false
   end

begin skip end
```

```
module "data streams"

* record stream (data: diskfile; head, length: position;
    block: page; newpage: bool)

* proc openread stream(var file: stream; title: name)
  begin open_file(file.data, title, file.length);
    file.head := position(1, 1) "reading(file)"
  end

* proc more stream(var file: stream): bool
  begin "reading(file)"
    if file.head.pages < file.length.pages do
      val more_stream := true
    else file.head.pages = file.length.pages do
      val more_stream :=
        file.head.words <= file.length.words
    else true do
      val more_stream := false
    end
  end

* proc read stream(var file: stream; var value: char)
  var x: int
  begin "more_stream(file)"
    x := file.head.words;
    if x = 1 do
      read_file(file.data, file.head.pages, file.block);
      file.head.words := 2
    else x = pagelength do
      file.head := position(file.head.pages + 1, 1)
    else true do
      file.head.words := x + 1
    end;
    value := file.block[x]
  end

* proc mark stream(var file: stream): position
  begin "more_stream(file) or writing(file)"
    val mark_stream := file.head
  end

* proc move stream(var file: stream; place: position)
  begin "reading(file)"
    if not ((file.head.pages = place.pages)
      and (file.head.words > 1)) do
        read_file(file.data, place.pages, file.block)
    end;
    file.head := place
  end
```

```
*  proc endread_stream(var file: stream)
   begin "reading(file)"
      end_file(file.data) "closed(file)"
   end

*  proc openwrite_stream(var file: stream; title: name)
   begin open_file(file.data, title, file.length);
      if file.length.pages = 0 do
         file.head := position(1, 1); file.newpage := true
      else file.length.words = pagelength do
         file.head := position(file.length.pages + 1, 1);
         file.newpage := true
      else true do
         read_file(file.data, file.length.pages, file.block);
         file.head := position(file.length.pages,
            file.length.words + 1); file.newpage := false
      end
      "writing(file)"
   end

*  proc write_stream(var file: stream;
      value: char)
   var x: int
   begin "writing(file)" x := file.head.words;
      file.block[x] := value;
      if x = pagelength do
         extend_file(file.data, file.newpage, pagelength);
         write_file(file.data, file.head.pages, file.block);
         file.head := position(file.head.pages + 1, 1);
         file.newpage := true
      else true do
         file.head.words := x + 1
      end
   end

*  proc endwrite_stream(var file: stream)
   begin "writing(file)"
      if file.head.words > 1 do
         extend_file(file.data, file.newpage,
            file.head.words - 1);
         write_file(file.data, file.head.pages, file.block)
      end;
      end_file(file.data) "closed(file)"
   end

begin skip end


module "standard commands"

*  proc readdrive(var drive: int)
```

```
  begin writeline_terminal(line('  Drive no = .'));
    readint_terminal(drive)
  end

* proc readfile(var title: name)
  begin writeline_terminal(line('  File name = .'));
    readname_terminal(title)
  end

* proc list
  var drive: int
  begin readdrive(drive);
    list_library(drive, write_terminal)
  end

* proc backup
  var drive: int
  begin readdrive(drive);
    writeline_terminal(
      line('insert blank disk in drive.'));
    writeint_terminal(1 - drive, 2);
    write_terminal(nl); pause_terminal;
    backup_library(drive)
  end

* proc create
  var drive: int; title: name
  begin readdrive(drive); readfile(title);
    create_library(drive, title)
  end

* proc delete
  var drive: int; title: name
  begin readdrive(drive); readfile(title);
    delete_library(drive, title)
  end

* proc protect(value: bool)
  var drive: int; title: name
  begin readdrive(drive); readfile(title);
    protect_library(drive, title, value)
  end

* proc rename
  var drive: int; old, new: name
  begin readdrive(drive);
    writeline_terminal(line('  Old name = .'));
    readname_terminal(old);
    writeline_terminal(line('  New name = .'));
    readname_terminal(new);
    rename_library(drive, old, new)
  end
```

```
* proc copy
  var drive: int; title1, title2, temp: name;
      file1, file2: diskfile; size1, size2: position;
      block: page
  begin
      writeline terminal(line('  Input name = .'));
      readname terminal(title1);
      writeline terminal(line('  Output name = .'));
      readname terminal(title2);
      writeline terminal(line('  Output drive = .'));
      readint terminal(drive); temp := name('temp1');
      delete library(drive, title2);
      create library(drive, temp);
      open file(file1, title1, size1);
      open file(file2, temp, size2);
      while size2.pages < size1.pages do
        size2.pages := size2.pages + 1;
        if size2.pages < size1.pages do
           size2.words := pagelength
        else true do size2.words := size1.words end;
        read file(file1, size2.pages, block);
        extend file(file2, true, size2.words);
        write file(file2, size2.pages, block)
      end;
      end file(file1); end file(file2);
      rename library(drive, temp, title2);
      protect library(drive, title2, true)
  end

* proc newsystem(kernel: bool)
  const kerneladdr = "pageno" 3;
        kernellimit = 4096 "words";
        systemaddr = "pageno" 11;
        systemlimit = 8192 "words"
  var drive, length, limit, pageno, wordno, value: int;
      title: name; file: stream; block: page
  begin readdrive(drive); readfile(title);
      openread stream(file, title); wordno := 0;
      if kernel do
        pageno := kerneladdr; limit := kernellimit
      else true do
        pageno := systemaddr; limit := systemlimit;
        while wordno < namelength do
           wordno := wordno + 1;
           block[wordno] := title[wordno]
        end
      end;
      length := wordno;
      while more stream(file) do
        assume2(length < limit, title,
           line('  too large.'));
        read stream(file, value:char);
```

```
      length := length + 1; wordno := wordno + 1;
      block[wordno] := char(value);
      if wordno = pagelength do
         write_page(drive, pageno, block);
         pageno := pageno + 1; wordno := 0
      end
   end;
   if wordno > 0 do write_page(drive, pageno, block) end;
   endread_stream(file)
end

begin skip end


module "library commands"

   const codelength = 24 "pages = 12288 words"
   array code [1:codelength] (page)
   record program (progname: name; progcode: code)

   proc load(title: name): program
   var file: diskfile; length: position; i: int
   begin open_file(file, title, length);
      assume2(length.pages > 0, title,
         line(' file empty.'));
      assume2(length.pages <= codelength, title,
         line(' code limit.'));
      val load.progname := title; i := 1;
      while i <= length.pages do
         read_file(file, i, val load.progcode[i]);
         i := i + 1
      end
   end

   lib proc prefix(
      progname: name;
      pdp11: bool;
      maxrow, maxcolumn: int;
      proc select(normal: bool);
      proc cursor(row, column: int);
      proc erase;
      proc display(value: char);
      proc assume(condition: bool; text: line);
      proc accept(var value: char);
      proc pause;
      proc print(value: char);
      proc openread(var file: stream; title: name);
      proc more(var file: stream): bool;
      proc read(var file: stream; var value: char);
      proc mark(var file: stream): position;
      proc move(var file: stream; place: position);
```

```
      proc endread(var file: stream);
      proc openwrite(var file: stream; title: name);
      proc write(var file: stream; value: char);
      proc endwrite(var file: stream);
      proc create(drive: int; title: name);
      proc delete(drive: int; title: name);
      proc locate(var drive: int; title: name);
      proc rename(drive: int; old, new: name);
      proc protect(drive: int; title: name; value: bool);
      proc readbool(proc read(var c: char); var value: bool);
      proc readint(proc read(var c: char); var value: int);
      proc readname(proc read(var c: char); var value: name);
      proc writebool(proc write(c: char); value: bool);
      proc writeint(proc write(c: char); value, length: int);
      proc writename(proc write(c: char); value: name);
      proc writeline(proc write(c: char); value: line);
      proc readsector(drive, sectorno: int;
        var value: sector);
      proc writesector(drive, sectorno: int; value: sector);
      proc subset(first, last: char): charset;
      proc load(title: name): program)
    [ load(progname) ]

  * proc call(progname: name)
    begin
        prefix(progname, pdp11, maxrow, maxcolumn,
          select_terminal, cursor, erase, write_terminal,
          assume1, read_terminal, pause_terminal, print,
          openread_stream, more_stream, read_stream,
          mark_stream, move_stream, endread_stream,
          openwrite_stream, write_stream, endwrite_stream,
          create_library, delete_library, locate_library,
          rename_library, protect_library, read_bool,
          read_int, read_name, write_bool, write_int,
          write_name, write_line, read_sector,
          write_sector, subset, load);
        select_terminal(true); display(bel)
    end

begin skip end

var op: name
begin
    while true do
        write_terminal(nl);
        writeline_terminal(line('Command = .'));
        readname_terminal(op);
        if op = name('backup') do backup
        else op = name('copy') do copy
        else op = name('create') do create
        else op = name('delete') do delete
```

```
      else op = name('insert') do insert_library
      else op = name('list') do list
      else op = name('newkernel') do newsystem(true)
      else op = name('newsystem') do newsystem(false)
      else op = name('protect') do protect(true)
      else op = name('rename') do rename
      else op = name('unprotect') do protect(false)
      else true do call(op) end;
      flush_library
   end
end "Edison operating system"
```

10

COMPILER

The user command that invokes compilation is described in Section 5.7.

The Edison compiler consists of a program named compile, which calls four passes one at a time. Each of the first three passes performs a sequential scan of the program text and outputs intermediate code to a temporary file. The output of one pass becomes the input of the next pass. The last pass scans its input twice and outputs final code on a given disk.

10.1 COMPILER ADMINISTRATION

This section contains the complete text of the compile program with some additional comments.

Program Prefix

The parameters of the compiler denote constants and procedures declared within the operating system. Every program that can be invoked by a user command uses the same prefix (Section 5.15).

Failures

This module handles compilation failures (Section 5.7.2).

Note Output

This module controls the output (by pass 4) of error messages and check sums to a disk file named notes (Section 5.7).

Text Input

This module defines the input (by pass 1) of program text from a given disk file. All control characters (except newline) are skipped (Section 3.19.1).

Code Output

This module deletes the final code file if the program text contains errors, and assigns a given name to it if the program is compiled successfully.

Symbol Input

This module controls the input of intermediate code from a disk file. The rewind procedure enables pass 4 to begin a second scan of its input. The endin procedure deletes the intermediate input file at the end of each pass.

Symbol Output

This module handles the output of intermediate (or final) code to a disk file and the computation of check sums (across all passes). The openout procedure creates an output file on a given disk at the beginning of each pass. A boolean named copied and a procedure named reopen enable pass 4 to suppress disk transfers during its first scan and activate them during the final scan.

Compiler Passes

This module describes the four passes as library procedures. A procedure parameter named rerun enables pass 4 to scan its input a second time.

Statement Part

The input and output files of a pass are placed on opposite drives to reduce disk arm movement. The temporary files are named temp1 and temp2. The boolean constant named trim determines whether or not the compiler optimizes the generated code as explained in Section 6.10.

Compiler Text

```
const nl = char(10); sp = ' ';
    linelength = 80 "characters";
    namelength = 12 "characters";
    sectorlength = 64 "integers"
set charset (char)
array line [1:linelength] (char)
array name [1:namelength] (char)
array sector [1:sectorlength] (int)
record position (pages, words: int)
enum word (sixteen_bits)
array program [1:12300] (word)
array stream [1:536] (word)

proc prefix(
    progname: name;
    pdp11: bool;
    maxrow, maxcolumn: int;
    proc select(normal: bool);
    proc cursor(row, column: int);
    proc erase;
    proc display(value: char);
    proc assume(condition: bool; text: line);
    proc accept(var value: char);
    proc pause;
    proc print(value: char);
    proc openread(var file: stream; title: name);
    proc more(var file: stream): bool;
    proc read(var file: stream; var value: char);
    proc mark(var file: stream): position;
    proc move(var file: stream; place: position);
    proc endread(var file: stream);
    proc openwrite(var file: stream; title: name);
    proc write(var file: stream; value: char);
    proc endwrite(var file: stream);
    proc create(drive: int; title: name);
    proc delete(drive: int; title: name);
    proc locate(var drive: int; title: name);
    proc rename(drive: int; old, new: name);
    proc protect(drive: int; title: name; value: bool);
    proc readbool(proc read(var c: char); var value: bool);
    proc readint(proc read(var c: char); var value: int);
    proc readname(proc read(var c: char); var value: name);
    proc writebool(proc write(c: char); value: bool);
    proc writeint(proc write(c: char); value, length: int);
    proc writename(proc write(c: char); value: name);
    proc writeline(proc write(c: char); value: line);
    proc readsector(drive, sectorno: int;
        var value: sector);
    proc writesector(drive, sectorno: int; value: sector);
    proc subset(first, last: char): charset;
    proc load(title: name): program)
```

```
"The Edison system: Edison compiler
            14 July 1981
 Copyright (c) 1981 Per Brinch Hansen"

module "failure"

* enum failure (blocklimit, charlimit, inputlimit,
     labellimit, namelimit, processlimit, wordlimit)

* proc fail(reason: failure)
  var text: line
  begin
     if reason = blocklimit do text := line('block.')
     else reason = charlimit do text := line('char.')
     else reason = inputlimit do text := line('input.')
     else reason = labellimit do text := line('label.')
     else reason = namelimit do text := line('name.')
     else reason = processlimit do text := line('process.')
     else reason = wordlimit do text := line('word.') end;
     display(nl); writeline(display, text);
     writeline(display, line(' limit.')); halt
  end

begin skip end

module "note output"

  const notedrive = 0

  var notes: name; file: stream

  proc print(c: char)
  begin write(file, c) end

* enum errorkind (ambiguous, call, cobeginx, constructor,
     funcval, incomplete, numeral, range, splitx, syntax,
     type, undeclared)

* var errors: bool

* proc noteerror(lineno: int; kind: errorkind)
  var text: line
  begin
     if kind = ambiguous do
        text := line('ambiguous name.')
     else kind = call do
        text := line('invalid procedure call.')
     else kind = cobeginx do
        text := line('invalid concurrent statement.')
     else kind = constructor do
        text := line('invalid constructor.')
```

```
        else kind = funcval do
            text := line('invalid use of function variable.')
        else kind = incomplete do
            text := line('invalid recursive use of name.')
        else kind = numeral do
            text := line('numeral out of range.')
        else kind = range do
            text := line('invalid range.')
        else kind = splitx do
            text := line('invalid split procedure.')
        else kind = syntax do
            text := line('invalid syntax.')
        else kind = type do
            text := line('invalid type.')
        else kind = undeclared do
            text := line('undeclared name.')
        end;
        writeline(print, line('line .'));
        writeint(print, lineno, 4); print(sp);
        writeline(print, text); print(nl);
        errors := true
    end

*   proc notesums(title: name; sum1, sum2: int)
    begin writename(print,title);
        writeline(print, line(' check sums = .'));
        writeint(print, sum1, 7);
        writeint(print, sum2, 7);
        print(nl); print(nl)
    end

*   proc endnotes(errors, summed: bool)
    begin endwrite(file);
        if errors do
            writeline(display, line(
                'compilation errors (see notes on disk)', nl))
        else summed do
            writeline(display, line(
                'check sums ready (see notes on disk)', nl))
        else true do delete(notedrive, notes) end
    end

begin notes := name('notes'); create(notedrive, notes);
    openwrite(file, notes); errors := false
end

module "text input"

    const em = char(25)

    var invisible: charset
```

```
*  var text: name; textdrive: int; input: stream

*  proc nextchar(var ch: char)
   begin
      if more(input) do
         read(input, ch);
         while ch in invisible do read(input, ch) end
         "display(ch)"
      else true do ch := em end
   end

*  proc endtext
   begin endread(input) end

begin writeline(display, line(' Text name = .'));
   readname(accept, text); locate(textdrive, text);
   invisible := subset(char(0), char(31)) -
      charset(nl) + charset(char(127));
   openread(input, text)
end


module "code output"

*  var code: name; codedrive: int

*  proc endcode(temp: name; errors: bool)
   begin
      if errors do delete(codedrive, temp)
      else true do rename(codedrive, temp, code) end
   end

begin writeline(display, line(' Code name = .'));
   readname(accept, code);
   writeline(display, line(' Code drive = .'));
   readint(accept, codedrive);
   delete(codedrive, code)
end


module "symbol input"

   var temp: name; pass: char; start: position

*  proc openin(title: name; scan: char)
   begin openread(input, title); temp := title;
      pass := scan; start := mark(input)
   end

*  proc next(var value: int)
   begin read(input, value:char) "display(pass);
      writeint(display, value, 7); display(nl)"
   end
```

```
* proc rewind(scan: char)
  begin move(input, start); pass := scan end

* proc endin
  var drive: int
  begin endread(input); locate(drive, temp);
     delete(drive, temp)
  end

begin skip end


module "symbol output"

  const n = 8191

  var output: stream; copied: bool;
     sum1, sum2: int

* var summed: bool

* proc openout(drive: int; title: name; normal: bool)
  begin create(drive, title); openwrite(output, title);
     copied := normal
  end

* proc emit(value: int)
  begin
     if copied do write(output, char(value)) end;
     if summed do
        sum1 := (sum1 + value mod n) mod n;
        sum2 := (sum2 + sum1) mod n
     end
  end

* proc reopen
  begin copied := true;
     if summed do notesums(text, sum1, sum2) end
  end

* proc endout
  begin endwrite(output);
     if summed do notesums(text, sum1, sum2) end
  end

begin
  writeline(display, line('  Compute check sums? .'));
  readbool(accept, summed); sum1 := 0; sum2 := 0
end


module "compiler passes"
```

```
*  lib proc pass1(
      proc next(var value: char);
      proc emit(value: int);
      proc fail(reason: failure))
   [ load(name('edison1')) ]

*  lib proc pass2(
      proc next(var value: int);
      proc emit(value: int);
      proc fail(reason: failure))
   [ load(name('edison2')) ]

*  lib proc pass3(
      proc next(var value: int);
      proc emit(value: int);
      proc fail(reason: failure))
   [ load(name('edison3')) ]

*  lib proc pass4(trim: bool;
      proc next(var value: int);
      proc emit(value: int);
      proc report(lineno: int; error: errorkind);
      proc rerun;
      proc fail(reason: failure))
   [ load(name('edison4')) ]

*  proc rerun
   begin rewind('5'); reopen end

begin skip end


const trim = true

var temp1, temp2: name; drive1, drive2: int
begin temp1 := name('temp1'); temp2 := name('temp2');
   drive1 := 1 - textdrive; drive2 := textdrive;
   openout(drive1, temp1, true);
   pass1(nextchar, emit, fail); endtext; endout;
   openin(temp1, '2'); openout(drive2, temp2, true);
   pass2(next, emit, fail); endin; endout;
   openin(temp2, '3'); openout(drive1, temp1, true);
   pass3(next, emit, fail); endin; endout;
   openin(temp1, '4'); openout(codedrive, temp2, false);
   pass4(trim, next, emit, noteerror, rerun, fail);
   endin; endout; endnotes(errors, summed);
   endcode(temp2, errors)
end
```

10.2 LEXICAL ANALYSIS

This section contains the complete text of pass 1 of the Edison compiler with some additional comments.

Basic Symbols

Pass 1 scans a program text once and outputs an intermediate form of the basic symbols of Edison (Section 3.2.3):

The special symbols and word symbols of the language are output as enumeration values of type symbol.

A name is output as a symbol value ("name") followed by a name index in the range 1:maxname. The standard names have fixed name indices (Section 3.19.2). This pass does not distinguish between different declarations of the same name in different blocks.

A numeral is output as a symbol value ("numeral") followed by the integer value denoted by the numeral (Section 3.19.3).

A graphic symbol is output as a symbol value ("graphic") followed by the ordinal value of the graphic character (Section 3.7.5).

A character string is output as a sequence of graphic symbols separated by commas (Section 3.2.5).

Spaces and comments are not output. A newline character is output as a symbol value ("newline") followed by a line number (Section 3.2.4).

An error detected in the program text is output as a symbol value ("error") followed by an enumeration value of type errorkind. (This symbol eventually produces an error message in pass 4.)

The output of pass 1 is terminated by a symbol value named "endtext."

So the output of pass 1 has practically the same syntactical structure as the program text itself. This simple form of intermediate code is also used by passes 2 and 3.

Word Symbols and Names

The characters of all words (that is, word symbols and names) are stored in a character table. A variable named top defines the total number of characters stored.

Each word is also described in a word table by three attributes:

(1) The alias of a word symbol is the ordinal value of the corresponding enumeration symbol. The alias of a name is the negative value of its name index.

(2) The word length defines the number of characters in a word.

(3) The lastchar is the index of the last of these characters (all of which are kept in the character table).

A variable named size defines the total number of words described. A variable called name defines the index of the next name to be inserted in the table.

The insert procedure inserts a word in the character table and describes it in a given entry of the word table.

The declare procedure describes a word symbol in the character and word tables.

The convert procedure looks up a word in the character and word tables using hashing. If the tables already contain the word, its alias is returned; otherwise, the word (which can only be a name) is inserted with a new (negative) name index which is then returned.

Symbol Look-Ahead

Pass 1 inputs a character to begin with. Whenever the pass has recognized the current character, it immediately inputs the next one. This principle of a single-symbol look-ahead is followed by all the passes.

Pass 1 Text

```
"Edison-11 Compiler: Pass 1

 Symbol analysis

 Per Brinch Hansen

 4 August 1980

 Copyright (c) 1980 Per Brinch Hansen"

enum symbol (also1, and1, array1, asterisk1, becomes1,
     begin1, cobegin1, colon1, comma1, const1, div1,
     do1, else1, end1, endtext1, enum1, equal1,
     error1, graphic1, greater1, if1, in1, lbracket1,
     less1, lib1, lparanth1, minus1, mod1, module1,
     name1, newline1, not1, notequal1, notgreater1,
     notless1, numeral1, or1, period1, plus1,
     pre1, post1, proc1, rbracket1, record1,
     rparanth1, semicolon1, set1, skip1, val1,
     var1, when1, while1)

enum failure (blocklimit, charlimit, inputlimit,
     labellimit, namelimit, outputlimit, processlimit,
     wordlimit)
```

```
proc pass1(
    proc next(var value: char);
    proc emit(value: symbol);
    proc fail(reason: failure))

const " table limits"
    maxchar = 6500; maxname = 750; maxword = 809

"maxword is a prime > maxname + number of word symbols"

const linelength = 132
array line [1:linelength] (char)

proc emit2(sym: symbol; arg: int)
begin emit(sym); emit(symbol(arg)) end


module "errors"

*   enum errorkind (ambiguous3, call3, cobegin3,
        constructor3, funcval3, incomplete3, numeral3,
        range3, split3, syntax3, type3, undeclared3)

*   proc error(kind: errorkind)
    begin emit2(error1, int(kind)) end

begin skip end


module "word table"

    const "standard names"
        bool1 = 1; char1 = 2; false1 = 3; int1 = 4;
        true1 = 5; univname1 = 6; univtype1 = 7;
        addr1 = 8; halt1 = 9; obtain1 = 10; place1 = 11;
        sense1 = 12; last_standard = 20;

        none = maxword

    array chartable [1:maxchar] (char)

    record wordattr (alias, wordlength, lastchar: int)

    array wordtable [1:maxword] (wordattr)

    var heap: chartable; top: int;
        table: wordtable; size, name: int

    proc key(word: line; length: int): int
    const span = 26 "letters"
    var hash, i: int
    begin hash := 1; i := 0;
```

```
    while i < length do
       i := i + 1;
       hash := hash *
          (int(word[i]) mod span + 1) mod maxword
    end;
    val key := hash + 1
end

proc insert(word: line; length, index, value: int)
var m, n: int
begin top := top + length;
    if top > maxchar do fail(charlimit) end;
    m := length; n := top - m;
    while m > 0 do
       heap[m + n] := word[m]; m := m - 1
    end;
    table[index] := wordattr(value, length, top);
    size := size + 1;
    if size = maxword do fail(wordlimit) end
end

proc found(word: line; length, index: int): bool
var same: bool; m, n: int
begin
    if table[index].wordlength <> length do same := false
    else true do
       same := true; m := length;
       n := table[index].lastchar - m;
       while same and (m > 0) do
          same := word[m] = heap[m + n]; m := m - 1
       end
    end;
    val found := same
end

proc declare(word: line; length, value: int)
var i: int
begin i := key(word, length);
    while table[i].alias <> none do
       i := i mod maxword + 1
    end;
    insert(word, length, i, value)
end

* proc convert(word: line; length: int;
       var value: int)
var i: int; more: bool
begin i := key(word, length); more := true;
    while more do
       if table[i].alias = none do
          if name = maxname do fail(namelimit) end;
          value := - name; name := name + 1;
```

```
                  insert(word, length, i, value); more := false
            else found(word, length, i) do
                  value := table[i].alias; more := false
            else true do i := i mod maxword + 1 end
         end
      end

begin top := 0; size := maxword;
   while size > 0 do
         table[size] := wordattr(none, 0, none);
      size := size - 1
   end;
   "word symbols"
   declare(line('ALSO'), 4, int(also1));
   declare(line('AND'), 3, int(and1));
   declare(line('ARRAY'), 5, int(array1));
   declare(line('BEGIN'), 5, int(begin1));
   declare(line('COBEGIN'), 7, int(cobegin1));
   declare(line('CONST'), 5, int(const1));
   declare(line('DIV'), 3, int(div1));
   declare(line('DO'), 2, int(do1));
   declare(line('ELSE'), 4, int(else1));
   declare(line('END'), 3, int(end1));
   declare(line('ENUM'), 4, int(enum1));
   declare(line('IF'), 2, int(if1));
   declare(line('IN'), 2, int(in1));
   declare(line('LIB'), 3, int(lib1));
   declare(line('MOD'), 3, int(mod1));
   declare(line('MODULE'), 6, int(module1));
   declare(line('NOT'), 3, int(not1));
   declare(line('OR'), 2, int(or1));
   declare(line('PRE'), 3, int(pre1));
   declare(line('POST'), 4, int(post1));
   declare(line('PROC'), 4, int(proc1));
   declare(line('RECORD'), 6, int(record1));
   declare(line('SET'), 3, int(set1));
   declare(line('SKIP'), 4, int(skip1));
   declare(line('VAL'), 3, int(val1));
   declare(line('VAR'), 3, int(var1));
   declare(line('WHEN'), 4, int(when1));
   declare(line('WHILE'), 5, int(while1));
   "standard names"
   declare(line('BOOL'), 4, - bool1);
   declare(line('CHAR'), 4, - char1);
   declare(line('FALSE'), 5, - false1);
   declare(line('INT'), 3, - int1);
   declare(line('TRUE'), 4, - true1);
   declare(line('ADDR'), 4, - addr1);
   declare(line('HALT'), 4, - halt1);
   declare(line('OBTAIN'), 6, - obtain1);
   declare(line('PLACE'), 5, - place1);
   declare(line('SENSE'), 5, - sense1);
   name := last_standard + 1
end
```

```
module "nextsym"

*  const newline = char(10); endmedium = char(25);
      space = ' '; quote = '"'; apostrophy = char(39);
      maxint = 32767

   set charset (char)

   var alphanum, comment, composite,
      capital_letters, digits, graphic, letters,
      octals, parantheses, punctuation, single,
      small_letters, special, stringchar: charset;

      lineno: int

*  var ch: char

*  proc nextsym
   var word: line; value, i: int
   begin
      while ch = space do next(ch)
      else ch = newline do
         lineno := lineno + 1; emit2(newline1, lineno);
         next(ch)
      else ch = quote do
         next(ch);
         while ch in comment do
            if ch = newline do lineno := lineno + 1 end;
            next(ch)
         end;
         if ch = quote do next(ch)
         else true do error(syntax3) end
      end;
      if ch in letters do
         i := 0;
         while ch in alphanum do
            if ch in small_letters do
               ch := char(int(ch) - 32)
            end;
            i := i + 1; word[i] := ch; next(ch)
         end;
         convert(word, i, value);
         if value < 0 do emit2(name1, - value)
         else true do emit(symbol(value)) end
      else ch in digits do
         value := 0;
         while ch in digits do
            i := int(ch) - int('0');
            if value <= (maxint - i) div 10 do
               value := 10 * value + i; next(ch)
            else true do
```

```
                error(numeral3);
                while ch in digits do next(ch) end
        end
    end;
    emit2(numeral1, value)
else ch in punctuation do
    if ch = ';' do emit(semicolon1)
    else ch = ',' do emit(comma1)
    else ch = '.' do emit(period1) end;
    next(ch)
else ch in parantheses do
    if ch = '(' do emit(lparanth1)
    else ch = ')' do emit(rparanth1)
    else ch = '[' do emit(lbracket1)
    else ch = ']' do emit(rbracket1) end;
    next(ch)
else ch in composite do
    if ch = ':' do
        next(ch);
        if ch = '=' do emit(becomes1); next(ch)
        else true do emit(colon1) end
    else ch = '>' do
        next(ch);
        if ch = '=' do emit(notless1); next(ch)
        else true do emit(greater1) end
    else ch = '<' do
        next(ch);
        if ch = '>' do emit(notequal1); next(ch)
        else ch = '=' do emit(notgreater1); next(ch)
        else true do emit(less1) end
    end
else ch in single do
    if ch = '+' do emit(plus1)
    else ch = '-' do emit(minus1)
    else ch = '*' do emit(asterisk1)
    else ch = '=' do emit(equal1) end;
    next(ch)
else ch = apostrophy do
    next(ch);
    if ch in stringchar do
        emit2(graphic1, int(ch)); next(ch);
        while ch in stringchar do
            emit(comma1); emit2(graphic1, int(ch));
            next(ch)
        end;
        if ch = apostrophy do next(ch)
        else true do error(syntax3) end
    else true do
        if ch = apostrophy do next(ch) end;
        error(syntax3)
    end
```

```
              else ch = '#' do
                value := 0; next(ch);
                if ch in octals do
                  while (ch in octals) and (value <= #7777) do
                    value := 8 * value + (int(ch) - int('0'));
                  next(ch)
                end;
                  if (ch in octals) and (value <= #17777) do
                    value := #100000 + 8 * (value - #10000)
                      + (int(ch) - int('0'));
                  next(ch)
                end;
                  if ch in octals do
                    error(numeral3);
                    while ch in octals do next(ch) end
                end
              else true do error(syntax3) end;
                emit2(numeral1, value)
            else ch = endmedium do skip
            else true do "ch in invalid_graphics"
              error(syntax3); next(ch)
            end
        end

  begin
    capital_letters :=
      charset('ABCDEFGHIJKLMNOPQRSTUVWXYZ');
    small_letters :=
      charset('abcdefghijklmnopqrstuvwxyz');
    letters := capital_letters + small_letters;
    digits := charset('0123456789');
    alphanum := letters + digits + charset('_');
    special := charset(apostrophy,
      '!"#$%&()*+,-./:;<=>?@[]_');
    graphic := alphanum + special + charset(space);
    comment :=
      graphic - charset(quote) + charset(newline);
    composite := charset(':<>');
    octals := charset('01234567');
    parantheses := charset('()[]');
    punctuation := charset(';,.');
    single := charset('+-*=');
    stringchar := graphic - charset(apostrophy);
    lineno := 1; emit2(newline1, 1);
    next(ch)
  end


  begin
    while ch <> endmedium do nextsym end;
    emit(endtext1)
  end
```

10.3 SYNTAX AND SCOPE ANALYSIS

This section contains the complete text of pass 2 of the Edison compiler with some additional comments.

Pass 2 scans the intermediate code output by pass 1 once and checks whether the syntax and scope rules of the Edison language are followed in the program text. Different uses of the same name in different blocks are distinguished by unique name indices. The output of pass 2 has the same syntactical structure as the output of pass 1 (Section 10.2).

Input

The skipsym procedure inputs the next symbol, which is not a newline or error symbol. The latter are treated as hidden symbols and are automatically copied into the output.

The nextsym procedure copies the last symbol and its argument (if any) into the output, and inputs the next symbol.

Initially, the module reads the first symbol (Section 10.2).

Scope Analysis

Pass 2 enforces the scope rules of Edison (Section 3.4).

The (possibly ambiguous) name indices generated by pass 1 are called original name indices. The unique name indices produced by pass 2 are called final name indices.

In order to distinguish between different uses of the same name in different blocks, nested blocks are assigned level numbers 0, 1, 2, . . . starting with the outermost block of the program.

A map table defines a mapping from original to final name indices.

A name table defines a mapping from final name indices to a set of name attributes. Each known name is described by the following attributes:

(1) The kind of entity denoted by a name is described as being either a constant, a type, a field, or other.

(2) The block levels at which a name is known are called the min and max levels of the name. If a name is local to a block at level n, minlevel = maxlevel = n. If a name is exported from a block at level n, minlevel = n - 1 and maxlevel = n within the given block. When the block ends, the maxlevel is changed to n - 1.

(3) The original name index is also stored as a name attribute.

A variable called nameno defines the total number of standard names and declarations recognized so far in the program text. Another variable defines the level of nesting of the current block.

Initially, all entries in the map and name tables are marked as undeclared. Following this, the standard names are entered at block level 0.

The procedure named newname introduces a new name of a given kind. The name is assigned a final index and is described by its attributes. Following this, the name is output with its final name index, and the next symbol is input. If the same name already has been declared within the given block (or has been exported to it), pass 2 reports the name as being ambiguous.

The procedure called oldname checks whether a name used in the current block is known within it. Following this, the name is output with its final index, and the next symbol is input. If the name is undeclared, an error message is output. Invalid recursive declarations of constants and data types are detected by marking these names as being incompletely declared while their declarations are being checked. At the end of the declarations, the kind attribute of these names is changed to either constant or type by means of a procedure called changed. When an undeclared or incompletely declared name has been reported, the name is then described as being of universal kind to suppress further error messages referring to the same name.

At the beginning of a block, the block level is incremented by one.

At the end of a block, the map and name tables are changed to describe only those names that are known in the immediately surrounding block. This is done by examining every declared name as follows:

(1) If a name is global to the given block (that is, if maxlevel < blocklevel), it is reentered in the map table.

(2) If a name is local to the given block (that is, if minlevel = maxlevel = blocklevel), it is marked as undeclared.

(3) If a name is exported from the given block (that is, if minlevel < maxlevel), it is reentered in the map table, and the maxlevel of the name is made equal to its minlevel. (This ensures that the name will be marked as undeclared at the end of the surrounding block as explained above.)

Finally, the block level is decreased by one.

A function variable **val** F is only known within the body of a function named F. The function name is, however, known both within the body and in the surrounding block (Sections 3.16.1 and 3.16.3). To enable the compiler to enforce these rules, the name of a complete procedure is marked as partially declared until the end of its body. The name kind is then changed to complete.

A split procedure is treated as follows (Section 3.16.4):

The predeclaration is initially marked as partially declared and is then changed to be of kind split.

The postdeclaration must refer to a known name of kind split declared at the same block level as the postdeclaration. The name kind is changed to postname at the beginning of the postdeclaration and to complete at the end of the body.

An unmatched predeclaration is detected when all the names are scanned at the end of a block.

Syntax Analysis

Each syntactic form of the Edison language is described by a procedure. When this procedure is called, it inputs and checks the syntax of a sentence that is supposed to be of that form. Since some of the syntactic forms are recursively defined, the corresponding procedures are also recursive. This compilation method is called *recursive descent* [Wirth, 1976a].

In general, a syntax expression E has the form

$$T1 \# T2 \# \ldots \# Tn$$

where T1, T2, ..., Tn stand for syntax terms that define other classes of sentences (Section 3.2.1).

A sentence of this form is recognized by a procedure named E that calls other procedures named T1, T2, ..., Tn:

```
proc E(succ: symbols)
begin
  if sym in first(T1) do T1(succ)
  else sym in first(T2) do T2(succ)
      . . .
  else sym in first(Tn) do Tn(succ)
  else true do syntax(succ) end;
  check(succ)
end
```

The current input symbol is called sym. The set of symbols that can occur at the beginning of a sentence of the form T is denoted first(T). When pass 2 recognizes one of these symbols, it calls a procedure named T that recognizes sentences of that form.

The procedure E has a parameter that defines the set of symbols that can occur after a sentence of the form E. When a syntax error is detected, pass 2 calls a procedure named syntax that outputs an error symbol and then skips further input symbols until it finds one of the possible successor symbols. Since the endtext symbol is included in all successor sets, the compiler will never attempt to scan past the end of the program text. This is known as *error recovery*.

If the syntax of a sentence is correct, pass 2 will still call a procedure to check whether or not the first symbol after the sentence is one of the possible successor symbols. If it is not, this is also treated as a syntax error.

A syntax term T has the form

$$F1 \quad F2 \quad \ldots \quad Fn$$

where F1, F2, . . . , Fn stand for syntax factors that define other classes of sentences.

A sentence of this form is recognized by a procedure named T that calls other procedures named F1, F2, . . . , Fn:

```
proc T(succ: symbols)
begin
    F1(first(F2) + . . . + first(Fn) + succ);
    F2(first(F3) + . . . + first(Fn) + succ);

        . . .
    Fn(succ);
    check(succ)
end
```

Since a syntax factor, such as F1, may describe empty sentences, it is necessary to stop a possible error recovery at the beginning of the next factor F2, or F3, . . . , or Fn. That is why the successor symbols of F1 are the union of the first symbols of F2, F3, . . ., Fn, and the successors of T itself.

A syntax factor F of the form

$$[\, E \,]*$$

is recognized by a procedure of the form

```
proc F(succ: symbols)
begin
    while sym in first(E) do
        E(first(E) + succ)
    end;
    check(succ)
end
```

A syntax factor F of the form

$$[\, E \,]$$

is recognized by a procedure of the form

```
proc F(succ: symbols)
begin
  if sym in first(E) do E(succ) end;
  check(succ)
end
```

A syntax factor F of the form

$$N$$

where N denotes the name of another syntactic form can be recognized by a
procedure of the form

```
proc F(succ: symbols)
begin N(succ);   check(succ) end
```

A syntax factor of the form

$$S$$

where S is a basic symbol, is recognized as follows:

```
proc checksym(s: symbol;   succ: symbols)
begin
  if sym = s do nextsym
  else true do syntax(succ) end
end
```

As these rules show, it is a fairly mechanical job to write a set of recursive procedures that correspond to the syntactic rules of the language.
The previous systematic rules are supplemented by a few heuristic rules:

(1) If a syntactic form includes names of different kinds (such as the
variable and type names in a variable group), the resulting error messages can
be very misleading if the error recovery stops on a name and gives it the
wrong interpretation (Section 2.2.5). In such cases, it is often advisable to
exclude names from the successor sets and skip them after a syntax error.

(2) If the declaration of an entity does not include a name for the
entity, the whole declaration is skipped.

(3) A missing semicolon in a statement list is such a frequent error that
it deserves a more careful form of error recovery.

Pass 2 Text

```
"Edison-11 Compiler: Pass 2

 Syntax and scope analysis

 Per Brinch Hansen

 7 July 1981

 Copyright (c) 1980 Per Brinch Hansen"

enum symbol (also1, and1, array1, asterisk1, becomes1,
    begin1, cobegin1, colon1, comma1, const1, div1,
    do1, else1, end1, endtext1, enum1, equal1, error1,
    graphic1, greater1, if1, in1, lbracket1, less1,
    lib1, lparanth1, minus1, mod1, module1, name1,
    newline1, not1, notequal1, notgreater1, notless1,
    numeral1, or1, period1, plus1, pre1, post1,
    proc1, rbracket1, record1, rparanth1, semicolon1,
    set1, skip1, val1, var1, when1, while1)

enum failure (blocklimit, charlimit, inputlimit,
    labellimit, namelimit, outputlimit, processlimit,
    wordlimit)

proc pass2(
    proc next(var value: symbol);
    proc emit(value: symbol);
    proc fail(reason: failure))

const "table limits" maxname = 750

proc emit2(sym: symbol; arg: int)
begin emit(sym); emit(symbol(arg)) end


module "symbol sets"

* set symbols (symbol)

* var addsym, constsym, declsym, exprsym,
    hiddensym, initdeclsym, literalsym, multsym,
    pairsym, procsym, relationsym, selectsym,
    signsym, statsym, typesym: symbols

begin
    addsym := symbols(minus1, or1, plus1);
    constsym := symbols(graphic1, name1, numeral1);
```

```
    declsym := symbols(array1, const1, enum1, lib1,
      module1, post1, pre1, proc1, record1, set1, var1);
    exprsym := symbols(graphic1, lparanth1, minus1, not1,
      numeral1, plus1, val1);
    hiddensym := symbols(error1, newline1);
    initdeclsym := symbols(array1, const1, enum1,
      record1, set1);
    literalsym := symbols(graphic1, numeral1);
    multsym := symbols(and1, asterisk1, div1, mod1);
    pairsym := symbols(graphic1, name1, numeral1);
    procsym := symbols(lib1, post1, pre1, proc1);
    relationsym := symbols(equal1, greater1, in1, less1,
      notequal1, notgreater1, notless1);
    selectsym := symbols(colon1, lbracket1, period1);
    signsym := symbols(minus1, plus1);
    statsym := symbols(cobegin1, if1, skip1, when1,
      while1);
    typesym := symbols(array1, enum1, record1, set1)
end


module "input"

* var sym: symbol; x: int

* proc skipsym
  begin next(sym);
    while sym in hiddensym do
      next(x:symbol); emit2(sym, x); next(sym)
    end;
    if sym in pairsym do next(x:symbol) end
  end

* proc nextsym
  begin emit(sym);
    if sym in pairsym do emit(x:symbol) end;
    skipsym
  end

begin skipsym end


module "errors"

* enum errorkind (ambiguous3, call3, cobegin3,
    constructor3, funcval3, incomplete3, numeral3,
    range3, split3, syntax3, type3, undeclared3)

* proc error(kind: errorkind)
  begin emit2(error1, int(kind)) end
```

```
* proc syntax(succ: symbols)
  begin "error(syntax3);"
    while not (sym in succ) do nextsym end";
    error(syntax3)"
  end

* proc check(succ: symbols)
  begin if not (sym in succ) do syntax(succ) end
  end

* proc checksym(s: symbol; succ: symbols)
  begin
    if sym = s do nextsym
    else true do syntax(succ) end
  end

begin skip end


module "names"

* const "standard names"
    bool1 = 1; char1 = 2; false1 = 3; int1 = 4;
    true1 = 5; univname1 = 6; univtype1 = 7;
    addr1 = 8; halt1 = 9; obtain1 = 10;
    place1 = 11; sense1 = 12; last_standard = 20;

    noname = 0

* enum namekind (undeclared, incomplete,
    universal, constant, type, field, variable,
    split, partial, complete)

  set namekinds (namekind)

  record nameattr (kind: namekind;
    minlevel, maxlevel, originalname: int)

  array nametable [0:maxname] (nameattr)

  array maptable [1:maxname] (int)

  var names: nametable; nameno: int;
    map: maptable; blocklevel: int

  proc predeclare(name: int; kind: namekind)
  begin map[name] := name;
    names[name] := nameattr(kind, blocklevel,
      blocklevel, name)
  end
```

```
* proc beginblock
  begin blocklevel := blocklevel + 1 end

* proc endblock
  var finalname: int; n: nameattr
  begin finalname := 0;
    while finalname < nameno do
      finalname := finalname + 1;
      n := names[finalname];
      if n.kind <> undeclared do
        if n.maxlevel < blocklevel do
          map[n.originalname] := finalname
        else true do
          if n.kind = split do error(split3) end;
          if n.maxlevel = n.minlevel do
            if map[n.originalname] = finalname do
              map[n.originalname] := noname
            end;
            n := nameattr(undeclared, 0, 0, 0)
          else true do
            n.maxlevel := n.minlevel;
            map[n.originalname] := finalname
          end;
          names[finalname] := n
        end
      end
    end;
    blocklevel := blocklevel - 1
  end

* proc newname(export: bool; mode: namekind)
  var origin, scope: int; n: nameattr
  begin "sym = name1"
    if nameno = maxname do fail(namelimit) end;
    nameno := nameno + 1; origin := blocklevel;
    if export do scope := origin - 1
    else true do scope := origin end;
    n := names[map[x]];
    if not (n.kind in namekinds(undeclared,
      universal)) and (n.maxlevel >= scope) do
        error(ambiguous3)
    end;
    names[nameno] := nameattr(mode, scope,
      origin, x);
    map[x] := nameno; emit2(name1, nameno);
    skipsym
  end

* proc change(name: int; newkind: namekind)
  begin
    if name <> univname1 do
```

```
            names[map[name]].kind := newkind
        end
    end

*   proc postname
    var finalname: int; n: nameattr
    begin "sym = name1"
        finalname := map[x]; n := names[finalname];
        if (n.kind = split) and (n.maxlevel = blocklevel) do
            names[finalname].kind := partial;
            emit2(name1, finalname); skipsym
        else true do
            error(split3); newname(false, partial)
        end
    end

*   proc ischar(name: int): bool
    begin val ischar := map[name] = char1 end

*   proc isproc(name: int): bool
    begin
        val isproc := names[map[name]].kind in
            namekinds(split, partial, complete)
    end

*   proc kindof(name: int): namekind
    begin val kindof := names[map[name]].kind end

*   proc oldname
    var n: nameattr
    begin "sym = name1"
        n := names[map[x]];
        if n.kind = undeclared do
            error(undeclared3); map[x] := univname1
        else n.kind = incomplete do
            error(incomplete3); map[x] := univname1
        end;
        emit2(name1, map[x]); skipsym
    end

*   proc valname
    var n: nameattr
    begin "sym = name1"
        n := names[map[x]];
        if n.kind in namekinds(split, complete) do
            error(funcval3); emit2(name1, univname1);
            skipsym
        else true do oldname end
    end

begin
```

```
      names[noname] := nameattr(undeclared, 0, 0, 0);
      nameno := 0;
      while nameno < maxname do
         nameno := nameno + 1;
         map[nameno] := noname;
         names[nameno] := nameattr(undeclared, 0, 0, 0)
      end;
      blocklevel := 0;
      "standard names"
      predeclare(bool1, type);
      predeclare(char1, type);
      predeclare(false1, constant);
      predeclare(int1, type);
      predeclare(true1, constant);
      predeclare(univname1, universal);
      predeclare(addr1, complete);
      predeclare(halt1, complete);
      predeclare(obtain1, complete);
      predeclare(place1, complete);
      predeclare(sense1, complete);
      nameno := last_standard
end


pre proc variable_list(export: bool; kind: namekind;
      succ: symbols)

pre proc procedure_heading(export, postx: bool;
      var name: int; succ: symbols)

pre proc declaration(export: bool; succ: symbols)

pre proc expression(succ: symbols)

pre proc procedure_call(succ: symbols)

pre proc statement_list(succ: symbols)

"control_symbol:
    'char' '(' numeral ')'"

proc control_symbol(succ: symbols)
begin "(sym = name1) and ischar(x)" nextsym;
   checksym(lparanth1, symbols(numeral1, rparanth1)
      + succ);
   if sym = numeral1 do nextsym
   else true do syntax(symbols(rparanth1) + succ) end;
   checksym(rparanth1, succ)
end

"constant_symbol:
```

```
        numeral # character_symbol # constant_name
    character_symbol:
        graphic_symbol # control_symbol"

proc constant_symbol(succ: symbols)
begin
    if sym = numeral1 do nextsym
    else sym = graphic1 do nextsym
    else sym = name1 do
        if ischar(x) do control_symbol(succ)
        else true do oldname end
    else true do syntax(succ) end;
    check(succ)
end

"constant_declaration:
    constant_name '=' constant_symbol"

proc constant_declaration(export: bool; succ: symbols)
var name: int
begin
    if sym = name1 do
        name := x; newname(export, incomplete);
        checksym(equal1, constsym + succ);
        constant_symbol(succ); change(name, constant)
    else true do syntax(succ) end;
    check(succ)
end

"constant_declaration_list:
    'const' constant_declaration
        [ ';' constant_declaration ]*"

proc constant_declaration_list(export: bool; succ: symbols)
var enddecl: symbols
begin "sym = const1" nextsym;
    enddecl := symbols(semicolon1) + succ;
    constant_declaration(export, enddecl);
    while sym = semicolon1 do
        nextsym; constant_declaration(export, enddecl)
    end
end

"enumeration_symbol:
    constant_name"

proc enumeration_symbol(export: bool; succ: symbols)
begin
    if sym = name1 do newname(export, constant)
    else true do syntax(succ) end;
    check(succ)
end
```

```
"enumeration_symbol_list:
   enumeration_symbol [ ',' enumeration_symbol ]*"

proc enumeration_symbol_list(export: bool;
   succ: symbols)
var endsym: symbols
begin endsym := symbols(comma1) + succ;
   enumeration_symbol(export, endsym);
   while sym = comma1 do
      nextsym; enumeration_symbol(export, endsym)
   end;
   check(succ)
end

"enumeration_type:
   'enum' type_name '(' enumeration_symbol_list ')'"

proc enumeration_type(export: bool; succ: symbols)
begin "sym = enum1" nextsym;
   if sym = name1 do
      newname(export, type);
      checksym(lparanth1, symbols(name1, rparanth1)
         + succ);
      enumeration_symbol_list(export,
         symbols(rparanth1) + succ);
      checksym(rparanth1, succ)
   else true do syntax(succ) end
end

"record_type:
   'record' type_name '(' field_list ')'
 field_list:
   variable_list"

proc record_type(export: bool; succ: symbols)
var name: int
begin "sym = record1" nextsym;
   if sym = name1 do
      name := x; newname(export, incomplete);
      checksym(lparanth1, symbols(name1, rparanth1)
         + succ);
      variable_list(false, field, symbols(rparanth1)
         + succ);
      checksym(rparanth1, succ);
      change(name, type)
   else true do syntax(succ) end
end

"range_symbol:

   constant_symbol ':' constant_symbol"
```

```
proc range_symbol(succ: symbols)
begin constant_symbol(symbols(colon1) + constsym + succ);
    checksym(colon1, constsym + succ);
    constant_symbol(succ)
end
```

"type_name:
    name"

```
proc type_name(succ: symbols)
begin
    if sym = name1 do oldname
    else true do syntax(succ) end
end
```

"array_type:
    'array' type_name '[' range_symbol ']'
    '(' element_type ')'
  element_type:
    type_name"

```
proc array_type(export: bool; succ: symbols)
var name: int
begin "sym = array1" nextsym;
    if sym = name1 do
        name := x; newname(export, incomplete);
        checksym(lbracket1, constsym + symbols(rbracket1,
            lparanth1, name1, rparanth1) + succ);
        range_symbol(symbols(rbracket1, lparanth1, name1,
            rparanth1) + succ);
        checksym(rbracket1, symbols(lparanth1, name1,
            rparanth1) + succ);
        checksym(lparanth1, symbols(name1, rparanth1)
            + succ);
        type_name(symbols(rparanth1) + succ);
        checksym(rparanth1, succ);
        change(name, type)
    else true do syntax(succ) end
end
```

"set_type:
    'set' type_name '(' base_type ')'
  base_type:
    type_name"

```
proc set_type(export: bool; succ: symbols)
var name: int
begin "sym = set1" nextsym;
    if sym = name1 do
        name := x; newname(export, incomplete);
        checksym(lparanth1, symbols(name1, rparanth1)
            + succ);
```

```
      type_name(symbols(rparanth1) + succ);
      checksym(rparanth1, succ);
      change(name, type)
   else true do syntax(succ) end
end


"type_declaration:
   enumeration_type # record_type #
   array_type # set_type"

proc type_declaration(export: bool; succ: symbols)
begin "sym in typesym"
   if sym = enum1 do enumeration_type(export, succ)
   else sym = record1 do record_type(export, succ)
   else sym = array1 do array_type(export, succ)
   else sym = set1 do set_type(export, succ) end
end

"variable_group:
   variable_name [ ',' variable_name ]* ':' type_name"

proc variable_group(export: bool; kind: namekind;
   succ: symbols)
begin
   if sym = name1 do
   newname(export, kind);
      while sym = comma1 do
         nextsym;
         if sym = name1 do newname(export, kind)
         else true do
            syntax(symbols(comma1, colon1) + succ)
         end
      end;
      checksym(colon1, succ);
      type_name(succ); check(succ)
   else true do syntax(succ) end
end

"variable_list:
   variable_group [ ';' variable_group ]*"

post proc variable_list(export: bool;
   kind: namekind; succ: symbols)
var endgroup: symbols
begin endgroup := symbols(semicolon1) + succ;
   variable_group(export, kind, endgroup);
   while sym = semicolon1 do
      nextsym;
      variable_group(export, kind, endgroup)
   end;
   check(succ)
end
```

```
"variable_declaration_list:
   'var' variable_list"

proc variable_declaration_list(export: bool;
   succ: symbols)
begin "sym = var1" nextsym;
   variable_list(export, variable, succ)
end

"parameter_group:
   [ 'var' ] variable_group # proc_heading"

proc parameter_group(succ: symbols)
var name: int
begin
   if sym = proc1 do
      procedure_heading(false, false, name, succ);
      endblock; change(name, complete)
   else true do
      if sym = var1 do nextsym end;
      variable_group(false, variable, succ)
   end;
   check(succ)
end

"parameter_list:
   parameter_group [ ';' parameter_group ]*"

proc parameter_list(succ: symbols)
var endgroup: symbols
begin endgroup := symbols(semicolon1) + succ;
   parameter_group(endgroup);
   while sym = semicolon1 do
      nextsym; parameter_group(endgroup)
   end;
   check(succ)
end

"procedure_heading:
   'proc' procedure_name [ '(' parameter_list ')' ]
   [ ':' type_name ]"

post proc procedure_heading(export, postx: bool; ·
   var name: int; succ: symbols)
begin
   checksym(proc1, symbols(name1, lparanth1, colon1)
      + succ);
   if sym = name1 do
      name := x;
      if postx do postname
      else true do newname(export, partial) end;
      beginblock;
```

```
        if sym = lparanth1 do
          nextsym;
          parameter_list(symbols(rparanth1, colon1) + succ);
          checksym(rparanth1, symbols(colon1) + succ)
        end;
        if sym = colon1 do
          nextsym; type_name(succ)
        end
      else true do
        name := univname1; beginblock; syntax(succ)
      end;
      check(succ)
end

"procedure_body:
   [ declaration ]* 'begin' statement_list 'end'"

proc procedure_body(succ: symbols)
begin
    while sym in declsym do
      declaration(false, declsym + symbols(begin1, end1)
        + statsym + succ)
    end;
    checksym(begin1, statsym + symbols(end1) + succ);
    statement_list(symbols(end1) + succ);
    checksym(end1, succ)
end

"complete_procedure:
   procedure_heading procedure_body"

proc complete_procedure(export, postx: bool;
    succ: symbols)
var name: int
begin
    procedure_heading(export, postx, name, declsym
      + symbols(begin1) + statsym + succ);
    procedure_body(succ);
    endblock; change(name, complete)
end

"preprocedure:
   'pre' procedure_heading"

proc preprocedure(export: bool; succ: symbols)
var name: int
begin "sym = pre1" nextsym;
    procedure_heading(export, false, name, succ);
    endblock; change(name, split)
end
```

```
"postprocedure:
   'post' complete_procedure"

proc postprocedure(export: bool; succ: symbols)
begin "sym = post1" nextsym;
   complete_procedure(false, true, succ)
end

"library_procedure:
   'lib' procedure_heading '[' expression ']'"

proc library_procedure(export: bool; succ: symbols)
var name: int
begin "sym =lib1" nextsym;
   procedure_heading(export, false, name,
     symbols(lbracket1, rbracket1) + exprsym + succ);
   checksym(lbracket1, exprsym + symbols(rbracket1)
     + succ);
   expression(symbols(rbracket1) + succ);
   checksym(rbracket1, succ);
   endblock; change(name, complete)
end

"procedure_declaration:
   complete_procedure # preprocedure #
   postprocedure # library_procedure"

proc procedure_declaration(export: bool;
   succ: symbols)
begin "sym in procsym"
   if sym = proc1 do
     complete_procedure(export, false, succ)
   else sym = pre1 do
     preprocedure(export, succ)
   else sym = post1 do
     postprocedure(export, succ)
   else sym = lib1 do
     library_procedure(export, succ)
   end
end

"module_declaration:
   'module' [ [ '*' ] declaration ]*
   'begin' statement_list 'end'"

proc module_declaration(succ: symbols)
var export: bool
begin "sym = module1" nextsym; beginblock;
   while sym in (symbols(asterisk1) + declsym) do
     if sym = asterisk1 do
       export := true; nextsym
```

```
    else true do export := false end;
    declaration(export, declsym + symbols(asterisk1,
      begin1, end1) + statsym + succ)
  end;
  checksym(begin1, statsym + symbols(end1) + succ);
  statement_list(symbols(end1) + succ);
  checksym(end1, succ);
  endblock
end

"declaration:
    constant_declaration_list # type_declaration #
    variable_declaration_list # proc_declaration #
    module_declaration"

post proc declaration(export: bool; succ: symbols)
begin
  if sym = const1 do
    constant_declaration_list(export, succ)
  else sym in typesym do
    type_declaration(export, succ)
  else sym = var1 do
    variable_declaration_list(export, succ)
  else sym in procsym do
    procedure_declaration(export, succ)
  else sym = module1 do
    module_declaration(succ)
  else true do syntax(succ) end;
  check(succ)
end

"function_variable:
    'val' procedure_name"

proc function_variable(succ: symbols)
begin "sym = val1" nextsym;
  if sym = name1 do valname
  else true do syntax(succ) end
end

"field_selector:
    '.' field_name"

proc field_selector(succ: symbols)
begin "sym = period1" nextsym;
  if sym = name1 do oldname; check(succ)
  else true do syntax(succ) end
end
```

```
"indexed_selector:
   '[' expression ']'"

proc indexed_selector(succ: symbols)
begin "sym = lbracket1" nextsym;
   expression(symbols(rbracket1) + succ);
   checksym(rbracket1, succ); check(succ)
end

"type_transfer:
   ':' type_name"

proc type_transfer(succ: symbols)
begin "sym = colon1" nextsym;
   type_name(succ); check(succ)
end

"variable_symbol:
   variable_name # function_variable #
   variable_symbol selector
 selector:
   field_selector # indexed_selector # type_transfer"

proc variable_symbol(succ: symbols)
var endvar: symbols
begin endvar := selectsym + succ;
   if sym = name1 do oldname
   else sym = val1 do function_variable(endvar)
   else true do syntax(endvar) end;
   while sym = period1 do field_selector(endvar)
   else sym = lbracket1 do indexed_selector(endvar)
   else sym = colon1 do type_transfer(endvar) end;
   check(succ)
end

"constructor:
   type_name [ '(' expression_list ')' ]
 expression_list:
   expression [ ',' expression ]*"

proc constructor(succ: symbols)
var endexpr: symbols
begin "(sym = name1) and (kindof(x) = type)"
   oldname;
   if sym = lparanth1 do
     nextsym;
     endexpr := symbols(comma1, rparanth1) + succ;
     expression(endexpr);
     while sym = comma1 do
       nextsym; expression(endexpr)
     end;
     checksym(rparanth1, succ)
```

```
      end;
      check(succ)
end

"factor:
    constant_symbol # variable_symbol #
    constructor # procedure_call #
    '(' expression ')' # 'not' factor #
    factor type_transfer"

proc factor(succ: symbols)
var endfactor: symbols; kind: namekind
begin endfactor := symbols(colon1) + succ;
    if sym in literalsym do constant_symbol(endfactor)
    else sym = name1 do
      kind := kindof(x);
      if kind = constant do constant_symbol(endfactor)
      else kind = type do constructor(endfactor)
      else kind = variable do variable_symbol(endfactor)
      else isproc(x) do procedure_call(endfactor)
      else true do oldname end
    else sym = val1 do variable_symbol(endfactor)
    else sym = lparanth1 do
      nextsym; expression(symbols(rparanth1) + succ);
      checksym(rparanth1, endfactor)
    else sym = not1 do nextsym; factor(endfactor)
    else true do syntax(endfactor) end;
    while sym = colon1 do
      type_transfer(endfactor)
    end;
    check(succ)
end

"term:
    factor [ multiplying_operator factor ]*"

proc term(succ: symbols)
var endfactor: symbols
begin endfactor := multsym + succ;
    factor(endfactor);
    while sym in multsym do
      nextsym; factor(endfactor)
    end;
    check(succ)
end

"simple_expression:
    [ sign_operator ] term
    [ adding_operator term ]*"
```

```
proc simple_expression(succ: symbols)
var endterm: symbols
begin endterm := addsym + succ;
   if sym in signsym do nextsym end;
   term(endterm);
   while sym in addsym do
      nextsym; term(endterm)
   end;
   check(succ)
end
```

"expression:
   simple_expression
   [relational_operator simple_expression]"

```
post proc expression(succ: symbols)
var endsimple: symbols
begin endsimple := relationsym + succ;
   simple_expression(endsimple);
   if sym in relationsym do
      nextsym; simple_expression(succ)
   end;
   check(succ)
end
```

"assignment_statement:
   variable_symbol ':=' expression"

```
proc assignment_statement(succ: symbols)
begin
   variable_symbol(symbols(becomes1) + exprsym
      + succ);
   checksym(becomes1, exprsym + succ);
   expression(succ)
end
```

"argument_list:
   expression [',' expression]*"

```
proc argument_list(succ: symbols)
var endexpr: symbols
begin endexpr := symbols(comma1) + succ;
   expression(endexpr);
   while sym = comma1 do
      nextsym; expression(endexpr)
   end;
   check(succ)
end
```

"procedure_call:
   procedure_name ['(' argument_list ')']"

```
post proc procedure_call(succ: symbols)
begin "(sym = name1) and isproc(x)"
   oldname;
   if sym = lparanth1 do
      nextsym;
      argument_list(symbols(rparanth1) + succ);
      checksym(rparanth1, succ)
   end
end

"conditional_statement :
   expression 'do' statement_list"

proc conditional_statement(succ: symbols)
var enddo: symbols
begin enddo := statsym + succ;
   expression(symbols(do1) + enddo);
   checksym(do1, enddo);
   statement_list(succ); check(succ)
end

"conditional_statement_list:
   conditional_statement
   [ 'else' conditional_statement ]*"

proc conditional_statement_list(succ: symbols)
var endstat: symbols
begin endstat := symbols(else1) + succ;
   conditional_statement(endstat);
   while sym = else1 do
      nextsym; conditional_statement(endstat)
   end;
   check(succ)
end

"if_statement:
   'if' conditional_statement_list 'end'"

proc if_statement(succ: symbols)
begin "sym = if1" nextsym;
   conditional_statement_list(symbols(end1) + succ);
   checksym(end1, succ)
end

"while_statement:
   'while' conditional_statement_list 'end'"

proc while_statement(succ: symbols)
begin "sym = while1" nextsym;
   conditional_statement_list(symbols(end1) + succ);
   checksym(end1, succ)
end
```

```
"when_statement:
   'when' conditional_statement_list 'end'"

proc when_statement(succ: symbols)
begin "sym = when1" nextsym;
   conditional_statement_list(symbols(end1) + succ);
   checksym(end1, succ)
end

"process_statement:
   constant_symbol 'do' statement_list"

proc process_statement(succ: symbols)
var enddo: symbols
begin enddo := statsym + succ;
   constant_symbol(symbols(do1) + enddo);
   checksym(do1, enddo);
   statement_list(succ); check(succ)
end

"process_statement_list:
   process_statement [ 'also' process_statement ]*"

proc process_statement_list(succ: symbols)
var endstat: symbols
begin endstat := symbols(also1) + succ;
   process_statement(endstat);
   while sym = also1 do
      nextsym; process_statement(endstat)
   end;
   check(succ)
end

"concurrent_statement:
   'cobegin' process_statement_list 'end'"

proc concurrent_statement(succ: symbols)
begin "sym = cobegin1" nextsym;
   process_statement_list(symbols(end1) + succ);
   checksym(end1, succ)
end

"statement:
   'skip' # assignment_statement #
   procedure_call # if_statement #
   while_statement # when_statement #
   concurrent_statement"

proc statement(succ: symbols)
begin
   if sym = skip1 do nextsym
```

```
      else sym = val1 do assignment_statement(succ)
      else sym = name1 do
         if isproc(x) do procedure_call(succ)
         else true do assignment_statement(succ) end
      else sym = if1 do if_statement(succ)
      else sym = while1 do while_statement(succ)
      else sym = when1 do when_statement(succ)
      else sym = cobegin1 do
         concurrent_statement(succ)
      else true do syntax(succ) end;
      check(succ)
end

"statement_list:
   statement [ ';' statement ]*"

post proc statement_list(succ: symbols)
var semistat, endstat: symbols
begin semistat := symbols(semicolon1) + statsym;
   endstat := semistat + succ;
   statement(endstat);
   while sym in semistat do
      checksym(semicolon1, statsym);
      statement(endstat)
   end;
   check(succ)
end

"program:
   [ initial_declaration ]* complete_procedure
 initial_declaration:
   constant_declaration_list # type_declaration"

proc program(succ: symbols)
var enddecl: symbols
begin
   enddecl := initdeclsym + symbols(proc1) + succ;
   while sym in initdeclsym do
      if sym = const1 do
         constant_declaration_list(false, enddecl)
      else sym in typesym do
         type_declaration(false, enddecl)
      end
   end;
   complete_procedure(false, false, succ);
   check(succ)
end

begin program(symbols(endtext1));
   emit(endtext1)
end
```

10.4 SEMANTIC ANALYSIS

This section contains the complete text of pass 3 of the Edison compiler with some additional comments.

Pass 3 scans the intermediate code output by pass 2 once and checks whether the semantic rules of the Edison language are satisfied by the program text.

Intermediate Code

The output of pass 3 is almost identical to the standard Edison code described in Chapter 6 with the following exceptions:

(1) The destinations of jump instructions are identified by numeric labels in the range 1:maxlabel. And so are the amounts of storage required to hold the variables and temporaries of procedures and processes.

(2) Call instances of procedures are identified by the level numbers of nested blocks starting with 0 (Sections 6.1 and 10.5).

(3) Procedure calls include the combined length of the arguments used.

(4) Whole variable symbols are output as instructions named variable, parameter, and funcval.

(5) While and if statements include pseudoinstructions named while and endif.

(6) Line numbers and program errors are output as pseudoinstructions named newline and error.

The operation codes are output as enumeration values of type operator. The output is terminated by an operator named endcode.

Name Table

All names have unique indices in the range 1:maxname generated by pass 2. A name table defines a mapping from name indices to name attributes.

The kind of entity denoted by a name is described as being either a constant, an elementary type, a record type, an array type, or other.

Each kind of name has a different set of attributes:

A constant is described by its value and the name index of its type (Section 3.6.1).

An elementary type is described by the length of its values (in words) (Section 3.7).

A record type is described by the length of its values (in words). A link attribute defines the name index of the first record field (Section 3.9).

An array type is described by the length of its values (in words). Two subtype attributes define the name indices of the index and element types. The bounds of the index range are also attributes of the array type (Sections 3.8 and 3.10).

A set type is described by the length of its values (in words). A subtype attribute defines the name index of the base type (Section 3.11).

A record field is described by its displacement within a record value and by the name index of its type. A link attribute defines the name index of the next field (if any) in the record value. If the given field is the last one, the link has the value none (Section 3.9).

A variable is described by its block level and displacement and by the name index of its type. The variables introduced by a variable declaration list (Section 3.13.1) are linked together in their order of declaration. And so are the parameters introduced by a parameter list (Section 3.16.2).

A procedure is described by its block level and symbolic address (a numeric label). If the procedure is a function, the name index of its type is defined by a type attribute. This attribute has the value none for a general procedure. An attribute named param defines the name index of its first parameter (if any) (Section 3.16). The symbolic address is irrelevant for a standard procedure (Section 3.19.7).

The address of a procedure parameter P is a displacement within a call instance. A link attribute defines the name index of the next parameter (if any) in the parameter list that includes P (Section 3.16.2).

The problem of storing different kinds of record types in the same name table is solved by means of dynamic retyping (Section 2.2.12).

Syntax Analysis

Pass 3 uses the same method of recursive descent as pass 2 to recognize the syntactic forms of the Edison language (Section 10.3). Although this duplicates the syntax analysis of pass 2, it also makes pass 3 (the most complicated pass) much simpler to understand.

Type Checking

Two operands are of the same type only if their types are denoted by the same name index (Section 3.1). This requirement is checked by a procedure called checktype. When an operand is of the wrong type, an error is reported, and the operand is then considered to be of a universal type to suppress further error messages referring to the same operand (see the procedure called typerror2).

Variable Addressing

The procedure that recognizes a variable group (Section 3.13.1) initially links the corresponding variable names in the name table. The displacements of the variables within the group are then computed by following the links and retrieving the lengths of the variable values (as defined by their types). The displacement of a whole group of variables is determined by the procedure that recognizes a variable declaration list consisting of one or more groups of variables. The displacement of a variable declaration list is, in turn, determined by the procedures that recognize a module declaration (Section 3.4.4) and a procedure body (Section 3.16.1). The same method is used to determine the displacements within a field list (Section 3.9) and a parameter list (Section 3.16.2).

Pass 3 Text

```
"Edison-11 compiler: Pass 3

 Syntax and semantic analysis

 Per Brinch Hansen

 6 July 1981

 Copyright (c) 1980 Per Brinch Hansen"

enum symbol (also1, and1, array1, asterisk1, becomes1,
    begin1, cobegin1, colon1, comma1, const1, div1,
    do1, else1, end1, endtext1, enum1, equal1, error1,
    graphic1, greater1, if1, in1, lbracket1, less1,
    lib1, lparanth1, minus1, mod1, module1, name1,
    newline1, not1, notequal1, notgreater1, notless1,
    numeral1, or1, period1, plus1, pre1, post1, proc1,
    rbracket1, record1, rparanth1, semicolon1, set1,
    skip1, val1, var1, when1, while1)

enum operator (add2, also2, and2, assign2, blank2,
    cobegin2, constant2, construct2, difference2,
    divide2, do2, else2, endcode2, endif2, endlib2,
    endproc2, endwhen2, equal2, error2, field2,
    funcval2, goto2, greater2, in2, index2,
    intersection2, less2, libproc2, minus2, modulo2,
    multiply2, newline2, not2, notequal2, notgreater2,
    notless2, or2, paramarg2, paramcall2, parameter2,
    procarg2, proccall2, procedure2, process2,
    subtract2, union2, valspace2, value2, variable2,
    wait2, when2, while2, addr2, halt2, obtain2,
    place2, sense2)
```

```
enum failure (blocklimit, charlimit, inputlimit,
    labellimit, namelimit, outputlimit, processlimit,
    wordlimit)

proc pass3(
    proc next(var value: symbol);
    proc emit(value: operator);
    proc fail(reason: failure))

const "table limits" maxlabel = 1000; maxname = 750;
    maxprocess = 20;

"standard names" bool1 = 1; char1 = 2; false1 = 3;
    int1 = 4; true1 = 5; univname1 = 6; univtype1 = 7;
    addr1 = 8; halt1 = 9; obtain1 = 10; place1 = 11;
    sense1 = 12;
    last_standard = 20;

"type lengths" elemlength = 1; liblength = 1;
    proclength = 2; setlength = 8 "words";
    setlimit = 127 " + 1 members";

    none = 0

enum namekind (univkind, constant, univtype,
    elemtype, recordtype, arraytype, settype,
    field, variable, valparam, varparam,
    procparam, procedur, standard)

"univkind variant:"

record nameattr (kind: namekind; link: int;
    none1, none2, none3, none4, none5: int)

"constant variant:"

record constattr (constkind: namekind; constlink: int;
    consttype, constvalue, none6, none7, none8: int)

"univtype, elemtype, recordtype, arraytype, and settype
    variant:"

record typeattr (typekind: namekind; typelink: int;
    length, subtype1, subtype2, bound1, bound2: int)

"field, variable, valparam, and varparam variant:"

record varattr (varkind: namekind; varlink,
    varlevel, vardispl, vartype, none9, none10: int)

"procparam, procedur, and standard variant:"
```

```
record procattr (prockind: namekind; proclink: int;
  proclevel, procaddr, proctype, param, none11: int)

array nametable [1:maxname] (nameattr)

record processattr (procconst, proclabel: int)

array processtable [1:maxprocess] (processattr)

set processset(int)

proc emit2(a: operator; b: int)
begin emit(a); emit(operator(b)) end

proc emit3(a: operator; b, c: int)
begin emit2(a, b); emit(operator(c)) end

proc emit4(a: operator; b, c, d: int)
begin emit3(a, b, c); emit(operator(d)) end

proc emit5(a: operator; b, c, d, e: int)
begin emit4(a, b, c, d); emit(operator(e)) end

module "symbol sets"

* set symbols (symbol)

* var addsym, constsym, declsym, equalitysym, exprsym,
    hiddensym, initdeclsym, literalsym, multsym,
    ordersym, pairsym, procsym, relationsym,
    selectsym, signsym, statsym, typesym: symbols

begin addsym := symbols(minus1, or1, plus1);
  constsym := symbols(graphic1, name1, numeral1);
  declsym := symbols(array1, const1, enum1, lib1,
    module1, post1, pre1, proc1, record1, set1, var1);
  equalitysym := symbols(equal1, notequal1);
  exprsym := symbols(graphic1, lparanth1, minus1,
    not1, numeral1, plus1, val1);
  hiddensym := symbols(error1, newline1);
  initdeclsym := symbols(array1, const1, enum1,
    record1, set1);
  literalsym := symbols(graphic1, numeral1);
  multsym := symbols(and1, asterisk1, div1, mod1);
  ordersym := symbols(greater1, less1, notgreater1,
    notless1);
  pairsym := symbols(graphic1, name1, numeral1);
  procsym := symbols(lib1, post1, pre1, proc1);
  relationsym := symbols(equal1, greater1, in1,
    less1, notequal1, notgreater1, notless1);
  selectsym := symbols(colon1, lbracket1, period1);
  signsym := symbols(minus1, plus1);
```

```
      statsym := symbols(cobegin1, if1, skip1, when1,
       while1);
      typesym := symbols(array1, enum1, record1, set1)
end

module "input"

*  var sym: symbol; x: int

*  proc nextsym
   begin next(sym);
       while sym in hiddensym do
         next(x:symbol);
         if sym = error1 do emit2(error2, x)
         else sym = newline1 do emit2(newline2, x) end;
         next(sym)
       end;
       if sym in pairsym do next(x:symbol) end
   end

begin nextsym end

module "names"

*  set namekinds (namekind)

*  var names: nametable;
      typekinds, varkinds, prockinds: namekinds

*  proc standard_names
   begin
       names[int1] := typeattr(elemtype, none, elemlength,
         none, none, none, none):nameattr;
       names[bool1] := names[int1];
       names[char1] := names[int1];
       names[false1] := constattr(constant, none, bool1,
         int(false), none, none, none):nameattr;
       names[true1] := constattr(constant, none, bool1,
         int(true), none, none, none):nameattr;
       names[univname1] := nameattr(univkind, none, none,
         none, none, none, none);
       names[addr1] := procattr(standard, none, 0, none,
         int1, none, none):nameattr;
       names[halt1] := procattr(standard, none, 0, none,
         univtype1, none, none):nameattr;
       names[obtain1] := names[halt1];
       names[place1] := names[halt1];
       names[sense1] := procattr(standard, none, 0, none,
         bool1, none, none):nameattr
   end
```

```
*  proc isfunction(x: int): bool
   begin
      if names[x].kind in prockinds do
         val isfunction :=
            names[x]:procattr.proctype <> univtype1
      else true do val isfunction := false end
   end

var i: int
begin i := 0;
   while i < maxname do
      i := i + 1;
      names[i] := nameattr(univkind, none, none, none,
         none, none, none)
   end;
   typekinds := namekinds(univtype, elemtype, recordtype,
      arraytype, settype);
   varkinds := namekinds(variable, valparam, varparam);
   prockinds := namekinds(procparam, procedur, standard)
end

module "labels"

   var labelno: int

*  proc newlabel(var value: int)
   begin
      if labelno = maxlabel do fail(labellimit) end;
      labelno := labelno + 1; value := labelno
   end

begin labelno := 0 end

module "errors"

*  enum errorkind (ambiguous3, call3, cobegin3,
      constructor3, funcval3, incomplete3, numeral3,
      range3, split3, syntax3, type3, undeclared3)

*  proc error(kind: errorkind)
   begin emit2(error2, int(kind)) end

*  proc syntax(succ: symbols)
   begin error(syntax3);
      while not (sym in succ) do nextsym end
   end

*  proc check(succ: symbols)
   begin if not (sym in succ) do syntax(succ) end end

*  proc checksym(s: symbol; succ: symbols)
   begin
```

```
        if sym = s do nextsym
        else true do syntax(succ) end
    end

*   proc kinderror1(name: int)
    begin if name <> univname1 do error(type3) end end

*   proc kinderror2(name: int; var typ: int)
    begin kinderror1(name); typ := univtype1 end

*   proc typerror1
    begin error(type3) end

*   proc typerror2(var typ: int)
    begin
        if typ <> univtype1 do
            typerror1; typ := univtype1
        end
    end

*   proc checkelem(var typ: int)
    begin
        if names[typ].kind <> elemtype do
            typerror2(typ)
        end
    end

*   proc checktype(var typ1: int; typ2: int)
    begin
        if typ1 <> typ2 do
            if typ2 = univtype1 do typ1 := univtype1
            else true do typerror2(typ1) end
        end
    end

begin skip end

pre proc variable_list(kind: namekind; level, displ: int;
    var first, length: int; succ: symbols)

pre proc procedure_heading(postx: bool; level: int;
    var name, paramlength: int; succ: symbols)

pre proc declaration(level, displ: int;
    var varlength: int; succ: symbols)

pre proc expression(var typ: int; succ: symbols)

pre proc procedure_call(succ: symbols)

pre proc statement_list(succ: symbols)
```

```
"control_symbol:
   'char' '(' numeral ')'"

proc control_symbol(var typ, value: int; succ: symbols)
begin "(sym = name1) and (x = char1)" nextsym;
   checksym(lparanth1, symbols(numeral1, rparanth1) + succ);
   if sym = numeral1 do
      typ := char1; value := x; nextsym
   else true do
      typ := univtype1; value := 0;
      syntax(symbols(rparanth1) + succ)
   end;
   checksym(rparanth1, succ)
end

"constant_symbol:
   numeral # character_symbol # constant_name
 character_symbol:
   graphic_symbol # control_symbol"

proc constant_symbol(var typ, value: int; succ: symbols)
var c: constattr
begin typ := univtype1; value := 0;
   if sym = numeral1 do
      typ := int1; value := x; nextsym
   else sym = graphic1 do
      typ := char1; value := x; nextsym
   else sym = name1 do
      if x = char1 do control_symbol(typ, value, succ)
      else names[x].kind = constant do
         c := names[x]:constattr; typ := c.consttype;
         value := c.constvalue; nextsym
      else true do
         kinderror1(x); nextsym
      end
   else true do syntax(succ) end;
   check(succ)
end

"constant_declaration:
   constant_name '=' constant_symbol"

proc constant_declaration(succ: symbols)
var name, typ, value: int
begin
   if sym = name1 do
      name := x; nextsym;
      checksym(equal1, constsym + succ);
      constant_symbol(typ, value, succ);
      names[name] := constattr(constant, none, typ, value,
         none, none, none):nameattr
```

```
      else true do syntax(succ) end;
      check(succ)
end

"constant_declaration_list:
   'const' constant_declaration
     [ ';' constant_declaration ]*"

proc constant_declaration_list(succ: symbols)
var enddecl: symbols
begin "sym = const1" nextsym;
   enddecl := symbols(semicolon1) + succ;
   constant_declaration(enddecl);
   while sym = semicolon1 do
     nextsym; constant_declaration(enddecl)
   end
end

"enumeration_symbol:
   constant_name"

proc enumeration_symbol(typ, value: int; succ: symbols)
begin
   if sym = name1 do
     names[x] := constattr(constant, none, typ, value,
       none, none, none):nameattr;
     nextsym
   else true do syntax(succ) end;
   check(succ)
end

"enumeration_symbol_list:
   enumeration_symbol [ ',' enumeration_symbol ]*"

proc enumeration_symbol_list(typ: int; succ: symbols)
var endsym: symbols; value: int
begin endsym := symbols(comma1) + succ; value := 0;
   enumeration_symbol(typ, value, endsym);
   while sym = comma1 do
     nextsym; value := value + 1;
     enumeration_symbol(typ, value, endsym)
   end;
   check(succ)
end

"enumeration_type:
   'enum' type_name '(' enumeration_symbol_list ')'"

proc enumeration_type(succ: symbols)
var typ: int
```

```
begin "sym = enum1" nextsym;
   if sym = name1 do
      typ := x; nextsym;
      checksym(lparanth1, symbols(name1, rparanth1) + succ);
      enumeration_symbol_list(typ,symbols(rparanth1)
         + succ);
      checksym(rparanth1, succ);
      names[typ] := typeattr(elemtype, none, elemlength,
         none, none, none, none):nameattr
   else true do syntax(succ) end
end

"record_type:
   'record' type_name '(' field_list ')'
 field_list:
   variable_list"

proc record_type(succ: symbols)
var typ, first, length: int
begin "sym = record1" nextsym;
   if sym = name1 do
      typ := x; nextsym;
      checksym(lparanth1, symbols(name1, rparanth1) + succ);
      variable_list(field, 0, 0, first, length,
         symbols(rparanth1) + succ);
      checksym(rparanth1, succ);
      names[typ] := typeattr(recordtype, none, length,
         first, none, none, none):nameattr
   else true do syntax(succ) end
end

"range_symbol:
   constant_symbol ':' constant_symbol"

proc range_symbol(var typ, lower, upper: int;
   succ: symbols)
var typ2: int
begin
   constant_symbol(typ, lower,
      symbols(colon1) + constsym + succ);
   checksym(colon1, constsym + succ);
   constant_symbol(typ2, upper, succ);
   checktype(typ, typ2);
   if lower > upper do
      error(range3); lower := upper
   end
end

"type_name:
   name"

proc type_name(var typ: int; succ: symbols)
begin
```

```
   if sym = name1 do
      if names[x].kind in typekinds do typ := x
      else true do kinderror2(x, typ) end;
      nextsym
   else true do syntax(succ); typ := univtype1 end
end

"array_type:
   'array' type name '[' range_symbol ']'
   '(' element_type ')'
 element_type:
   type_name"

proc array_type(succ: symbols)
var typ, rangetype, lower, upper, elemtype: int
begin "sym = array1" nextsym;
   if sym = name1 do
      typ := x; nextsym;
      checksym(lbracket1, constsym + symbols(rbracket1,
        lparanth1, name1, rparanth1) + succ);
      range_symbol(rangetype, lower, upper,
        symbols(rbracket1, lparanth1, name1, rparanth1)
           + succ);
      checksym(rbracket1, symbols(lparanth1, name1,
        rparanth1) + succ);
      checksym(lparanth1, symbols(name1, rparanth1) + succ);
      type_name(elemtype, symbols(rparanth1) + succ);
      checksym(rparanth1, succ);
      names[typ] := typeattr(arraytype, none,
        (upper - lower + 1) *
           names[elemtype]:typeattr.length, rangetype,
             elemtype, lower, upper):nameattr
   else true do syntax(succ) end
end

"set_type:
   'set' type_name '(' base_type ')'
 base_type:
   type_name"

proc set_type(succ: symbols)
var typ, basetype: int
begin "sym = set1" nextsym;
   if sym = name1 do
      typ := x; nextsym;
      checksym(lparanth1, symbols(name1, rparanth1) + succ);
      type_name(basetype, symbols(rparanth1) + succ);
      checkelem(basetype);
      checksym(rparanth1, succ);
      names[typ] := typeattr(settype, none, setlength,
        basetype, none, none, none):nameattr
   else true do syntax(succ) end
end
```

```
"type_declaration:
   enumeration_type # record_type #
   array_type ≠ set_type"

proc type_declaration(succ: symbols)
begin "sym in typesym"
   if sym = enum1 do enumeration_type(succ)
   else sym = record1 do record_type(succ)
   else sym = array1 do array_type(succ)
   else sym = set1 do set_type(succ) end
end

"variable_group:
   variable_name [ ',' variable_name ]* ':' type_name"

proc variable_group(kind: namekind;
   level, addr: int; var first, last, size: int;
   succ: symbols)
var typ, varlength, nextvar, i: int
begin first := none; last := none; size := 0;
   if sym = name1 do
      first := x; last := x; nextsym;
      while sym = comma1 do
         nextsym;
         if sym = name1 do
            names[last].link := x; last := x; nextsym
         else true do
            syntax(symbols(comma1, colon1) + succ)
         end
      end;
      names[last].link := none;
      checksym(colon1, succ); type_name(typ, succ);
      if kind = varparam do varlength := elemlength
      else true do
         varlength := names[typ]:typeattr.length
      end;
      i := first;
      while i <> none do
         nextvar := names[i].link;
         names[i] := varattr(kind, nextvar, level,
            addr + size, typ, none, none):nameattr;
         size := size + varlength; i := nextvar
      end;
      check(succ)
   else true do syntax(succ) end
end

"variable_list:
   variable_group [ ';' variable_group ]*"

post proc variable_list(kind: namekind; level, displ: int;
   var first, length: int; succ: symbols)
var last, first2, last2, length2: int; endgroup: symbols
```

```
begin endgroup := symbols(semicolon1) + succ;
  variable_group(kind, level, displ, first, last,
    length, endgroup);
  while sym = semicolon1 do
    nextsym;
    variable_group(kind, level, displ + length,
      first2, last2, length2, endgroup);
    if length2 > 0 do
      if length = 0 do first := first2
      else true do names[last].link := first2 end;
      last := last2; length := length + length2
    end
  end;
  check(succ)
end

"variable_declaration_list:
  'var' variable_list"

proc variable_declaration_list(level, displ: int;
  var length: int; succ: symbols)
var first: int
begin "sym = var1" nextsym;
  variable_list(variable, level, displ, first,
    length, succ)
end

"parameter_group:
  [ 'var' ] variable_group # procedure_heading"

proc parameter_group(level, displ: int;
  var first, last, length: int; succ: symbols)
var name, paramlength: int; varkind: namekind
begin
  if sym = proc1 do
    procedure_heading(false, level, name,
      paramlength, succ);
    if name <> univname1 do
      names[name].kind := procparam;
      names[name]:procattr.procaddr := displ;
      first := name; last := name; length := proclength
    else true do
      first := none; last := none; length := 0
    end
  else true do
    if sym = var1 do varkind := varparam; nextsym
    else true do varkind := valparam end;
    variable_group(varkind, level, displ, first,
      last, length, succ)
  end;
  check(succ)
end
```

```
"parameter_list:
    parameter_group [ ';' parameter_group ]*"

proc parameter_list(level: int;
    var first, length: int; succ: symbols)
var last, first2, last2, length2: int; endgroup: symbols
begin endgroup := symbols(semicolon1) + succ;
    parameter_group(level, 0, first, last,
    length, endgroup);
    while sym = semicolon1 do
        nextsym;
        parameter_group(level, length, first2, last2,
            length2, endgroup);
        if length2 > 0 do
            if length = 0 do first := first2
            else true do names[last].link := first2 end;
            last := last2; length := length + length2
        end
    end;
    check(succ)
end

"procedure_heading:
    'proc' procedure_name [ '(' parameter_list ')' ]
    [':' type_name ]"

post proc procedure_heading(postx: bool; level: int;
    var name, paramlength: int; succ: symbols)
var proclabel, firstparam, typ: int
begin
    checksym(proc1, symbols(name1, lparanth1, colon1)
        + succ);
    if sym = name1 do
        name := x; nextsym;
        if postx and (name <> univname1) do
            proclabel := names[name]:procattr.procaddr
        else true do newlabel(proclabel) end;
        if sym = lparanth1 do
            nextsym;
            parameter_list(level + 1, firstparam, paramlength,
                symbols(rparanth1, colon1) + succ);
            checksym(rparanth1, symbols(colon1) + succ)
        else true do
            firstparam := none; paramlength := 0
        end;
        if sym = colon1 do nextsym; type_name(typ, succ)
        else true do typ := univtype1 end;
        names[name] := procattr(procedur, none, level,
            proclabel, typ, firstparam, none):nameattr
    else true do
        name := univname1; paramlength := 0;
        syntax(succ)
    end;
```

```
    check( succ)
end


"procedure_body:
   [ declaration ]* 'begin' statement_list 'end'"

proc procedure_body(level: int; var varlength: int;
   succ: symbols)
var sublength: int
begin varlength := 0;
   while sym in declsym do
      declaration(level, varlength, sublength,
         declsym + symbols(begin1, end1) + statsym + succ);
      varlength := varlength + sublength
   end;
   checksym(begin1, statsym + symbols(end1) + succ);
   statement_list(symbols(end1) + succ);
   checksym(end1, succ)
end


"complete_procedure:
   procedure_heading procedure_body"

proc complete_procedure(postx: bool; level: int;
   succ: symbols)
var name, proclabel, paramlength, endlabel, varlabel,
   templabel, varlength: int
begin
   procedure_heading(postx, level, name, paramlength,
      declsym + symbols(begin1) + statsym + succ);
   if name <> univname1 do
      proclabel := names[name]:procattr.procaddr
   else true do newlabel(proclabel) end;
   newlabel(endlabel); newlabel(varlabel);
   newlabel(templabel);
   if level > 0 do emit2(goto2, endlabel) end;
   emit5(procedure2, proclabel, paramlength,
      varlabel, templabel);
   procedure_body(level + 1, varlength, succ);
   emit5(endproc2, varlabel, varlength,
      templabel, endlabel)
end


"preprocedure:
   'pre' procedure_heading"

proc preprocedure(level: int; succ: symbols)
var name, paramlength: int
begin "sym = pre1" nextsym;
   procedure_heading(false, level, name,
      paramlength, succ)
end
```

```
"postprocedure:
   'post' complete_procedure"

proc postprocedure(level: int; succ: symbols)
begin "sym = post1" nextsym;
   complete_procedure(true, level, succ)
end

"library_procedure:
   'lib' procedure_heading '[' expression ']'"

proc library_procedure(level: int; succ: symbols)
var name, paramlength, proclabel, endlabel,
   templabel, exprtype: int
begin "sym = lib1" nextsym;
   procedure_heading(false, level, name, paramlength,
      symbols(lbracket1, rbracket1) + exprsym + succ);
   if name <> univname1 do
      proclabel := names[name]:procattr.procaddr
   else true do newlabel(proclabel) end;
   newlabel(endlabel); newlabel(templabel);
   emit2(goto2, endlabel);
   emit4(libproc2, proclabel, paramlength, templabel);
   checksym(lbracket1, symbols(rbracket1) + exprsym + succ);
   expression(exprtype, symbols(rbracket1) + succ);
   checksym(rbracket1, succ);
   emit3(endlib2, templabel, endlabel)
end

"procedure_declaration:
   complete_procedure # preprocedure #
   postprocedure # library_procedure"

proc procedure_declaration(level: int; succ: symbols)
begin "sym in procsym"
   if sym = proc1 do
      complete_procedure(false, level, succ)
   else sym = pre1 do preprocedure(level, succ)
   else sym = post1 do postprocedure(level, succ)
   else sym = lib1 do library_procedure(level, succ) end
end

"module_declaration:
   'module' [ [ '*' ] declaration ]*
   'begin' statement_list 'end'"

proc module_declaration(level, displ: int;
   var varlength: int; succ: symbols)
var sublength: int
```

```
begin "sym = module1" nextsym;
   varlength := 0;
   while sym in (symbols(asterisk1) + declsym) do
      if sym = asterisk1 do nextsym end;
      declaration(level, displ + varlength, sublength,
        declsym + symbols(asterisk1, begin1, end1)
           + statsym + succ);
      varlength := varlength + sublength
   end;
   checksym(begin1, statsym + symbols(end1) + succ);
   statement_list(symbols(end1) + succ);
   checksym(end1, succ)
end

"declaration:
   constant_declaration_list # type_declaration #
   variable_declaration_list # procedure_declaration #
   module_declaration"

post proc declaration(level, displ: int;
   var varlength: int; succ: symbols)
begin varlength := 0;
   if sym = const1 do constant_declaration_list(succ)
   else sym in typesym do type_declaration(succ)
   else sym = var1 do
      variable_declaration_list(level, displ,
        varlength, succ)
   else sym in procsym do
      procedure_declaration(level, succ)          .
   else sym = module1 do
      module_declaration(level, displ, varlength, succ)
   else true do syntax(succ) end;
   check(succ)
end

"function_variable:
   'val' procedure_name"

proc function_variable(var typ: int; succ: symbols)
var p: procattr
begin "sym = val1" nextsym;
   if sym = name1 do
      if isfunction(x) do
         p := names[x]:procattr; typ := p.proctype;
         emit3(funcval2, p.proclevel,
           names[typ]:typeattr.length)
      else true do kinderror2(x, typ) end;
      nextsym
   else true do typ := univtype1; syntax(succ) end
end
```

```
"field_selector:
   '.' field_name"

proc field_selector(var typ: int; succ: symbols)
var t: typeattr; v: varattr; i: int
begin "sym = period1" nextsym;
  if sym = name1 do
    t := names[typ]:typeattr;
    if t.typekind = recordtype do
      i := t.subtype1;
      while (i <> none) and (i <> x) do
        i := names[i].link
      end;
      if i = x do
        v := names[x]:varattr; typ := v.vartype;
        emit2(field2, v.vardispl)
      else true do kinderror2(x, typ) end
    else true do typeerror2(typ) end;
    extsym; check(succ)
  else true do typ := univtype1; syntax(succ) end
end

"indexed_selector:
   '[' expression ']'"

proc indexed_selector(var typ: int; succ: symbols)
var t: typeattr; exprtype: int
begin "sym = lbracket1" nextsym;
  t := names[typ]:typeattr;
  expression(exprtype, symbols(rbracket1) + succ);
  if t.typekind = arraytype do
    if exprtype = t.subtype1 do
      typ := t.subtype2;
      emit4(index2, t.bound1, t.bound2,
        names[typ]:typeattr.length)
    else true do typeerror2(typ) end
  else true do typeerror2(typ) end;
  checksym(rbracket1, succ); check(succ)
end

"type_transfer:
   ':' type_name"

proc type_transfer(var typ: int; succ: symbols)
var typ2: int
begin "sym = colon1" nextsym;
  type_name(typ2, succ);
  if names[typ]:typeattr.length =
    names[typ2]:typeattr.length do typ := typ2
  else true do typeerror2(typ) end;
  check(succ)
end
```

```
"variable_symbol:
   variable_name # function_variable #
   variable_symbol selector
 selector:
   field_selector # indexed_selector # type_transfer"

proc variable_symbol(var typ: int; succ: symbols)
var v: varattr; endvar: symbols
begin endvar := selectsym + succ;
   if sym = name1 do
     if names[x].kind in varkinds do
       v := names[x]:varattr; typ := v.vartype;
       if v.varkind = variable do
         emit3(variable2, v.varlevel, v.vardispl)
       else v.varkind = valparam do
         emit3(parameter2, v.varlevel, v.vardispl)
       else v.varkind = varparam do
         emit3(parameter2, v.varlevel, v.vardispl);
         emit2(value2, elemlength)
       end
     else true do kinderror2(x, typ) end;
     nextsym
   else sym = val1 do function_variable(typ, endvar)
   else true do typ := univtype1; syntax(endvar) end;
   while sym = period1 do field_selector(typ, endvar)
   else sym = lbracket1 do indexed_selector(typ, endvar)
   else sym = colon1 do type_transfer(typ, endvar) end;
   check(succ)
end

"constant_factor:
   constant_symbol"

proc constant_factor(var typ: int; succ: symbols)
var value: int
begin constant_symbol(typ, value, succ);
   emit2(constant2, value)
end

"variable_factor:
   variable_symbol"

proc variable_factor(var typ: int; succ: symbols)
begin variable_symbol(typ, succ);
   emit2(value2, names[typ]:typeattr.length)
end

"elementary_expression:
   expression"

proc elementary_expression(typ: int; succ: symbols)
var exprtype: int
begin expression(exprtype, succ);
   checkelem(exprtype)
end
```

```
"field_expression:
   expression"

proc field_expression(var name: int; succ: symbols)
var typ: int; f: varattr
begin expression(typ, succ);
   if name <> none do
      f := names[name]:varattr;
      checktype(typ, f.vartype);
      name := f.varlink
   else true do error(constructor3) end
end

"field_expression_list:
   field_expression [ ',' field_expression ]*"

proc field_expression_list(typ: int; succ: symbols)
var name: int; endexpr: symbols
begin endexpr := symbols(comma1) + exprsym + succ;
   name := names[typ]:typeattr.subtype1;
   field_expression(name, endexpr);
   while sym = comma1 do
      nextsym; field_expression(name, endexpr)
   end;
   if name <> none do error(constructor3) end
end

"element_expression_list:
   expression [ ',' expression ]*"

proc element_expression_list(typ: int; succ: symbols)
var t: typeattr; exprtype, no, max: int;
   endexpr: symbols
begin endexpr := symbols(comma1) + succ;
   t := names[typ]:typeattr; no := 1;
   expression(exprtype, endexpr);
   checktype(exprtype, t.subtype2);
   while sym = comma1 do
      nextsym; no := no + 1;
      expression(exprtype, endexpr);
      checktype(exprtype, t.subtype2)
   end;
   max := t.bound2 - t.bound1 + 1;
   if (t.subtype2 = char1) and (no < max) do
      emit2(blank2, max - no); no := max
   end;
   if no <> max do error(constructor3) end
end
```

```
"member_expression_list:
   expression [ ',' expression ]*"

proc member_expression_list(typ: int; succ: symbols)
var t: typeattr; exprtype, no: int; endexpr: symbols
begin endexpr := symbols(comma1) + succ;
   t := names[typ]:typeattr; no := 1;
   expression(exprtype, endexpr);
   checktype(exprtype, t.subtype1);
   while sym = comma1 do
     nextsym; no := no + 1;
     expression(exprtype, endexpr);
     checktype(exprtype, t.subtype1)
   end;
   emit2(construct2, no)
end

"constructor:
   elementary_constructor # record_constructor #
   array_constructor # set_constructor
 elementary_constructor:
   type_name '(' elementary_expression ')'
 record_constructor:
   type_name '(' field_expression_list ')'
 array_constructor:
   type_name '(' element_expression_list ')'
 set_constructor:
   type_name [ '(' member_expression_list ')' ]"

proc constructor(var typ: int; succ: symbols)
var mode: namekind; endexpr: symbols
begin "(sym = name1) and (names[x].kind in typekinds)"
   typ := x; mode := names[x].kind; nextsym;
   if sym = lparanth1 do
     nextsym; endexpr := symbols(rparanth1) + succ;
     if mode = elemtype do
       elementary_expression(typ, endexpr)
     else mode = recordtype do
       field_expression_list(typ, endexpr)
     else mode = arraytype do
       element_expression_list(typ, endexpr)
     else mode = settype do
       member_expression_list(typ, endexpr)
     end;
     checksym(rparanth1, succ)
   else true do
     if mode = settype do emit2(construct2, 0)
     else true do error(constructor3) end
   end;
   check(succ)
end
```

```
"function_call:
   procedure_call"

proc function_call(var typ: int; succ: symbols)
begin "(sym = name1) and (names[x].kind in prockinds)"
   if isfunction(x) do
      typ := names[x].procattr.proctype;
      emit2(valspace2, names[typ].typeattr.length)
   else true do kinderror2(x, typ) end;
   procedure_call(succ)
end

"factor:
   constant_factor # variable_factor # constructor #
   function_call # '(' expression ')' #
   'not' factor # factor type_transfer"

proc factor(var typ: int; succ: symbols)
var mode: namekind; endfactor: symbols
begin endfactor := symbols(colon1) + succ;
   if sym in literalsym do
      constant_factor(typ, endfactor)
   else sym = name1 do
      mode := names[x].kind;
      if mode = constant do
         constant_factor(typ, endfactor)
      else mode in typekinds do
         constructor(typ, endfactor)
      else mode in varkinds do
         variable_factor(typ, endfactor)
      else mode in prockinds do
         function_call(typ, endfactor)
      else true do
         kinderror2(x, typ); nextsym
      end
   else sym = val1 do variable_factor(typ, endfactor)
   else sym = lparanth1 do
      nextsym;
      expression(typ, symbols(rparanth1) + endfactor);
      checksym(rparanth1, endfactor)
   else sym = not1 do
      nextsym; factor(typ, endfactor);
      if typ = bool1 do emit(not2)
      else true do typerror2(typ) end
   else true do
      typ := univtype1; syntax(endfactor)
   end;
   while sym = colon1 do
      type_transfer(typ, endfactor)
   end;
   check(succ)
end
```

```
"term:
   factor [ multiplying_operator factor ]*"

proc term(var typ: int; succ: symbols)
var op: symbol; typ2: int; endfactor: symbols
begin endfactor := multsym + succ;
   factor(typ, endfactor);
   while sym in multsym do
      op := sym; nextsym; factor(typ2, endfactor);
      if typ = int1 do
         checktype(typ, typ2);
         if op = asterisk1 do emit(multiply2)
         else op = div1 do emit(divide2)
         else op = mod1 do emit(modulo2)
         else true do typerror2(typ) end
      else typ = bool1 do
         checktype(typ, typ2);
         if op = and1 do emit(and2)
         else true do typerror2(typ) end
      else names[typ].kind = settype do
         checktype(typ, typ2);
         if op = asterisk1 do emit(intersection2)
         else true do typerror2(typ) end
      else true do typerror2(typ) end
   end;
   check(succ)
end

"signed_term:
   [ sign_operator ] term"

proc signed_term(var typ: int; succ: symbols)
var op: symbol
begin
   if sym in signsym do
      op := sym; nextsym; term(typ, succ);
      if typ = int1 do
         if op = plus1 do skip
         else op = minus1 do emit(minus2) end
      else true do typerror2(typ) end
   else true do term(typ, succ) end
end

"simple_expression:
   signed_term [ adding_operator term ]*"

proc simple_expression(var typ: int; succ: symbols)
var op: symbol; typ2: int; endterm: symbols
begin endterm := addsym + succ;
   signed_term(typ, endterm);
   while sym in addsym do
      op := sym; nextsym; term(typ2, endterm);
```

```
   if typ = int1 do
      checktype(typ, typ2);
      if op = plus1 do emit(add2)
      else op = minus1 do emit(subtract2)
      else true do typerror2(typ) end
   else typ = bool1 do
      checktype(typ, typ2);
      if op = or1 do emit(or2)
      else true do typerror2(typ) end
   else names[typ].kind = settype do
      checktype(typ, typ2);
      if op = plus1 do emit(union2)
      else op = minus1 do emit(difference2)
      else true do typerror2(typ) end
   else true do typerror2(typ) end
end;
check(succ)
end

"expression:
   simple_expression
   [ relational_operator simple_expression ]"

post proc expression(var typ: int; succ: symbols)
var op: symbol; typ2: int; t: typeattr;
   endsimple: symbols
begin endsimple := relationsym + succ;
   simple_expression(typ, endsimple);
   if sym in relationsym do
      op := sym; nextsym;
      simple_expression(typ2, succ);
      t := names[typ2]:typeattr;
      if op in equalitysym do
         checktype(typ, typ2);
         if op = equal1 do emit2(equal2, t.length)
         else true do emit2(notequal2, t.length) end
      else op in ordersym do
         checktype(typ, typ2); checkelem(typ);
         if op = less1 do emit(less2)
         else op = greater1 do emit(greater2)
         else op = notless1 do emit(notless2)
         else op = notgreater1 do emit(notgreater2) end
         else op = in1 do
            if t.typekind = settype do
               checktype(typ, t.subtype1); emit(in2)
            else true do typerror2(typ) end
         end;
         if typ <> univtype1 do typ := bool1 end
      end;
      check(succ)
   end
```

```
"assignment_statement:
   variable_symbol ':=' expression"

proc assignment_statement(succ: symbols)
var vartype, exprtype: int
begin
   variable_symbol(vartype, symbols(becomes1)
     + exprsym + succ);
   checksym(becomes1, exprsym + succ);
   expression(exprtype, succ);
   checktype(vartype, exprtype);
   emit2(assign2, names[vartype]:typeattr.length)
end

"standard_call:
   'addr' '(' variable_symbol ')' #
   'halt' #
   'obtain' '(' expression ',' variable_symbol ')' #
   'place' '(' expression ',' expression ')' #
   'sense' '(' expression ',' expression ')'"

proc standard_call(succ: symbols)
var endarg1, endarg2: symbols; typ: int
begin "(sym = name1) and (names[x].kind = standard)"
   endarg2 := symbols(rparanth1) + succ;
   endarg1 := symbols(comma1) + endarg2;
   if x = addr1 do
      nextsym; checksym(lparanth1, endarg2);
      variable_symbol(typ, endarg2);
      checksym(rparanth1, succ); emit(addr2)
   else x = halt1 do
      nextsym; emit(halt2)
   else x = obtain1 do
      nextsym; checksym(lparanth1, endarg1);
      expression(typ, endarg1); checktype(typ, int1);
      checksym(comma1, endarg2);
      variable_symbol(typ, endarg2); checktype(typ, int1);
      checksym(rparanth1, succ); emit(obtain2)
   else x = place1 do
      nextsym; checksym(lparanth1, endarg1);
      expression(typ, endarg1); checktype(typ, int1);
      checksym(comma1, endarg2);
      expression(typ, endarg2); checktype(typ, int1);
      checksym(rparanth1, succ); emit(place2)
   else x = sense1 do
      nextsym; checksym(lparanth1, endarg1);
      expression(typ, endarg1); checktype(typ, int1);
      checksym(comma1, endarg2);
      expression(typ, endarg2); checktype(typ, int1);
      checksym(rparanth1, succ); emit(sense2)
   end
end
```

```
"procedure_argument:
   procedure_name"

proc procedure_argument(succ: symbols)
var length: int; p: procattr
begin
  if sym = name1 do
    if names[x].kind in prockinds do
      p := names[x]:procattr;
      if p.prockind = standard do kinderror1(x)
      else p.prockind = procedur do
        emit3(procarg2, p.proclevel, p.procaddr)
      else p.prockind = procparam do
        emit3(paramarg2, p.proclevel, p.procaddr)
      end
    else true do kinderror1(x) end;
    nextsym
  else true do syntax(succ) end;
  check(succ)
end

"argument:
   expression # variable_symbol # procedure_argument"

proc argument(var param, size: int; succ: symbols)
var typ: int; n: nameattr
begin
  if param <> none do
    n := names[param];
    if n.kind = valparam do
      expression(typ, succ);
      checktype(typ, n:varattr.vartype);
      size := names[typ]:typeattr.length
    else n.kind = varparam do
      variable_symbol(typ, succ);
      checktype(typ, n:varattr.vartype);
      size := elemlength
    else n.kind = procparam do
      procedure_argument(succ);
      size := proclength
    end;
    param := n.link
  else true do
    expression(typ, succ); size := 0;
    error(call3)
  end
end

"argument_list:
   argument [ ',' argument ]*"

proc argument_list(name: int; var length: int;
   succ: symbols)
```

```
var par, length2: int; endarg: symbols
begin endarg := symbols(comma1) + succ;
  par := names[name]:procattr.param;
  argument(par, length, endarg);
  while sym = comma1 do
    nextsym; argument(par, length2, endarg);
    length := length + length2
  end;
  if par <> none do error(call3) end;
  check(succ)
end

"procedure_call:
  standard_call #
  procedure_name [ '(' argument_list ')' ]"

post proc procedure_call(succ: symbols)
var name, length: int; p: procattr
begin "(sym = name1) and (names[x].kind in prockinds)"
  name := x; p := names[x]:procattr;
  if p.prockind = standard do standard_call(succ)
  else true do
    nextsym;
    if sym = lparanth1 do
      nextsym;
      argument_list(name, length, symbols(rparanth1)
        + succ);
      checksym(rparanth1, succ)
    else true do
      if p.param <> none do error(call3) end;
      length := 0
    end;
    if p.prockind = procedur do
      emit4(proccall2, p.proclevel, p.procaddr, length)
    else p.prockind = procparam do
      emit4(paramcall2, p.proclevel, p.procaddr, length)
    end
  end
end

"conditional_statement:
  expression 'do' statement_list"

proc conditional_statement(truelabel: int; succ: symbols)
var typ, falselabel: int; enddo: symbols
begin enddo := statsym + succ;
  expression(typ, symbols(do1) + enddo);
  if typ <> bool1 do typerror2(typ) end;
  newlabel(falselabel);
  checksym(do1, enddo);
  emit2(do2, falselabel);
  statement_list(succ);
```

```
    emit3(else2, truelabel, falselabel);
    check(succ)
end

"conditional_statement_list:
    conditional_statement
    [ 'else' conditional_statement ]*"

proc conditional_statement_list(truelabel: int;
    succ: symbols)
var endstat: symbols
begin endstat := symbols(else1) + succ;
    conditional_statement(truelabel, endstat);
    while sym = else1 do
        nextsym;
        conditional_statement(truelabel, endstat)
    end;
    check(succ)
end

"if_statement:
    'if' conditional_statement_list 'end'"

proc if_statement(succ: symbols)
var truelabel: int
begin "sym = if1" nextsym; newlabel(truelabel);
    conditional_statement_list(truelabel, symbols(end1)
        + succ);
    checksym(end1, succ);
    emit2(endif2, truelabel)
end

"while_statement:
    'while' conditional_statement_list 'end'"

proc while_statement(succ: symbols)
var truelabel: int
begin "sym = while1" nextsym; newlabel(truelabel);
    emit2(while2, truelabel);
    conditional_statement_list(truelabel, symbols(end1)
        + succ);
    checksym(end1, succ)
end

"when_statement:
    'when' conditional_statement_list 'end'"

proc when_statement(succ: symbols)
var waitlabel, truelabel: int
begin "sym = when1" nextsym; newlabel(waitlabel);
    emit2(when2, waitlabel); newlabel(truelabel);
    conditional_statement_list(truelabel, symbols(end1)
        + succ);
```

```
    emit2(wait2, waitlabel);
    checksym(end1, succ);
    emit2(endwhen2, truelabel)
end

"process_statement:
   constant_symbol 'do' statement_list"

proc process_statement(endlabel: int;
   var p: processattr; succ: symbols)
var typ, procconst, proclabel, templabel: int;
   enddo: symbols
begin enddo := statsym + succ;
   constant_symbol(typ, procconst, symbols(do1) + enddo);
   if (procconst < 0) or (procconst > setlimit) do
      error(cobegin3); procconst := 1
   end;
   newlabel(proclabel); newlabel(templabel);
   checksym(do1, enddo);
   emit3(process2, proclabel, templabel);
   statement_list(succ);
   emit3(also2, endlabel, templabel);
   p := processattr(procconst, proclabel);
   check(succ)
end

"process_statement_list:
   process_statement [ 'also' process_statement ]*"

proc process_statement_list(endlabel: int;
   var tasks: processtable; var count: int;
   succ: symbols)
var used: processset; p: processattr; endstat: symbols
begin endstat := symbols(also1) + succ;
   process_statement(endlabel, p, endstat);
   used := processset(p.procconst);
   count := 1; tasks[1] := p;
   while sym = also1 do
      nextsym;
      process_statement(endlabel, p, endstat);
      if p.procconst in used do error(cobegin3)
      else true do
         used := used + processset(p.procconst);
         if count = maxprocess do
            fail(processlimit)
         end;
         count := count + 1; tasks[count] := p
      end
   end;
   check(succ)
end
```

```
"concurrent_statement:
   'cobegin' process_statement_list 'end'"

proc concurrent_statement(succ: symbols)
var beginlabel, endlabel, count, i: int;
   tasks: processtable
begin "sym = cobegin1" nextsym;
   newlabel(beginlabel); newlabel(endlabel);
   emit2(goto2, beginlabel);
   process_statement_list(endlabel, tasks, count,
     symbols(end1) + succ);
   checksym(end1, succ);
   emit4(cobegin2, beginlabel, endlabel, count);
   i := 0;
   while i < count do
     i := i + 1; emit(operator(tasks[i].procconst));
     emit(operator(tasks[i].proclabel))
   end
end

"statement:
   'skip' # assignment_statement # procedure_call #
   if_statement # while_statement #
   when_statement # concurrent_statement"

proc statement(succ: symbols)
begin
   if sym = skip1 do nextsym
   else sym = val1 do assignment_statement(succ)
   else sym = name1 do
     if names[x].kind in prockinds do
       if isfunction(x) do kinderror1(x)
       else true do procedure_call(succ) end
     else true do assignment_statement(succ) end
   else sym = if1 do if_statement(succ)
   else sym = while1 do while_statement(succ)
   else sym = when1 do when_statement(succ)
   else sym = cobegin1 do concurrent_statement(succ)
   else true do syntax(succ) end;
   check(succ)
end

"statement_list
   statement [ ';' statement ]*"

post proc statement_list(succ: symbols)
var semistat, endstat: symbols
begin semistat := symbols(semicolon1) + statsym;
   endstat := semistat + succ;
   statement(endstat);
   while sym in semistat do
     checksym(semicolon1, statsym);
     statement(endstat)
```

```
    end;
    check( succ)
end

"program:
    [ initial_declaration ]* complete_procedure
 initial_declaration:
    constant_declaration_list # type_declaration"

proc programx( succ: symbols)
var enddecl: symbols
begin standard_names;
    enddecl := initdeclsym + symbols( proc1) + succ;
    while sym in initdeclsym do
        if sym = const1 do
            constant_declaration_list( enddecl)
        else sym in typesym do
            type_declaration( enddecl)
        end
    end;
    complete_procedure( false, 0, succ);
    check( succ)
end

begin programx( symbols( endtext1));
    emit( endcode2)
end
```

10.5 CODE GENERATION

This section contains the complete text of pass 4 of the Edison compiler with some additional comments.

Pass 4 scans the intermediate code output by pass 3 twice and generates optimized Edison code (Section 6.10).

Input

Like all the other passes, pass 4 uses a single-symbol look-ahead method of input (Section 10.2). The nextop procedure inputs the next operator and its arguments (if any).

Labels

During the first scan of the input, pass 4 builds a table that maps numeric labels into the addresses, displacements, or lengths of stored entities expressed in words. During the second scan of the input, the labels are replaced by the corresponding values.

Output

The final code is well suited to interpretation on a byte-addressable computer, such as the PDP 11:

Operation codes are represented by consecutive even numbers beginning with #400 (Chapter 8).

Displacements of variables (called "offsets") are expressed in bytes.

Jump destinations are expressed (in bytes) relative to the jump instructions to make the code relocatable in the store.

The compiler will generate efficient code for a word-addressable computer if the spacing of consecutive words is changed from its present value of 2 to 1. The range of values used to represent the operation codes can be changed by using a different value of the operation base (which is currently #400). It is then necessary to recompile all the Edison programs on an existing system.

Errors

Error messages for incorrect programs are output to a disk file named notes (Section 10.1). To suppress redundant error messages, the compiler outputs at most one error message per line.

Parameters

During the first scan of the input, pass 4 builds a table that defines the length of the parameters of nested procedures. The current level of nesting is defined by a variable. The parameter lengths are used as arguments of the instruction named procedure during the second scan (Section 6.5).

Temporaries

During the first scan, pass 4 also builds a table that defines the current (and the maximum) lengths of the temporaries needed to execute nested procedures. This is done by keeping track of how the length of the variable stack will change when the Edison instructions are executed. The maximum lengths of the temporaries are used as arguments of the instruction named procedure during the second scan.

Code Optimization

Pass 4 includes a procedure for each instruction of the Edison code defined in Chapter 6. Pass 4 inputs one standard instruction at a time from pass 3 and calls the corresponding procedure with the arguments of that instruction (Section 2.3.5).

When a procedure, such as the one named whole variable, recognizes that a given instruction can be combined with the next one (Section 6.10), it calls another procedure, in this case the one named nearby variable. This procedure may then find that it is possible to combine the first two instructions with a third one by calling yet another procedure named nearby elementary variable, which finally replaces three standard instructions, such as

$$\text{instance}(0) \text{ variable}(\text{displ}) \text{ value}(1)$$

by a single extra instruction

$$\text{localvalue}(\text{displ})$$

This is the method by which the Edison code is optimized.

If the boolean parameter named trim is changed from true to false, the compiler only emits standard instructions.

Pass 4 Text

```
"Edison - 11 Compiler: Pass 4

Code generation

Per Brinch Hansen

4 August 1980

Copyright (c) 1980 Per Brinch Hansen"

enum operator (add2, also2, and2, assign2, blank2,
   cobegin2, constant2, construct2, difference2,
   divide2, do2, else2, endcode2, endif2, endlib2,
   endproc2, endwhen2, equal2, error2, field2,
   funcval2, goto2, greater2, in2, index2,
   intersection2, less2, libproc2, minus2, modulo2,
   multiply2, newline2, not2, notequal2, notgreater2,
   notless2, or2, paramarg2, paramcall2, parameter2,
   procarg2, proccall2, procedure2, process2,
   subtract2, union2, valspace2, value2, variable2,
   wait2, when2, while2, addr2, halt2, obtain2,
   place2, sense2)

enum errorkind (ambiguous3, call3, cobegin3,
   constructor3, funcval3, incomplete3,
   numeral3, range3, split3, syntax3, type3,
   undeclared3)
```

```
enum failure (blocklimit, charlimit, inputlimit,
    labellimit, namelimit, outputlimit, processlimit,
    wordlimit)

proc pass4(trim: bool;
    proc next(var op: operator);
    proc emit(value: int);
    proc report(lineno: int; error: errorkind);
    proc rerun;
    proc fail(reason: failure))

const "table limits"
    maxblock = 10; maxlabel = 1000;

    "type lengths" elemlength = 1; liblength = 1;
    linklength = 5; proclength = 2;
    setlength = 8 "words";
    setlimit = 127 "+ 1 members";
    none = 0

enum opcode ("standard codes" add4, also4, and4,
    assign4, blank4, cobegin4, constant4, construct4,
    difference4, divide4, do4, else4, endcode4,
    endlib4, endproc4, endwhen4, equal4, field4,
    goto4, greater4, in4, index4, instance4,
    intersection4, less4, libproc4, minus4,
    modulo4, multiply4, newline4, not4, notequal4,
    notgreater4, notless4, or4, paramarg4,
    paramcall4, procarg4, proccall4, procedure4,
    process4, subtract4, union4, valspace4, value4,
    variable4, wait4, when4, addr4, halt4, obtain4,
    place4, sense4,
    "extra codes" elemassign4, elemvalue4, localcase4,
    localset4, localvalue4, localvar4, outercall4,
    outercase4, outerparam4, outerset4, outervalue4,
    outervar4, setconst4, singleton4, stringconst4)

var final: bool


module "input"

  set operators (operator)

  var no_arguments, one_argument, two_arguments,
      three_arguments, four_arguments: operators

* var op: operator; a, b, c, d: int;
      lineno: int

* proc nextop
  begin next(op);
      while op = newline2 do
```

```
            next(lineno:operator); next(op)
         end;
         if op in no_arguments do skip
         else op in one_argument do next(a:operator)
         else op in two_arguments do
            next(a:operator); next(b:operator)
         else op in three_arguments do
            next(a:operator); next(b:operator);
            next(c:operator)
         else op in four_arguments do
            next(a:operator); next(b:operator);
            next(c:operator); next(d:operator)
         end
      end

begin
   no_arguments := operators(add2, and2, difference2,
      divide2, endcode2, greater2, in2, intersection2,
      less2, minus2, modulo2, multiply2, not2,
      notgreater2, notless2, or2, subtract2, union2,
      addr2, halt2, obtain2, place2, sense2);
   one_argument := operators(assign2, blank2,
      constant2, construct2, do2, endif2, endwhen2,
      equal2, error2, field2, goto2, newline2,
      notequal2, valspace2, value2, wait2, when2,
      while2);
   two_arguments := operators(also2, else2, endlib2,
      funcval2, paramarg2, parameter2, procarg2,
      process2, variable2);
   three_arguments := operators(cobegin2, index2,
      libproc2, paramcall2, proccall2);
   four_arguments := operators(endproc2, procedure2)
end


module "labels"

   array labeltable [1:maxlabel] (int)

   var labels: labeltable; i: int

*  proc define(index, value: int)
   begin labels[index] := value end

*  proc valueof(index: int): int
   begin val valueof := labels[index] end

begin i := 0;
   while i < maxlabel do
      i := i + 1; labels[i] := none
   end
end
```

```
module "output"

  const opbase = #400; spacing = 2

  var pointer, wordno: int

* var codelength: int

* proc oper(op: opcode)
  begin pointer := wordno;
    emit(opbase + spacing * int(op));
    wordno := wordno + 1
  end

* proc offset(value: int)
  begin emit(spacing * value);
    wordno := wordno + 1
  end

* proc literal(value: int)
  begin emit(value);
    wordno := wordno + 1
  end

* proc label(index: int)
  begin emit(spacing * (valueof(index) - pointer));
    wordno := wordno + 1
  end

* proc defaddr(label: int)
  begin define(label, wordno) end

* proc out again
  begin codelength := wordno - 1;
    pointer := 1; wordno := 1
  end

begin codelength := 0; pointer := 1;
  wordno := 1
end


module "errors"

  var errorline: int

* proc error(kind: errorkind)
  begin
    if not final and (lineno <> errorline) do
      report(lineno, kind); errorline := lineno
    end;
    nextop
  end
```

```
begin errorline := none end

module "parameters"

    array paramtable [1:maxblock] (int)

    var procs: paramtable; level: int

*   proc newproc(paramlength: int)
    begin
        if level = maxblock do fail(blocklimit) end;
        level := level + 1;
        procs[level] := paramlength
    end

*   proc thislevel: int
    begin val thislevel := level end

*   proc paramlength(level: int): int
    begin val paramlength := procs[level] end

*   proc endprocx
    begin level := level - 1 end

*   proc initparam
    begin level := 0 end

begin initparam end

module "temporaries"

    record tempattr (temp, maxtemp: int)

    array temptable [1:maxblock] (tempattr)

    var temps: temptable; level: int

*   proc newtemp
    begin
        if level = maxblock do fail(blocklimit) end;
        level := level + 1;
        temps[level] := tempattr(0, 0)
    end

*   proc push(length: int)
    var t: tempattr
    begin t := temps[level];
        t.temp := t.temp + length;
        if t.maxtemp < t.temp do
            t.maxtemp := t.temp
        end;
```

```
      temps[level] := t
   end

*  proc pop(length: int)
   begin
      temps[level].temp := temps[level].temp - length
   end

*  proc endtemp(var templength: int)
   begin templength := temps[level].maxtemp;
      level := level - 1
   end

*  proc inittemp
   begin level := 0 end

begin inittemp end


proc again
begin rerun; out again;
   initparam; inittemp
end

proc in_setrange(value: int): bool
begin
   val in_setrange :=
      (0 <= value) and (value <= setlimit)
end


"extra codes:"

pre proc constlist(value: int)

"nearby_case(steps, displ, value, falselabel);
   nearby_equal(steps, displ, value) 'do(falselabel)'"

proc nearby_case(steps, displ, value, falselabel: int)
begin "0 <= steps <= 1"
   if steps = 0 do oper(localcase4)
   else true do oper(outercase4) end;
   offset(displ); literal(value); label(falselabel);
   nextop
end

"nearby_equal(steps, displ, value):
   nearby_elem_const(steps, displ, value) 'equal(1)'"

proc nearby_equal(steps, displ, value: int)
begin "0 <= steps <= 1" nextop;
   if op = do2 do
      nearby_case(steps, displ, value, a)
```

```
      else true do
         if steps = 0 do oper(localvalue4)
         else true do oper(outervalue4) end;
         offset(displ); push(1);
         oper(constant4); literal(value); push(1);
         oper(equal4); offset(1); pop(1)
      end
end

"nearby_elem_const(steps, displ, value):
   nearby_elem(steps, displ) 'constant(value)'"

proc nearby_elem_const(steps, displ, value: int)
begin "0 <= steps <= 1" nextop;
   if (op = equal2) and (a = 1) do
      nearby_equal(steps, displ, value)
   else true do
      if steps = 0 do oper(localvalue4)
      else true do oper(outervalue4) end;
      offset(displ); push(1);
      if in_setrange(value) and (op = constant2) do
         constlist(value)
      else in_setrange(value) and (op = construct2)
         and (a = 1) do
         oper(singleton4); literal(value);
         push(setlength); nextop
      else true do
         oper(constant4); literal(value); push(1)
      end
   end
end

"nearby_elem(steps, displ):
   localvalue(displ) # outervalue(displ)
 localvalue(displ):
   localvar(displ) 'value(1)'
 outervalue(displ):
   outervar(displ) 'value(1)'"

proc nearby_elem(steps, displ: int)
begin "0 <= steps <= 1" nextop;
   if op = constant2 do
      nearby_elem_const(steps, displ, a)
   else true do
      if steps = 0 do oper(localvalue4)
      else true do oper(outervalue4) end;
      offset(displ); push(1)
   end
end
```

```
"nearby_set(steps, displ):
    localset(displ) # outerset(displ)
  localset(displ):
    localvar(displ) 'value(setlength)'
  outerset(displ):
    outervar(displ) 'value(setlength)'"

proc nearby_set(steps, displ: int)
begin "0 <= steps <= 1" nextop;
    if steps = 0 do oper(localset4)
    else true do oper(outerset4) end;
    offset(displ); push(setlength)
end

"nearby_variable(steps, displ):
    localvar(displ) # outervar(displ)
  localvar(displ):
    'instance(0)' 'variable(displ)'
  outervar(displ):
    'instance(1)' 'variable(displ)'"

proc nearby_variable(steps, displ: int)
begin "0 <= steps <= 1, nextop already called"
    if (op = value2) and (a = 1) do
        nearby_elem(steps, displ)
    else (op = value2) and (a = setlength) do
        nearby_set(steps, displ)
    else true do
        if steps = 0 do oper(localvar4)
        else true do oper(outervar4) end;
        offset(displ); push(1)
    end
end

"constlist(n, value1, ..., valuen):
    setconst(n, value1, ..., valuen) #
    stringconst(n, value1, ..., valuen)
  setconst(n, value1, ..., valuen):
    stringconst(n, value1, ..., valuen)
    'construct(n, lineno)'
  stringconst(n, value1, ..., valuen):
    'constant(value1)' ... 'constant(valuen)'"

post proc constlist(value1: int)
const maxn = 80
array table [1:maxn] (int)
var list: table; n, i: int
begin
    "in_setrange(value1) and (op = constant2)
        and (a = value2)"
    n := 1; list[1] := value1;
    while (op = constant2) and in_setrange(a)
```

```
        and (n < maxn) do
        n := n + 1; list[n] := a; nextop
      end;
      if (op = construct2) and (a <= n) do
        i := 0;
        while i < n - a do
          i := i + 1; oper(constant4); literal(list[i])
        end;
        push(n - a);
        if a = 1 do
          oper(singleton4); literal(list[n])
        else true do
          oper(setconst4); literal(a);
          while i < n do
            i := i + 1; literal(list[i])
          end
        end;
        push(setlength); nextop
      else true do
        oper(stringconst4); literal(n); i := 0;
        while i < n do
          i := i + 1; literal(list[i])
        end;
        push(n)
      end
  end
end

"singleton(value):
   smallconst(value) 'construct(1, lineno)'"

proc singleton(value: int)
begin oper(singleton4); literal(value);
   push(setlength); nextop
end

"one:
   'constant(1)'"

proc one
begin "nextop already called"
   if op = do2 do nextop
   else true do
     oper(constant4); literal(1); push(1)
   end
end

"smallconst(value):
   'constant(value)'"

proc smallconst(value: int)
begin "in_setrange(value)" nextop;
   if op = constant2 do constlist(value)
```

```
      else (op = construct2) and (a = 1) do
         singleton(value)
      else value = 1 do one
      else true do
         oper(constant4); literal(value); push(1)
      end
end

"elemvalue:
    'value(1)'"

proc elemvalue
begin oper(elemvalue4); nextop end

"elemassign:
    'assign(1)'"

proc elemassign
begin oper(elemassign4); pop(2); nextop end

"outercall(displ):
    'instance(1)' 'proccall(displ)'"

proc outercall(proclabel, arglength: int)
begin oper(outercall4); label(proclabel);
   push(linklength); pop(arglength + linklength);
   nextop
end

"outerparam(displ):
    'instance(1)' 'paramcall(displ)'"

proc outerparam(displ, arglength: int)
begin oper(outerparam4); offset(displ);
   push(linklength); pop(arglength + linklength);
   nextop
end


"standard code"

"library_procedure:
    'goto' 'libproc' expression 'endlib'"

proc goto(endlabel: int)
begin oper(goto4); label(endlabel); nextop end

proc libproc(proclabel, paramlength, templabel: int)
begin defaddr(proclabel); oper(libproc4);
   offset(paramlength); offset(valueof(templabel));
   literal(lineno); newproc(paramlength);
   newtemp; nextop
end
```

```
proc endlib(templabel, endlabel: int)
var templength: int
begin endtemp(templength); endprocx;
  define(templabel, templength);
  oper(endlib4); literal(lineno);
  defaddr(endlabel); nextop
end
```

```
"complete_procedure:
  [ 'goto' ] 'procedure' [ declaration ]*
  statement_part 'endproc'"
```

```
proc procedure(proclabel, paramlength, varlabel,
  templabel: int)
begin defaddr(proclabel); oper(procedure4);
  offset(paramlength); offset(valueof(varlabel));
  offset(valueof(templabel)); literal(lineno);
  newproc(paramlength); newtemp; nextop
end
```

```
proc endproc(varlabel, varlength, templabel,
  endlabel: int)
var templength: int
begin endtemp(templength); endprocx;
  define(templabel, templength);
  define(varlabel, varlength); oper(endproc4);
  defaddr(endlabel); nextop
end
```

```
"procedure_declaration:
  complete_procedure # library_procedure
 module_declaration:
  [ declaration ]* statement_part
 declaration:
  empty # procedure_declaration #
  module_declaration"
```

```
"variable_symbol:
  whole_variable #
  variable_symbol [ 'field' ] #
  variable_symbol expression 'index'
 whole_variable:
  'instance' 'variable' [ 'value' ]"
```

```
proc field(displ: int)
begin nextop;
  while op = field2 do
    displ := displ + a; nextop
  end;
  if displ <> 0 do
    oper(field4); offset(displ)
  end
end
```

```
proc index(lower, upper, length: int)
begin oper(index4); literal(lower);
  literal(upper); offset(length); literal(lineno);
  pop(1); nextop
end

proc whole_variable(level, displ: int)
var steps: int
begin "op in operators(variable2, parameter2, funcval2)"
  steps := thislevel - level; nextop;
  while op = field2 do
    displ := displ + a; nextop
  end;
  if trim and (steps <= 1) do
    nearby_variable(steps, displ)
  else true do
    oper(instance4); literal(steps);
    oper(variable4); offset(displ);
    push(1)
  end
end

proc variable(level, displ: int)
begin whole_variable(level, linklength + displ) end

proc parameter(level, displ: int)
begin
  whole_variable(level, - paramlength(level) + displ)
end

proc funcval(level, length: int)
begin
  whole_variable(level + 1,
    - paramlength(level + 1) - length)
end

"constructor:
  elementary_constructor # record_constructor #
  array_constructor # set_constructor
 elementary_constructor:
  expression
 record_constructor:
  expression [ expression ]*
 array_constructor:
  expression [ expression ]* [ 'blank' ]
 set_constructor:
  [ expression ]* 'construct'"

proc blank(number: int)
begin oper(blank4); literal(number);
  push(number); nextop
end
```

```
proc construct(number: int)
begin oper(construct4); literal(number);
    literal(lineno); pop(number);
    push(setlength); nextop
end

"factor:
    'constant' # constructor # variable_symbol 'value' #
    'valspace' procedure_call # expression #
    factor 'not' # factor"

proc constant(value: int)
begin
    if trim and in_setrange(value) do
        smallconst(value)
    else true do
        oper(constant4); literal(value);
        push(1); nextop
    end
end

proc value(length: int)
begin
    if trim and (length = 1) do elemvalue
    else true do
        oper(value4); offset(length);
        pop(1); push(length); nextop
    end
end

proc valspace(length: int)
begin oper(valspace4); offset(length);
    push(length); nextop
end

proc notx
begin oper(not4); nextop end

"term:
    factor [ factor multiplying_operator ]*
 multiplying_operator:
    'multiply' # 'divide' # 'modulo' #
    'and' # 'intersection'"

proc multiply
begin oper(multiply4); literal(lineno);
    pop(1); nextop
end

proc divide
begin oper(divide4); literal(lineno);
    pop(1); nextop
end
```

```
proc modulo
begin oper(modulo4); literal(lineno);
  pop(1); nextop
end

proc andx
begin oper(and4); pop(1); nextop end

proc intersection
begin oper(intersection4); pop(setlength);
  nextop
end
```

"signed_term:
   term [empty # 'minus']"

```
proc minus
begin oper(minus4); literal(lineno); nextop end
```

"simple_expression:
   signed_term [term adding_operator]*
  adding_operator:
   'add' # 'subtract' # 'or' # 'union' #
   'difference'"

```
proc add
begin oper(add4); literal(lineno);
  pop(1); nextop
end

proc subtract
begin oper(subtract4); literal(lineno);
  pop(1); nextop
end

proc orx
begin oper(or4); pop(1); nextop end

proc union
begin oper(union4); pop(setlength); nextop end

proc difference
begin oper(difference4); pop(setlength); nextop end
```

"expression:
  simple_expression
  [simple_expression relational_operator]
relational_operator:
  'equal' # 'notequal' # 'less' # 'notless' #
  'greater' # 'notgreater' # 'in'"

```
proc equal(length: int)
begin oper(equal4); offset(length);
  pop(2 * length); push(1); nextop
end

proc notequal(length: int)
begin oper(notequal4); offset(length);
  pop(2 * length); push(1); nextop
end

proc less
begin oper(less4); pop(1); nextop end

proc notless
begin oper(notless4); pop(1); nextop end

proc greater
begin oper(greater4); pop(1); nextop end

proc notgreater
begin oper(notgreater4); pop(1); nextop end

proc inx
begin oper(in4); literal(lineno);
  pop(setlength); nextop
end

"assignment_statement:
   variable_symbol expression 'assign'"

proc assign(length: int)
begin
  if trim and (length = 1) do elemassign
  else true do
    oper(assign4); offset(length);
    pop(1 + length); nextop
  end
end

"standard_call:
   variable_symbol 'addr' #
   'halt' #
   expression variable_symbol 'obtain' #
   expression expression 'place' #
   expression expression 'sense'"

proc addrx
begin oper(addr4); pop(1); nextop end

proc haltx
begin oper(halt4); literal(lineno); nextop end
```

```
proc obtainx
begin oper(obtain4); pop(2); nextop end

proc placex
begin oper(place4); pop(2); nextop end

proc sensex
begin oper(sense4); pop(2); nextop end

"procedure_argument:
   'procarg' # 'paramarg'"

proc procarg(level, proclabel: int)
begin oper(instance4); literal(thislevel - level);
   oper(procarg4); label(proclabel);
   push(proclength); nextop
end

proc paramarg(level, displ: int)
begin oper(instance4); literal(thislevel - level);
   oper(paramarg4);
   offset(- paramlength(level) + displ);
   push(proclength); nextop
end

"argument:
   expression # variable_symbol # procedure_argument
 argument_list:
   argument [ argument ]*
 procedure_call:
   standard_call #
   [ argument_list ] 'proccall' #
   [ argument_list ] 'paramcall'"

proc proccall(level, proclabel, arglength: int)
var steps: int
begin steps := thislevel - level;
   if trim and (steps = 1) do
      outercall(proclabel, arglength)
   else true do
      oper(instance4); literal(steps);
      oper(proccall4); label(proclabel);
      push(linklength); pop(arglength + linklength);
      nextop
   end
end

proc paramcall(level, displ, arglength: int)
var steps: int
begin steps := thislevel - level;
   displ := - paramlength(level) + displ;
   if trim and (steps = 1) do
      outerparam(displ, arglength)
```

```
      else true do
         oper(instance4); literal(steps);
         oper(paramcall4); offset(displ);
         push(linklength); pop(arglength + linklength);
         nextop
      end
   end

"conditional_statement:
   expression 'do' statement_list 'else'
 conditional_statement_list:
   conditional_statement [ conditional_statement ]*"

proc dox(falselabel: int)
begin oper(do4); label(falselabel); pop(1);
   nextop
end

proc elsex(truelabel, falselabel: int)
begin nextop;
   if op <> endif2 do
      oper(else4); label(truelabel)
   end;
   defaddr(falselabel)
end

"if_statement:
   conditional_statement_list 'endif'"

proc endif(truelabel: int)
begin defaddr(truelabel); nextop end

"while_statement:
   'while' conditional_statement_list"

proc whilex(truelabel: int)
begin defaddr(truelabel); nextop end

"when_statement:
   'when' conditional_statement_list 'wait'
   'endwhen'"

proc whenx(waitlabel: int)
begin oper(when4); defaddr(waitlabel); nextop end

proc wait(waitlabel: int)
begin oper(wait4); label(waitlabel); nextop end

proc endwhen(truelabel: int)
begin defaddr(truelabel); oper(endwhen4);
   nextop
end
```

```
"process_statement:
   'process' statement_list 'also'"

proc process(proclabel, templabel: int)
begin defaddr(proclabel); oper(process4);
   offset(valueof(templabel)); literal(lineno);
   newtemp; nextop
end

proc alsox(endlabel, templabel: int)
var templength: int
begin endtemp(templength);
   define(templabel, templength);
   oper(also4); label(endlabel); nextop
end

"process_statement_list:
   process_statement [ process_statement ]*
 concurrent_statement:
   'goto' process_statement_list 'cobegin'"

proc cobeginx(beginlabel, endlabel, number: int)
var procconst, proclabel, i: int
begin defaddr(beginlabel); oper(cobegin4);
   literal(number); literal(lineno); i := 0;
   while i < number do
      next(procconst:operator); literal(procconst);
      next(proclabel:operator); label(proclabel);
      i := i + 1
   end;
   defaddr(endlabel); nextop
end

"statement:
   empty # assignment_statement #
   procedure_call # if_statement #
   while_statement # when_statement #
   concurrent_statement
 statement_list:
   statement [ statement ]*
 statement_part:
   statement_list
 program:
   complete_procedure 'endcode'"

proc endcode
begin oper(endcode4); literal(lineno - 1) end

proc assemble(last_scan: bool)
var more: bool
begin final := last_scan; more := true;
   offset(codelength); nextop;
```

```
while more do
   if op <= construct2 do
      if op = add2 do add
      else op = also2 do alsox(a, b)
      else op = and2 do andx
      else op = assign2 do assign(a)
      else op = blank2 do blank(a)
      else op = cobegin2 do cobeginx(a, b, c)
      else op = constant2 do constant(a)
      else op = construct2 do construct(a) end
   else op <= endproc2 do
      if op = difference2 do difference
      else op = divide2 do divide
      else op = do2 do dox(a)
      else op = else2 do elsex(a, b)
      else op = endcode2 do
         endcode; more := false
      else op = endif2 do endif(a)
      else op = endlib2 do endlib(a, b)
      else op = endproc2 do endproc(a, b, c, d) end
   else op <= in2 do
      if op = endwhen2 do endwhen(a)
      else op = equal2 do equal(a)
      else op = error2 do error(errorkind(a))
      else op = field2 do field(a)
      else op = funcval2 do funcval(a, b)
      else op = goto2 do goto(a)
      else op = greater2 do greater
      else op = in2 do inx end
   else op <= not2 do
      if op = index2 do index(a, b, c)
      else op = intersection2 do intersection
      else op = less2 do less
      else op = libproc2 do libproc(a, b, c)
      else op = minus2 do minus
      else op = modulo2 do modulo
      else op = multiply2 do multiply
      else op = not2 do notx end
   else op <= procarg2 do
      if op = notequal2 do notequal(a)
      else op = notgreater2 do notgreater
      else op = notless2 do notless
      else op = or2 do orx
      else op = paramarg2 do paramarg(a, b)
      else op = paramcall2 do
         paramcall(a, b, c)
      else op = parameter2 do parameter(a, b)
      else op = procarg2 do procarg(a, b) end
   else op <= variable2 do
      if op = proccall2 do proccall(a, b, c)
      else op = procedure2 do
         procedure(a, b, c, d)
```

```
            else op = process2 do process(a, b)
            else op = subtract2 do subtract
            else op = union2 do union
            else op = valspace2 do valspace(a)
            else op = value2 do value(a)
            else op = variable2 do variable(a, b) end
        else op <= sense2 do
            if op = wait2 do wait(a)
            else op = when2 do whenx(a)
            else op = while2 do whilex(a)
            else op = addr2 do addrx
            else op = halt2 do haltx
            else op = obtain2 do obtainx
            else op = place2 do placex
            else op = sense2 do sensex end
        end
    end
end

begin assemble(false); again; assemble(true) end
```

REFERENCES

BELL, J. R., "Threaded code," *Comm. ACM 16*, 6, pp. 370–72, June 1973.

BOWLES, K. L., *Beginner's Guide for the UCSD Pascal System*. McGraw-Hill, New York, 1980.

BRINCH HANSEN, P., "The nucleus of a multiprogramming system," *Comm. ACM 13*, 4, pp. 238–50, April 1970.

BRINCH HANSEN, P., "Structured multiprogramming," *Comm. ACM 15*, 7, pp. 574–78, July 1972.

BRINCH HANSEN, P., *Operating System Principles*. Prentice-Hall, Englewood Cliffs, NJ, July 1973.

BRINCH HANSEN, P., "The programming language Concurrent Pascal," *IEEE Trans. on Software Engineering 1*, 2, pp. 199–207, June 1975.

BRINCH HANSEN, P., *The Architecture of Concurrent Programs*. Prentice-Hall, Englewood Cliffs, NJ, July 1977.

BRINCH HANSEN, P., "Edison programs," *Software—Practice and Experience 11*, 4, pp. 397–414, August 1981.

BRINCH HANSEN, P., and FELLOWS, J., "The Trio operating system," *Software—Practice and Experience 10*, pp. 943–948, 1980.

DAHL, O.-J., DIJKSTRA, E. W., and HOARE, C. A. R., *Structured Programming*. Academic Press, New York, 1972.

378 REFERENCES

DIGITAL EQUIPMENT CORPORATION, *PDP 11 Processor Handbook*. Maynard, MA, 1975.

DIGITAL EQUIPMENT CORPORATION, *PDP 11 Peripherals Handbook*. Maynard, MA, 1976.

DIJKSTRA, E. W., "Cooperating sequential processes," *Programming Languages*. Academic Press, New York, 1968.

DIJKSTRA, E. W., "Guarded commands, nondeterminism, and formal derivation," *Comm. ACM 18*, 8, pp. 453-57, August 1975.

HABERMANN, A. N., "Critical comments on the programming language Pascal," *Acta Informatica 3*, pp. 47-57, 1973.

HARTMANN, A. C., *A Concurrent Pascal Compiler for Minicomputers* (Lecture Notes in Computer Science 50). Springer-Verlag, New York, 1977.

HOARE, C. A. R., "The quality of software," *Software—Practice and Experience 2*, pp. 103-5, 1972a.

HOARE, C. A. R., "Towards a theory of parallel programming," *Operating Systems Techniques*. Academic Press, New York, pp. 61-71, 1972b.

HOARE, C. A. R., *Hints on Programming Language Design*. Computer Science Department, Stanford University, Stanford, CA, December 1973.

HOARE, C. A. R., "Monitors: an operating system structuring concept," *Comm. ACM 14*, 10, pp. 549-57, October 1974.

JENSEN, K., and WIRTH, N., *Pascal—User Manual and Report* (Lecture Notes in Computer Science 18), 2nd ed. Springer-Verlag, New York, 1975.

KNUTH, D. E., "The remaining trouble spots in Algol 60," *Comm. ACM 10*, pp. 611-18, October 1967.

McNEILL, W. H., *The Shape of European History*. Oxford University Press, New York, 1967.

NAUR, P. (ed.), *Revised Report on the Algorithmic Language Algol 60*. Regnecentralen, Copenhagen, 1962.

OWICKI, S., and GRIES, D., "An axiomatic proof technique for parallel programs," *Acta Informatica 6*, pp. 319-40, 1976.

WELSH, J., and McKEAG, M., *Structured System Programming*. Prentice-Hall, Englewood Cliffs, NJ, 1980.

WELSH, J., SNEERINGER, W. J., and HOARE, C. A. R., "Ambiguities and insecurities in Pascal," *Software—Practice and Experience 7*, pp. 685-96, 1977.

WIRTH, N., "The programming language Pascal," *Acta Informatica 1*, pp. 35-63, 1971.

WIRTH, N., *Systematic Programming: An Introduction*. Prentice-Hall, Englewood Cliffs, NJ, 1973.

WIRTH, N., *Algorithms + Data Structures = Programs*. Prentice-Hall, Englewood Cliffs, NJ, 1976a.

WIRTH, N., *Programming Languages: What to Demand and How to Assess Them.* Institut für Informatik, Eidgenössiche Technische Hochschule, Zurich, March 1976b.

WIRTH, N., "Modula: a language for modular multiprogramming," *Software—Practice and Experience 7*, 2, pp. 3-35, March-April 1977.

ZAKS, R., *The CP/M Handbook.* Sybex, Berkeley, CA, 1980.

SOFTWARE DISTRIBUTION

The Edison system is a portable software system for personal computers written by Per Brinch Hansen and described in this book.

The Edison system supports the development of programs written in the programming language Edison, a Pascal-like language that supports program modularity and concurrent execution.

The Edison system includes an operating system, an Edison compiler, a screen editor, a text formatter, a print program, and an assembler written in the Edison language.

The program text and portable code of the software are available on diskettes for the following microcomputers:

IBM Personal Computer	*PDP 11/23 Computer*
32 K words and Keyboard	(or LSI 11) 28 K words
Dual 5¼" Diskette Drive	Dual 8" Diskette Drive
single (or double) sided	RX02 (or RX01)
Monochrome Display	Terminal
Printer	VT 100 (or VT 52)
Display/Printer Adapter	Printer

The software can be edited and recompiled on these machine configurations. It can also be moved to other similar microcomputers by rewriting a kernel of 2 K words.

Please use the reverse side of this form to obtain more information on the distribution of the Edison System by the author.

Per Brinch Hansen (author)
c/o Computer Science Editor
Prentice-Hall, Inc.
Englewood Cliffs
New Jersey 07632
U.S.A.

INFORMATION REQUEST

THE PORTABLE CODE OF THE EDISON SYSTEM IS AVAILABLE FOR THE IBM PERSONAL COMPUTER AND THE COMPAQ PORTABLE COMPUTER FOR $37. (This price may change.)
    If you wish to use both the program text and the portable code of the Edison System on one or more machines, you must sign a software license agreement and pay a license fee of $300 for each machine. (This price may also change.)
    To receive more information on how to order the Edison System simply fill out this form and send it to Per Brinch Hansen. Please, send *no money* with this form.

[   ]   Check here, if you want the portable code only on double-sided 5¼″ diskettes for an IBM Personal Computer (or a Compaq). Price: $37.

[   ]   Check here, if you want the program text and portable code on single-sided 5¼″ diskettes for an IBM Personal Computer (or a Compaq). Price: $300.

[   ]   Check here, if you want the program text and portable code on 8″ diskettes for a PDP 11/23 Computer. Price: $300.

_____   Show the number of machines on which you plan to use the software.

Name _____

Address _____

_____

_____

_____

_____

INDEX